A Treatise on 2nd Amendment Rights in the 21st Century

A Treatise on 2ⁿᵈ Amendment Rights in the 21ˢᵗ Century

Containing an inquiry into the current legislation, perceptions and necessity of the 2nd Amendment right, together with a critical and chronological view of how the people's rights and perceptions have changed over time.

Doug Hawk

FIRST EDITION

UNEQUA
PRESS

Unequa Press
P.O. Box 668
Asheville, NC 28802

Unequa Press books may be purchased in bulk at special discounts for sales promotion, corporate gifts, fund-raising, or educational purposes. For details, contact Unequa Press, P.O. Box 668, Asheville NC, 28802 or info@unequa.com.

Printed in the United States of America

Library of Congress Control Number: 2016909970

ISBN 13: 978-0-9977121-0-0 (pb)
ISBN 13: 978-0-9977121-1-7 (ebook)

10 9 8 7 6 5 4 3 2 1

This book is dedicated to each and every human being who has taken the time to evaluate their own belief system and takes responsibility for their own life.

Acknowledgments

First and foremost, I want to thank M. Dawson Holland for his continuous and ongoing persuasion to develop this project from what began as a few blog posts into what has ultimately become this book, and his self-driven devotion to attempt to publicly promote the book long before it was ever completed. If it were not for Dawson, this book would truly not exist.

Having undergone that which is required to complete a publication such as this, I now distinctly understand why many authors thank their spouse and/or immediate family. I have an incredible wife who is a much better writer than I, and I want to thank Lydia for tolerating the most idiotic requests for validation; which I'm certain were often along the lines of "do you think this period (.) looks okay in this font?" I should probably also thank Shadow, Ferdinand and Jonnie Awesome; as I'm pretty sure I asked each of them similar questions during the writing process expecting credible feedback from two cats and a rabbit. Then again, the bunny is pretty damn sharp.

I would like to thank the staff at International Tactical Training Seminars (ITTS), not only for the exceptional firearms training provided, but also for the subsequent insights into topics and scenarios to research which I became aware of during that training. For those seeking firearms training, I could never recommend ITTS highly enough. Scott Reitz, Brett McQueen, Ray Komoorian, Jordan Weiss, Dane Hurst and Troy Thomas among others.

Shannon Frazier at WNC Center for Personal Protection also played a large part in motivating me to finish this project. I would also highly recommend his services.

I sincerely want to thank Jim Fields, Kevin Keith, Dale Adams, Mark Lucas and Kemuel Ronis; who have all set eyes upon some draft of this book and yet somehow still decided to remain my friend.

I would like to thank Sarah Hawley for insights into all things "publishing" and Karin Tobiason for insights into all things "public relations."

Though I have never had the honor of meeting the man personally, I feel compelled to thank James Williams Sensei of the Dojo of the Four Winds. Having poured through all of his digital content (numerous times), I'm certain he has had an impact on refining my ideologies toward self-defense as they pertain to this book, as well as providing a wealth of other insights I'm not sure I could describe in just a few words here. It is probably most evident in the final paragraph of this book.

If I have quoted (or perceptively over-quoted) people favorably, possibly without their express permission as the content was in the public domain, I want to thank them as well. If I did so, it was because I thought your words were extremely important for the people of this nation to read and they were not included merely for my economic gain. I sincerely hope you understand the use of your words and the respect I intend and don't attempt to sue me. As for those I have quoted unfavorably, it was probably long overdue.

Any errors, unintended misinterpretations or omissions of fact, improper formatting, aesthetic discontent due to bland cover design and any possible inappropriate references to Michael Bloomberg's genitals are my responsibility alone. Otherwise, any discontent you have with the factual content of this book falls upon you.

For those readers finding a familiar name here: the contents of this book don't necessarily represent the ideologies or views of those referenced in this acknowledgment.

Table of Contents

Introduction

"In order to form an immaculate member of a flock of sheep one must, above all, be a sheep."- Albert Einstein [1]

Has there been a shift away from the Constitution in regards to the powers of the government and rights of the people, creating an increasing threat of government tyranny and oppression, while subsequently restricting and prohibiting the right of the people to keep and bear arms through perceptual manipulation and circumvention?

First, let me start off by saying that I am not currently, nor have I ever been, a member of the National Rifle Association. That statement is not intended to either denounce or support the NRA in any way. I just want to be clear that what I write in the following pages is not being skewed in support of the NRA and is what I find to be legitimate facts pertaining to the Second Amendment in as unbiased manner as possible. I can't seem to stop myself from presenting the occasional smart-ass comment now and then though, so if you truly feel the comment is not reflective of the facts at hand then by all means refrain from being amused and feel free to redact my sarcasm from the overall analysis as it should not change the nature of any conclusions.

I am not involved in the military or law enforcement nor do I have any type of obsessive fascination with either of those occupations. Again, I do not intend to denounce the actions of those brave men and women who defend our country collectively or its citizens individually in those capacities. Other than dictated by U.S. law, I am not a member of any militia. I would also like to say that I am not a hunter nor am I a vegetarian or vegan either. And once again, I do not intend in any way to denounce or support those who choose to hunt for food and the other resources it can provide nor those who denounce the use of that food or resource. I do not compete in firearms related sporting events and have never done so. I am not a felon, a fugitive, a drug addict, or a mental defective; though I can't deny that my wife on occasion has attempted to form such an argument regarding the latter. I am a U.S. citizen and have not renounced my citizenship, I am subject to no court-ordered restraints and I have never been a party to domestic violence, let alone convicted of it; so I have no secret agenda in writing this to somehow argue I should have rights "restored" by any conclusions this writing ultimately makes. I do not subscribe to any organized religion and since the definition of "deity" includes the preternatural where there is presumed to be a rational explanation for the unknown phenomenon, such as being nothing more than an advanced life form, and I believe that in time all truths can eventually be discovered and explained rationally, then by definition I am also neither an Atheist nor Agnostic.[2] I think it is ridiculous that I even have to address this next issue but since it has been a documented argument as to why people desire to own firearms, I begrudgingly have to concede that genetics have been favorable to me and I am modestly endowed above the statistical average so I do not suffer from Penis Envy.[3] I am neither a Democrat nor a Republican and I evaluate my positions on matters of concern on a specific issue by issue basis. Though I have had experience with firearms since I was a youth, I did not feel compelled to own a firearm until I was 43 years old. All these points of things I am not a member of, being made to show that my life does not revolve around the use of firearms and I have not been programmed to be of any specific belief regarding firearms due to being a member of any subset of our society that appears to profess an ideology as a collective whole. Therefore, most importantly what I am not, is a sheep.

The sad truth is that most people have become sheep. People no longer want to think, they want to be led. Many in our society seem to have lost the concept of critical thinking and cognitive ability for them has atrophied. They want their government, their "God", their investment broker, their therapist, their television, their computer, their peers on Facebook and sometimes now it seems even their Chihuahuas, to think for them. And why not, that's a very easy life to have in some ways isn't it, when you can blame the outcome of your life on other people's decisions and sidestep any personal responsibility for the present state of your own existence? Even when life is hard, it's just not your fault. I've never quite understood the world those people choose to live in, but then again I've never found the sight of a sheep's ass all that appealing.

There is also a more subtle version of the personal responsibility problem such as when someone sees a random and unverified news article, maybe even a viral Facebook post, and then comes to a conclusion from what they've seen with no further research. Are they presented with all the facts or even any legitimate facts at all? Often not, yet they believe they have made an informed decision and would adamantly deny they were staring at the tail end of another lamb. On many occasions these seem to be the very same people, who after having taken someone else's word for something as mere fact, will not change their belief system even after they are shown the actual facts do not support their belief. They will go on and on finding one illogical reason after another as to why their belief is still correct in spite of all the contrary evidence...and yet they never truly formed that belief on their own to begin with, it was given to them. Apparently our 40th President Ronald Reagan was notorious for holding a belief long after it had been proven wrong and even embellishing the facts to justify his belief.[4] The problem being, that belief has somehow become a part of "who they are" as a human being, and we're just not supposed to say things that make people question their own belief systems.

We seem to have become a society who, through some type of misunderstanding of the First Amendment, has decided that because someone else has the Constitutional right of Free Speech it is somehow politically incorrect to point out when that speech is bat shit crazy. The right to express your opinion is protected by the First Amendment but contrary to current ideology the invalidity of your speech has no such protection. In fact, in many cases like libel and subversive speech that right is specifically denied. It becomes a little more muddled when someone says they've personally spoken to Jesus Christ or are full of Thetans. They are well within their First Amendment rights to say so and even for them personally to hold such a belief but it is somehow politically incorrect to question the sanity of those people as if the First Amendment also protects them from being diagnosed as delusional and a potential threat to society. I mean, who knows, maybe they really are telling the truth, right? What is bizarre is that once you say you "are" Jesus Christ or the reincarnation of L. Ron Hubbard's Thetan, you are deemed to be suffering from a psychosis even though that is entirely in line with the beliefs held in the previous statement and would be confirmation that those beliefs are at least potentially sound. How is it that we can hold beliefs that appear to be virtually impossible and in defiance of all known facts and conclude that is sanity, but when someone comes along and claims to be proof of that which we believe, at that point we finally conclude they are insane?

If pointing out when a belief may not be supported by facts is insensitive and thus politically incorrect, what false beliefs start slipping through the cracks as accepted truths...doomsday prophecies, witches in Salem, Occupy Wall Street? Does the First Amendment protect against delusions in speech, does it protect against any portion of religious beliefs that might be deemed delusions, or does calling out delusions impede the free exercise of religion or abridge the freedom of speech? This is something people need to decide, and though the topic of this writing is not about the First Amendment, maybe our acceptance of certain, let me call them "quirks," in society perpetuate belief systems that make a lone gunman conclude they are justified in killing innocent school children, thus leading us to debate the validity of and continued need for the Second Amendment by subsequent necessity? If I see false information being spread and can provide the facts to dispute it and take no action towards doing so, am I any less responsible for the persistence of the misinformation or delusion through society than the person from where it originated? Have we become so lackadaisical in regards to faith vs. fact, or logic vs. emotion, that many in society no longer have the ability to judge fiction from non-fiction or sound logic from spin or pure fallacy? Are we, as a society, enabling some people's false beliefs and therefore contributing to the misinformation problem?

Misinformation appears to be a major problem in society. I'm not suggesting it is a new phenomenon by any means, but recent technology has increased the spread of it exponentially. With the speed at which false propaganda can now be spread one might argue that we need to be more diligent in verification of the information, but that does not appear to be the result. Facebook certainly has not helped the situation any. People seem to hit "share" faster than their brains can think "to think" about what they are sharing. In my opinion, misinformation is a virtual plague on our society; garbage in, garbage out so to speak. Excluding organized religion, nowhere does this seem more present than in gun rights arguments in the United States; which brings me to the reason I decided to write this.

Though somewhat out of chronological order, the topic of why I began to look at Second Amendment rights will follow. It is no secret that gun rights have been a major issue in the U.S. for the past few decades. To some degree maybe they always were. When I first started to inquire as to what the actual current interpretations of the Second Amendment were I found so much conflicting information that I couldn't make heads or tails of any of it. Somewhere along the line it seemed someone had the "baffle them with bullshit" philosophy, and much of that bullshit stuck. I found ambiguous and conflicting references to court cases, conflicting information on pro- and anti-gun rights forums and conflicting quotes from those who signed the Declaration of Independence and those considered the "Framers" of the United States Constitution. What I found is that there is an abundance of information out there that you might call "a stretch" at best and a blatant lie at worst. The latter, however, is what initially left me dumbfounded.

Time and time again I would see these quotes by Framers of the Constitution, some extremely pro and others extremely anti firearms (or militia etc.), and wonder how the same person could hold two dramatically conflicting ideologies at the same point in time...and of course they typically didn't. I had a hard time finding quotes that were legitimate and had any valid reference. Many quotes that had a valid reference had basically been put together by someone for a specific intent and had been so chopped up and pieced together with ellipses that when you finally read the whole quote it wasn't even about the issue at all. Yet these were the quotes scattered around firearm discussion sites adamantly supporting or denying the intent of the Second Amendment.

There were other quotes I started to notice that appeared to make certain arguments as well. I had to find a gunsmith to install tritium sights on my wife's handgun. When I walked into the gunsmith's shop, the first thing I saw was a 2' x 3' poster with a picture of Adolph Hitler and the quote dated 1935, "This year will go down in history. For the first time, a civilized nation has full gun registration! Our streets will be safer, our police more efficient, and the world will follow our lead into the future!" Wow, that makes a lot of implications about the need for citizens to retain their gun rights.

Maybe Hitler at one point did make some kind of similar comment, there's just no real way to know at this point. But taken as a whole and in context with the intended meaning it is total bullshit. The date doesn't make any sense in correlation to the intent of the quote as there is no documented legislation in Germany to match the year. The *Regulations on Weapons Ownership* in 1919 literally made 'all' firearms and ammunition illegal in Germany.[5] In 1928 the *Law on Firearms and Ammunition* created a system of permits to allow people to own or sell, carry, manufacture and professionally deal in firearms and ammunition, ending the complete ban of firearms and ammo. The closest regulation to 1935 was three years later when the *German Weapons Act* was passed in 1938 dramatically easing firearm laws in Germany overall.[6,7] Now you may argue that the quote specifically referenced the disarming of Jews but some restrictions were already in place for them due to a previous "trustworthiness" clause. The *Regulations Against Jews' Possession of Weapons* which actually banned all Jewish right of possession was also not until 1938.[8]

Here is what is really interesting: If Hitler were to have really made the statement verbally but just cannot be validated and the quote merely has the year wrong as 1935 instead of 1938; look at how that reverses the entire context of the quote. Everything in the quote is now understood from the context that gun rights were just restored with a registration, ending the complete ban of weapons, and that is why the streets would be safer and the police more efficient. Research this one yourself, it should be enlightening. What an argument it would have made for the right of the people to be armed and maintain militias for the purposes of insurrection against a tyrannical government if it were true though, huh?…and thus pro gun rights supporters still take the bait and spread it like wildfire.

Even as I sit here and write this, I had a friend post something on Facebook about gun rights to which I made a comment regarding statistics I have in front of me, which pertained to machine guns and their specific comment. A woman immediately came on and started misquoting past legislation saying machine guns were banned in 1934 and since there are actually very few reported machine gun homicides since that time, gun control is confirmed to work. As I continued to correct and provide references for her misstatements, in one case I actually found the very reference she was copying and pasting where she had intentionally removed the 2 lines that would have killed her own argument and verified mine, she resorted more and more to passive aggressive responses and suggested that I must have no life since I had more time to do research than she did, with an overall tone that I was somehow an asshole because she couldn't accept that her facts were clearly being discredited and were not in line with what she "wanted" the facts to be.

It is because of an abundance of people who argue "what they wish the facts were" instead of "what the facts appear to be" that I finally decided to undertake this task. I started this project as unbiased and open minded as I possibly could and honestly wanted to learn, once and for all, what was truth and what was fiction in what I had previously been reading. By the end of my research, I have to admit that I noticed some definite trends.

So why did I become interested in aspects of the Second Amendment as they were intended, and as they stand today? A little over a decade ago I decided to make a career change. I had always been fairly good at un-spinning media stories and seeing trends and patterns. To make a long story short, as pretty much everyone is aware of the stock and housing bubbles which were created due to the investment mindset of people at the time, I decided to educate myself in all things investment related. I went back to college and took a number of classes on Economics and International Trade, and began to consume anything I could get my hands on related to such a mindset. This included a range of Psychology books, Statistics and Probability Theory, Military Strategy, History, Game Theory, Sociology, Logic, Venture Capital, Business Law (etc.)...anything and everything that could help decipher trends in global investments. Needless to say, I acquired at least a general background in a lot of related areas. It was the peripheral information to investing where I seemed to learn the most about the actions governments and members of society take at certain points during the economic life cycle of a nation.

Other than a recent hiatus, my company had a contract providing foreign exchange services for another firm for roughly 5 years. I was constantly in front of the news and I started noticing, what at least from my own perception, appeared to be some specific patterns both from a shift in political ideology toward accepted extremism and what appeared to be legislation that was questionably unconstitutional. At first my concerns were only economic in nature, noticing a trend towards witch hunt mentality such as after the bursting of the housing bubble where nobody wanted to take responsibility for their own actions and legislation was acknowledging that argument and being built around that mentality.

I had mentioned to a CNBC journalist in roughly 2006 that social unrest would become the new 'bubble.' As it appears I was correct and social unrest is having more of a direct impact on societal trends, my focus started to shift slightly. Having read how many of these particular trends in society end horribly time and time again throughout history, I began to take serious notice. It appeared to me at the time that the Second Amendment right applied to the importance of personal self-defense such as a direct personal attack or when the local community riots and loots its own neighborhood, to foreign invaders when the military is not sufficient, and also to the military itself when it has been misappropriated against the people it was intended to defend. Though it may be argued that insurrection was not the sole intent of the Second Amendment, we were clearly coming off of an event that shaped our nation that would suggest it was securing the means to choose that approach if the Republic had failed the people and that solution became necessary.

With this initial mindset, I began to feel it was not only prudent for self-defense but also a responsibility as a citizen of the United States to acknowledge my Second Amendment rights and not only acquire a few firearms but also take the training necessary to use them properly in case things should happen to go horribly astray. I began to wonder if the facts revolving around the Second Amendment really provide us any or all of the rights mentioned above. It was at this point that I started noticing the conflicts of information in Second Amendment arguments I mentioned earlier, needless to say exacerbated by emotional charge after a couple of recent mass killings, and decided to do the research myself to see what I could find.

The more I dove into the research, the more I realized looking at recent court cases and legislation did nothing but confuse the problem further as everything referenced or denied something that came before it, and many pieces of legislation just didn't make any initial sense until taken in context with a specific event that had happened at the time which led to its sudden creation. One of the biggest mistakes I found in other Second Amendment books is that the authors did not read the entire Court decisions and merely read the summaries or previous interpretations of the summaries. Since many of the earlier cases weren't truly about the Second Amendment, you need to read the entire decision to understand the Court's perception of the Second Amendment right itself.

It finally became clear that the entry point into the discussion of present day Second Amendment rights is located in 17th century England. Any full evaluation of the Second Amendment today would need to begin during the monarchical rule of the Stuarts in England, most specifically with events leading to the overthrow of King James II. By the same token, no evaluation would be fully complete unless ending with some indications of the ideology of the current administration of the President of the United States, Barack Hussein Obama II (no implications intended regarding the similar suffix of both men) and the current administration.

Hopefully looking at the evolution of interpretations of the Second Amendment in chronological order, and in some cases interpretations of the Constitution itself, will be enlightening to our cause. There seems to be little dispute that the Bill of Rights attached to the United States Constitution was inspired by the English Bill of Rights of 1689. We'll start by looking at what led to the English Bill of Rights initially and the parallels between it and the U.S. Bill of Rights. We'll also look at references to the Laws of England by the Framers of our Constitution which may have had some impact on how they adopted some of the English Laws while avoiding some implementations of it, when creating the U.S. Constitution and the Bill of Rights which was subsequently attached. There is sufficient correspondence from the time to look at the ideologies of the Framers of the Constitution, in their own words, and see the topics where there was some debate and those where there was general consensus in areas such as standing armies, militias, federal and state powers, the concept of insurrection and the right of the people generally to possess arms. We'll take a look at court decisions that have had some impact on Second Amendment rights, how they were interpreted and discuss what relevance they really have. There are a number of pieces of legislation that have been passed over the years, many in regards to specific events that took place, and we'll see if the legislation was in line with the Second Amendment ideologies of the Framers, interpretations in standing court precedent at the time, or possibly just blatant attempts to restrict firearms from society. There are a number of military conflicts that have changed the course of Second Amendment rights as well; we'll insert those in their proper chronological order. By the end we should have a good understanding of the Second Amendment and the main issues being debated.

After we have an understanding of the history, we'll cover the concept of Insurrection. We'll then focus more specifically on the current gun debate itself. We'll address whether "God" (or Jesus, Allah, Muhammad, Shiva, Zeus, Buddha, Jim Jones, Aleister Crowley ...you get the point) has a place in the Second Amendment debate. I won't dive into a mass of general statistics because there are sufficient books which address those up until relatively recently and there are references to some of those statistics throughout much of this writing. The point I really want to drive home is that you truly need to look at the source of the data yourself and determine what the data set actually represents. You cannot rely on third party evaluations of that data to make accurate conclusions in such a politically polarized debate. Therefore, what we will discuss are ways in which statistics and semantics are often manipulated and framed in a way as to intentionally deceive the people in the Second Amendment debate.

We'll look at other things which might manipulate the public perception as well, and see if those perceptions are in line with historical and, if verifiable, statistical fact. Then we'll take a look further into how some of the legislation has been applied and possibly misapplied over time. We'll see if the legislation is applied due to either rational argument or fallacious logic and semantics tricks used to insight an emotional response...such as arguments regarding "assault weapons" and "hunting and sporting" purposes. We'll try to discover if the media has any effect on the perceptions of legislators and the general public, maybe even on distorting statistics themselves. We'll look for any situations where laws have been "stacked" to effectively remove gun rights from groups of people. We'll see if there is a level of ignorance among citizens and legislators regarding the weapons themselves that create false assumptions. We'll check out some parallel logic for similar situations and see if the same logic would hold true regarding the gun debate.

I'll give you what I believe is a logical conclusion and summary of the facts. This is one man's research and one man's conclusion, and I hope it is a sound one. However, anyone can misinterpret data, anyone can be subject to unknowingly seeing things with a bias, and anyone can miss a vital piece of information in their diagnosis. What I would ask is that you think logically about anything addressed in this writing and its conclusion while setting personal emotions aside, and if my logic does not seem sound based on anything I have presented or facts you can find and verify on your own, then by all means make a logical rebuttal for the benefit of us all. I will be the first to change my beliefs if the facts in the situation dictate they must.

Though I have somewhat facetiously titled this book as a treatise, I will stick to documentable references as much as possible. There is an element to this writing that will remain somewhat informal as I want it not only to be informative but also a pleasurable experience which is not so clinical that you feel like you've just had a pap smear or prostate exam.

𝔓art I

Historical Progression of the Second Amendment Ideology

Chapter I

Protestant Subjects Only

"Those who cannot remember the past are condemned to repeat it."
- George Santayana [1]

Though the ideology it describes has likely existed for centuries, the quote by George Santayana leading into this chapter has been referenced and reworded for the past hundred years. It could also be suggested that those who are intentionally misinformed about the past are being manipulated to repeat it. Having found a lot of misinformation being spread regarding the Second Amendment and the current debate on gun control, I felt it necessary to do some historical research. I've found a number of events in history which have specifically changed the course of gun rights over time. Some of those events are directly related to the right to bear arms, such as Supreme Court cases and specific legislation regarding gun rights. Others are more indirectly related, which ultimately create shifts in perception by either the government or the people themselves, which subsequently led to changes in legislation. I have to concede that there is really not much new information being presented here. Versions of many of these events have previously been referenced in relation to Second Amendment rights, and in fact some previously occurring events are even directly cited in subsequent events. In many cases though, these same events have been presented with severely different conclusions. In some cases it is clear that the past event is being filtered through a perception of recent legislation as opposed to whether recent legislation actually follows the intent created in the past event...putting the cart before the horse, so to speak. However, I have not found an accounting of Second Amendment rights in a full chronological representation of the changing ideologies in both government and the people over time to completely address the progressive nature of those changes in sentiment and law. Also, what I read in the legislation and what I see resulting from an event may be different than past evaluations, and I'll attempt to explain my reasoning. Where wars are brought up, or possibly not brought up at all, please do not assume the length of the discussion under the topic is meant as any implication of its historical importance to society overall as I only intend to cover aspects that appear to have had an impact on gun rights philosophy or legislation in some manner. As such, the English Bill of Rights, though being from England, may be a lengthier discussion than WWII in regards to our specific topic at hand. If there is an overall evaluation regarding one of the events that will be better served in remaining sections of this book, I will save the evaluation for that time; if those evaluations are best described while accounting the event itself and merely prefatory to other events or topics in other sections of this book, then I will address them here. Since arguments are often made that the right to bear arms is specific to the militia, legislation regarding changes in the militia and its use will be included here as well. In some cases militia regulation may appear to directly pertain to the right to bear arms itself, at other times it may appear to suggest the reason to desire the right, but both are pertinent to the discussion. When legislation is presented, I will show the legislation as it was adopted. If there are subsequent amendments to the law that would later effect our discussion, I'll try to attempt to present them the best I can. Since new legislation is often intermixed into previous legislation and becomes quite convoluted, I will not reference any subsequent amendments that do not alter the points at hand. Though there is a long history of an armed populace prior, the relevant past regarding the Second Amendment in the United States appears to begin with events leading up to the passing of the English Bill of Rights of 1689, so that is where we will begin.

The English Bill of Rights of 1689

Though the term "militia" did not arise until the end of the 16th century, the concept that it was the duty of every able-bodied free man to defend his society and provide his own weapons to fulfill that obligation had existed for roughly a millennium.[2] This was not only seen as a civil liberty, but as a means of suppressing a monarchical ruler, as the concept of divine right of rule was on the rise. Much of the conflict leading to the English Bill of Rights of 1689 actually revolved around religious beliefs under monarchical power, but played itself out through restrictions on arms and a monarchical authority over the militia. Under Charles II, the Stuarts had begun to restrict the right of the people to have arms through legislation but did not enforce it heavily so backlash was initially moderate. Much of this was through registration of sales and possession, forest and game laws placing restrictions on illegal hunting, and eventually leading to warrantless searches and seizures by the militia for the enforcement of those restrictions.[3]   Under the Militia Act of 1662, the militia had been given broad powers to disarm otherwise law abiding citizens and placed the control of the militia exclusively under the King, and not that of Parliament.   Can you imagine if one man, such as the President, had exclusive control over state militias like that in the United States? The Game Act of 1671 restricted anyone without a specific amount of income from land from possessing firearms and many other tools for hunting. This effectively removed the right to own firearms from roughly 95 percent of the population, leaving the right to virtually only the nobility, and provided for Gamekeepers who could obtain warrants to search any home suspected of harboring weapons and seize any firearms they found.[4]   James II, a Roman Catholic, was seen as religiously tolerant by the Protestant majority of the people. In the few short years of rule by James II, the kingdom was perceived as having effectively restricted Protestants from the right to have arms through strict enforcement of both the previously existing Militia Act of 1662 and the Game Act of 1671.   The heir apparent of the throne was Mary II who was the daughter of James II, but more importantly a Protestant. Mary II was married to William of Orange. James II then gave birth to a son, James Francis Edward Stuart, and Protestants saw this new heir apparent as a sign of extended Roman Catholic rule, bringing the situation to a climax.[5]   James II was overthrown (actually declared to be an abdication of the thrown) in the Glorious Revolution with the help of William of Orange and would prove to be the last Roman Catholic monarch to reign over England. Don't worry; the Roman Catholic Church seems to be doing just fine.

The English Bill of Rights of 1689 was implemented after James II of England was overthrown in the Glorious Revolution, and was a restatement in statutory form of the "declaration of right" presented by the Convention Parliament to William and Mary in March 1689, inviting them to become joint sovereigns of England under the specific terms of this agreement.[6] A few of the provisions of the act include:

- "That the subjects which are protestants, may have arms for their defense suitable to their conditions, and as allowed by law,"

- no standing army may be maintained during a time of peace without the consent of parliament,

- freedom to petition the monarch without fear of retribution,

- "the freedom of speech, and debates or proceedings in parliament, ought not to be impeached or questioned in any court or place out of Parliament,"

- no excessive bail or "cruel and unusual" punishments may be imposed.

Any of these sound familiar to you? However, In distinct contrast to what we find in the U.S. Bill of Rights, the English Bill of Rights eventually barred Roman Catholics from the throne of England as "it hath been found by experience that it is inconsistent with the safety and welfare of this Protestant kingdom to be governed by a papist prince", as stated in a prelude to the Act of Settlement of 1701 to follow 12 years later.[7] Maybe the Framers of the U.S. Constitution saw rights based on religious preference such as historically evidenced in England to be a problem and is why the First Amendment's prohibition on a government religion precedes the right to bear arms in the

Bill of Rights of the United States Constitution? I know, I know..."In God We Trust" on our 21st century U.S. currency proves that ideology didn't exist when the Bill was drafted at the end of the 18th century.

It is important to point out something about the arms clause in the English Bill of Rights; there is no mention of a militia and no actual reference to a collective right, only an individual right. This was actually debated by the members of Convention Parliament. The first draft of the clause reads, "It is necessary for the publick Safety, that the Subjects which are Protestants, should provide and keep Arms for their common Defence. And that the Arms which have been seized, and taken from them, be restored."[8] Subsequent versions dropped both the public safety phrase, and then the common defense phrase to the final drafting listed above. At the time of the Convention Parliament, the concern regarding the militia was less about that of the collective defense and more about the extremely broad powers given to the militia under the Militia Act of 1662 to effectively disarm law abiding citizens, so protecting the militia in order to protect the right to have arms would have created a paradox. Attempts were made to present this clause as both an individual right and a collective right, but it is very important to understand here that though the collective right was ultimately dropped in the final draft, the individual right is clearly stated. It should also be noted that the Game Act of 1671 was subsequently amended in 1692, and more distinctly in 1706, removing guns from the "tools" of hunting definitions and thus from hunting restrictions.[9,10] By the time we reach the late 1700's the circumvention of the right to bear arms in England through hunting restrictions had been resolved, though not (yet) forgotten.

We should take a moment to explain some concepts on rights and individual and collective rights specifically. The Declaration of Independence states that all men are endowed with "unalienable" rights.[11] An unalienable (or inalienable) right is incapable of being alienated, surrendered, or transferred.[12] It is a natural right which is a right conferred upon man by natural law.[13] A Legal right is a claim recognized and delimited by law for the purpose of securing it.[14] An individual right is one held by a person individually, a collective right is one of a group of people in their entirety, either could be a natural right or a legal right. An individual legal right might be a right to vote in an election, however individually you do not have the power to elect a President. A legal collective right might therefore be that of a majority of society electing a President through all members expressing their individual right to vote in a democracy. In this example, an individual right is prefatory and necessary for the collective right; a majority cannot elect a president if individuals are not allowed to vote. One right might be prefatory to another, the right may be held both individually and collectively in sovereignty or they may not coexist in any capacity. While I may have a natural individual right to urinate in private, there is no natural collective right which allows a group of people to pee in public. The right to bear arms becomes an issue from two perspectives: One, is the right to bear arms a natural right or merely a legal right; and two, is the right to bear arms an individual right, a collective right, or both? At one extreme, a natural and individual right to bear arms cannot be taken away from that individual. At the other, a legal and strictly collective right to bear arms could be removed from law and thus the right removed from every member of society without recourse. This is really the essence of the debate at hand.

Sir William Blackstone's *The Commentaries on the Laws of England* was a popular treatise on English law during the late 18th century.[15] There is a lot of debate on how much the Framers actually followed Blackstone's interpretations during debates surrounding our Constitution and Bill of Rights, but his Commentaries are the second most referenced writing in the transcripts of the debates.[16] I'm not going to suggest the Framers built our Constitution or Bill of Rights directly around Blackstone's interpretations of English Law, as it is not necessary for our purposes since it is already quite evident the Framers took the lead from the English Bill of Rights of 1689. However it is important to note that they were distinctly aware of Blackstone's interpretations. Blackstone's comments are often said to have been quite lenient on the throne in regards to civil liberties, and maybe his interpretations were not entirely accurate in a true civil liberties capacity, but the Framers did seem to embody a desire for civil liberties that were consistent, at least, with Blackstone's interpretation of them in England. It is a couple of Blackstone's interpretations of the laws of England themselves that are relevant in regards to understanding people's perception of the right to bear arms under English Law during the late 18th century. Blackstone writes:

> The fifth and last auxiliary right of the subject, that I shall at present mention, is that of having arms for their defence, suitable to their condition and degree, and such as are allowed by law. Which is also declared by the same statute I W. & M. st.2. c.2. and is indeed a public allowance, under due restrictions, of the natural right of resistance and self-preservation, when the sanctions of society and laws are found insufficient to restrain the violence of oppression.[17]

He clearly says here that resistance and self-preservation is a natural right and thus an individual right conferred upon each man, just as Convention Parliament had debated and resolved it to be. There are historians that argue that Blackstone only means a collective right which is not absolute here, but the history shows that evaluation would be entirely contrary to the debates during the English Bill of Rights drafting and contrary to his use of "natural right." Does he imply a public allowance for the use of that natural right in a societal context, thus a collective right, to restrain the violence of oppression? Possibly, but that is not as clear. We cannot assume that because he merely uses the words public and society in his analysis, he means a public or societal collective right as opposed to the rights of the members of the public and society to have the individual right. I have a public allowance, under due restrictions, to kiss my wife in public...it does not mean the public has a collective right to kiss my wife as well. Maybe other quotes from Blackstone will clarify his intent:

> In these several articles consist the rights, or, as they are frequently termed, the liberties of Englishmen: liberties more generally talked of, than thoroughly understood; and yet highly necessary to be perfectly known and considered by every man of rank or property, left his ignorance of the points whereon it is founded should hurry him into faction and licentiousness on the one hand, or a pusillanimous indifference and criminal submission on the other. And we have seen that these rights consist, primarily, in the free enjoyment of personal security, of personal liberty, and of private property. So long as these remain inviolate, the subject is perfectly free; for every species of compulsive tyranny and oppression must act in opposition to one or other of these rights,

having no other object upon which it can possibly be employed. To preserve these from violation, it is necessary that the constitution of parliaments be supported in it's full vigor; and limits certainly known, be set to the royal prerogative. And, lastly, to vindicate these rights, when actually violated or attacked, the subjects of England are entitled, in the first place, to the regular administration and free course of justice in the courts of law; next to the right of petitioning the king and parliament for redress of grievances; and lastly to the right of having and using arms for self-preservation and defence. And all these rights and liberties it is our birthright to enjoy entire; unless where the laws of our country have laid them under necessary restraints.[18]

Well, we have a birthright in the free enjoyment of personal security against tyranny and oppression, confirming a natural and individual right, but by whom and against whom may that birthright be defended is still left relatively vague. Blackstone clearly states the need for laws to protect liberties while also a right of using arms for self-preservation and defense, but does every law necessarily supersede the right to use arms for self preservation and defense of liberties against the government (in Blackstone's case that being either the monarchy or the legislature) specifically? Here, Blackstone gives further clarification:

Political therefore, or civil, liberty, which is that of a member of society, is no other than natural liberty so far restrained by human laws (and no farther) as is necessary and expedient for the general advantage of the publick. Hence we may collect that the law, which restrains a man from doing mischief to his fellow citizens, though it diminishes the natural, increases the civil liberty of mankind: but every wanton and causeless restraint of the will of the subject, whether practiced by a monarch, a nobility, or a popular assembly, is a degree of tyranny.[19]

This holds that civil liberties are that of a member of society, built around the natural rights of an individual, only being restricted to such degree as it keeps one man from doing mischief to a fellow citizen for the overall public good, and any further suppression of natural rights of the members of society by a monarchy or legislature is tyranny. That clearly seems to state a collective right of society to preserve their natural liberties.

Okay, I think we have a more complete understanding of Blackstone's views in regards to individual and collective rights at the time. Blackstone does concede at one point "that the prevention of popular insurrections and resistance to government by disarming the bulk of the people, is a reason oftener meant than avowed by the makers of the forest and game laws."[20] So while Blackstone contends that the purpose of the natural right to bear arms is to restrain the violence of tyranny and oppression, he clearly states that the previously noted hunting restrictions were designed to circumvent that very right should the source of the tyranny and oppression be the government. The circumvention of arms rights due to hunting restrictions was also confirmed by George St. Tucker in annotating Blackstone's *Commentaries on the Laws of England* in 1803.[21] Tucker's annotations are often regarded as being the first publication of interpretation of the Second Amendment, with his notation, "The right of the people to keep and bear arms shall not be infringed. Amendments to C. U. S. Art. 4, and this without any qualification as to their condition or degree, as is the case in the British government" and stating further to our present point, "whoever exams the forest, and game laws in the British code, will readily perceive that the right of keeping arms is effectually taken away from the people of England."[22-24]   The restrictions were further referenced in 1809 by Willam Rawle in *A View of the Constitution of the United States of America,* 'In England, a country which boasts so much of its freedom, the right was secured to protestant subjects only, on the revolution of 1688; and it is cautiously described to be that of bearing arms for their defence, 'suitable to their conditions, and as allowed by law.' An arbitrary code for the preservation of game in that country has long disgraced them."[25]

We've seen acknowledgment of the risks to liberty through circumventions of the right to bear arms, through such measures as historical hunting restrictions, but what was the overall mindset of the citizens of England, including those in English colonies fighting for independence, in the late 1700's? Is there any evidence others felt as Blackstone did? This may best be addressed by comments in 1780 by the Recorder of London, the chief legal adviser to the mayor and council:

> The right of his majesty's Protestant subjects, to have arms for their own defence, and to use them for lawful purposes, is most clear and undeniable. It seems, indeed, to be considered, by the ancient laws of this kingdom, not only as a right, but as a duty; for all the subjects of the realm, who are able to bear arms, are bound to be ready, at all times, to assist the sheriff, and other civil magistrates, in the execution of the laws and the preservation of the public peace. And that right, which every Protestant most unquestionably possesses, individually, may, and in many cases must, be exercised collectively, is likewise

a point which I conceive to be most clearly established by the authority of judicial decisions and ancient acts of parliament, as well as by reason and common sense.[26]

We appear to have some consensus which suggests that both individual and collective rights were seen as being intended in the right to bear arms as demanded of William and Mary in the English Bill of Rights …at least as perceived by the people in the late 18th century. As long as you're Protestant, of course.

In summary: We have a religious conflict in England between the standing Roman Catholic King and the Protestant social majority; being fought through the restriction of a right to bear arms diminishing the ability of Protestants to rebel; being enforced by a monarchical control of the militia given great latitude in disarming civilians; a subsequent shift in religious power in England to the Protestants; a return of civil liberties which includes the right to bear arms to Protestant subjects only now restricting Catholics from having arms with no mention of the militia in doing so; and then finally the removal of the gun inclusions in game laws for real restoration of the right to possess arms. The issue here was that the Protestant majority of the people had civil liberties taken away so they could not instigate an act of insurrection against the monarch who ruled by a belief in Catholicism not supported by that majority. Neither side in this wanted to overthrow 'monarchical rule' itself or even the ruling family; it was to preserve the monarchical power under a specific religion by removing the threat of insurrection. Remember, Mary II is still a Stuart… just not a Catholic.

The restrictions on the right to bear arms had been held to be a wanton and causeless restraint imposed by Catholic monarchical power. Once Protestants were returned to the throne, gun rights were effectively returned to Protestants within a few years. Since the Protestants turned around and applied the same restrictions on the Catholics, this is certainly not an "equality" of civil rights issue or Catholics would have subsequently been allowed to have arms. This would suggest the issue at hand regarding the English Bill of Rights was clearly about the power of insurrection, which appears to have been seen as both an individual and collective right of the people in times of oppression. If you were Protestant in 1780s England, you probably did think you were the freest people on earth. If you were Catholic, maybe you weren't feeling the freedom quite so much.

Did the Framers see the benefit of the English Bill of Rights while trying to avoid making these mistakes: Creating a religious government leading directly to oppression of a group of its subjects and thus no overall "equality" of civil rights among the people; leaving unalienable rights open to subjective interpretation by future government, such as circumventing the natural right to possess arms; and giving the power over the militia to one man, while still preserving the militia concept itself? We'll try to determine if there is any evidence in the late 1780s of the Framers having perceived the right as Blackstone did in 1765 and the Recorder of London did in 1780; both an individual right and a collective right of the people.

Chapter II

Governments Can't Be Trusted...
Let's Start One

"To preserve liberty, it is essential that the whole body of people always possess arms, and be taught alike especially when young, how to use them." - Richard Henry Lee [1]

Debate between Federalists / Anti-Federalists

"In 1787 I'm told our founding fathers did agree, to write a list of principles for keepin' people free."[2] Sorry, I just couldn't resist a *Schoolhouse Rock!* reference. The United States of America had already declared its independence as free states no longer under British rule and subsequently confirmed that independence having been victorious in the American Revolutionary War ending in 1783. The fighting is over and our free nation lives happily ever after, right? No, not exactly.   After the war, there developed two political parties with dissimilar ideologies.   The Federalists were those who wanted to amend and strengthen the government as previously formed under the Articles of Confederation.

The Federalists then dubbed anyone who did not support them, Anti-Federalists. Anti-Federalists comprised people of many concerns: some feeling the stronger government threatened the sovereignty of the states, effectively creating more of a Central Government than a Federal Government; some feeling the new government would be so strong as to effectively be a new monarchic power; and others who seem to feel that any government at all threatened their personal liberties.

Those of the Constitutional Congress, eventually referred to as the Framers of our Constitution, were comprised of representatives of both new political parties. Many were not only involved in the debates directly, but also through subsequent writings to support ratification of the Constitution. Among the Federalists were Alexander Hamilton, James Madison and John Jay. These three would later be known for the Federalist Papers written to support the strong government provided for in the Constitution and push for its ratification by the states. George Washington and John Hancock were other notable Federalists. Anti-Federalists were comprised of such names as Patrick Henry, Samuel Adams, Robert Lee and James Warren. As a note, we should mention that Thomas Jefferson was stationed as Ambassador to France during the debate over federalism. Though Jefferson expressed many anti-federalist thoughts over the years, indications are that he supported the Constitution so long as a Bill of Rights was added.[3] Among these two political parties there were points of agreement and points of dissension regarding such concepts as state representation, standing armies, strength of militia, a right to bear arms and civil liberties in general.

One of the first problems addressed was state representation. The smaller states favored the New Jersey Plan, which called for a one-house legislature with representatives selected by the state legislatures and each state casting one vote. The larger states favored the Virginia Plan with three branches of government and a bicameral (two house) legislature with representatives being based on a state's population or money contributions. In what has been called "The Great Compromise" they decided on a bicameral legislature, where the House of Representatives would have members apportioned among the states by population and elected by the people, and a Senate with an equal number of representatives from each state who are chosen by the state legislatures. In spite of this compromise, many states still held a fear of a large federal government restricting state's rights.

Another issue the Framers had to debate was the common defense. To some degree, the common defense was addressed in Article I, Section 8 of the Constitution itself. The Constitution gives Congress the power to: Declare war; Raise and support Armies; Provide and maintain a Navy; make rules for the government and regulation of the land and naval forces; to provide for calling forth the militia to execute the laws of the union, suppress Insurrections and repel invasions; and to provide for organizing, arming, and disciplining the Militia, and for governing such part of them as may be employed in the service to the United States. The President is made Commander in Chief of the Army and Navy, and of the militia of the several states when called into the actual service of the United States.[4] This became a problem in attempting to ratify the Constitution, as many states saw an inherent risk of creating a standing army designed into the document.

In Convention during the drafting of the Constitution, while professing the value of both a common government and a militia, James Madison made this reference to standing armies:

> As the greatest danger is that of disunion of the States, it is necessary to guard [against] it by sufficient powers to the Common Government and as the greatest danger to liberty is from large standing armies, it is best to prevent them, by an effectual provision for a good Militia."[5]

Thomas Jefferson expressed his concerns directly to Madison in a letter dated December 20, 1787:

> I will now tell you what I do not like. First, the omission of a bill of rights, providing clearly and without the aid of sophism for freedom of religion, freedom of the press, protection against standing armies, restriction of monopolies, the eternal and unremitting force of the habeas corpus laws, and trials by jury in all matters of fact triable by the laws of the land and not by the laws of nations.[6]

To temper the length of the discussion slightly, let us concede from here that there was a general mistrust of standing armies at the time and thus focus on comments from a few Federalists clearly attempting to tame those fears in order to achieve full ratification of the Constitution by the states. One of those Federalists is again James Madison. In Federalist Number 46, Madison addresses the fear of a standing army by pointing out the overwhelming strength of the armed militia. Note here that Madison clearly segregates the militia as being independent of the regular army clearly discounting any arguments made that suggest the Framers intended the army and the militia to be one and the same. Madison also points out how those state militias would in fact be a defense against the threats of tyranny from a federal standing army, discounting any future arguments made that suggest the Framers did not consider the militia to be a tool of insurrection against evident government tyranny, as Madison here expressly argues that intent:

> Let a regular army, fully equal to the resources of the country, be formed; and let it be entirely at the devotion of the federal government; still it would not be going too far to say, that the State governments, with the people on their side, would be able to repel the danger. The highest number to which, according to the best computation, a standing army can be carried in any country, does not exceed one hundredth part of the whole number of souls; or one twenty-fifth part of the number able to bear arms. This proportion would not yield, in the United States, an army of more than twenty-five or thirty thousand men. To these would be opposed a militia amounting to near half a million of citizens with arms in their hands, officered by men chosen from among themselves, fighting for their common liberties, and united and conducted by governments possessing their affections and confidence. It may well be doubted, whether a militia thus circumstanced could ever be conquered by such a proportion of regular troops.[7]

In Federalist Number 29 Alexander Hamilton addresses the fear of a standing army and also professes the strength of the militia as being a security against one:

> But though the scheme of disciplining the whole nation must be abandoned as mischievous or impracticable; yet it is a matter of the utmost

importance that a well-digested plan should, as soon as possible, be adopted for the proper establishment of the militia. The attention of the government ought particularly to be directed to the formation of a select corps of moderate extent, upon such principles as will really fit them for service in case of need. By thus circumscribing the plan, it will be possible to have an excellent body of well-trained militia, ready to take the field whenever the defense of the State shall require it. This will not only lessen the call for military establishments, but if circumstances should at any time oblige the government to form an army of any magnitude that army can never be formidable to the liberties of the people while there is a large body of citizens, little, if at all, inferior to them in discipline and the use of arms, who stand ready to defend their own rights and those of their fellow-citizens. This appears to me the only substitute that can be devised for a standing army, and the best possible security against it, if it should exist.[8]

Noah Webster (yes, the man whose name is on your dictionary) was also a Federalist and in support of the Constitution. He is often labeled as the forgotten founding father.[9] In his pamphlet titled "An Examination into the Leading Principles of the Federal Constitution Proposed by the Late Convention Held at Philadelphia" Webster says:

Before a standing army can rule, the people must be disarmed; as they are in almost every kingdom of Europe. The supreme power in America cannot enforce unjust laws by the sword; because the whole body of the people are armed, and constitute a force superior to any bands of regular troops that can be, on any pretense, raised in the United States.[10]

Here we clearly have three Federalists at the time, in support of the provisions of maintaining a Navy and raising an Army provided in the Constitution, attempting to squelch the fears of creating a standing army, while confirming the risks inherent in a standing army. All point out the strength of an armed militia and the ideology that a standing army could never defeat a militia of the people. Is there any doubt here that this is what the Federalists are selling to the states in opposition to any potential standing army and the subsequent fear of a tyrannical government; the power of an armed militia of the people? We have Jefferson proposing a Bill of Rights to restrain the threat of a standing army, among other threats to personal liberties. What we do not yet have is a real understanding of what constitutes a militia and under what circumstances the people may be armed.

"I ask, sir, what is the militia? They consist now of the whole people, except a few public officers" as stated by George Mason during debates in Virginia Convention on Ratification of the Constitution.[11] Well, that seems to align with the ideologies of Jefferson, Madison, Hamilton and Webster that the militia is all of the people. They all speak of an armed militia as though it is one of those unalienable rights addressed in the Declaration of Independence, never questioning the right as though it cannot be taken away. They all speak of the militia as being entirely different than Congress' raised army. The Constitution itself distinctly segregates the rights of Congress to call up the militia from the right to raise and support an army. There is no semantic confusion suggesting that they meant that the militia was the army, they call the army the army and call the militia the militia. There is no debate about whether a militia should exist, the debate is about a federal army and the answer is unequivocally that the armed militia of the people would have the ability to overpower any standing army possibly established in the Constitution. They clearly state the militia would be the strongest defense against a standing army used for government tyranny, clearly addressing the right of the people to seek relief through insurrection under such circumstances. The question then becomes; Can you ever remove the right to bear arms from the citizens of the United States without also effectively removing the safeguard against tyranny the militia is intended to preserve in the eyes of the Framers of the Constitution and the Bill of Rights?

Many over the years have argued that the right to bear arms was strictly for militia purposes. Some will attempt to use this concept to restrict the right to bear arms to include military style weapons only, including the U.S. government, and we'll look at how that plays out later. Of course they then argue that the militia now means either the Army or National Guard and if you aren't in one of those organizations, you have no right to bear arms. Even Alexander Hamilton, though he was pointing out the futility in attempting to train the entire body of people composing the militia, does conclude; "Little more can reasonably be aimed at, with respect to the people at large, than to have them properly armed and equipped."[12] We've just seen how both of those two assumptions above are false, the Framers clearly supported an armed militia independent of the federal Army comprised of all the people.

Let's look at the right to keep and bear arms more specifically though. What about the beginning statement in the first argument on its own, is the right to bear arms only for militia purposes? At this point, it appears to be mostly an irrelevant argument. If the Framers believed a militia of all the people was a natural human right which cannot be taken away as they imply, taking away the arms of those people would immediately take away the ability to organize a militia. If you cannot remove the right of the people to organize an armed militia it seems to logically follow that you can never remove the arms without removing the militia right.

Just in case, sans the militia, let's see if there is any evidence that the Framers of the Constitution and Bill of Rights felt that the right to keep and bear arms was, in and of itself, also an unalienable right that cannot be taken away. Jefferson, in the first draft of his proposal for the Virginia Constitution in 1776 writes; "No Free man shall ever be debarred the use of arms."[13] In 1788, Richard Henry Lee, one of the initiators of the Declaration of Independence, and member of the first Senate which passed the Bill of Rights gave us the quote leading us into this chapter, "To preserve liberty, it is essential that the whole body of people always possess arms, and be taught alike especially when young, how to use them."[14] At Virginia's U.S. Constitution ratification convention in 1788, Patrick Henry asks; "[W]here and when did freedom exist when the power of the sword and purse were given up from the people? Unless a miracle in human affairs interposed, no nation ever retained its liberty after the loss of the sword and purse."[15] Henry argues that freedom itself is dependent upon the people bearing arms. In February 6, 1788 during Massachusetts convention Samuel Adams states "and that the said Constitution shall never be construed to authorize Congress to infringe the just liberty of the press or the rights of conscience; or to prevent the people of The United States who are peaceable citizens from keeping their own arms."[16] That seems to be an argument for the right to arms independent of the militia. In fact, this led to the Massachusetts convention creating what ultimately became the language of the initial proposal for the Second Amendment during the first session of Congress on June 8,

1789. Though Adams mentions Congress in his statement, notice that the word "Congress" is not present in the language proposed:

> The right of the people to keep and bear arms shall not be infringed; a well armed and well regulated militia being the best security of a free country; but no person religiously scrupulous of bearing arms shall be compelled to render military service in person.[17]

Fisher Ames served in the Massachusetts House of Representatives in 1788 and was a member of the Massachusetts convention that ratified the Constitution. He became a member of the First United States Congress where the Second Amendment was born in 1789.[18] In response to the amendments proposed by Madison, Ames wrote, "The rights of conscience, of bearing arms, of changing the government, are declared to be inherent in the people." This is a member of the first Congress while debating language for the Second Amendment stating the intent of Madison's proposal is that the right of bearing arms is inherent in the people.[19]

There is clearly an understanding that the right of bearing arms is an unalienable right. However, there were other proposals after the initial draft of the Second Amendment we should look at. Robert Whitehill, a delegate from Pennsylvania, attempted to offer at least two hunting related inclusions, "That the people have a right to bear arms for the defense of themselves and their own state, or the United States, or for the purposes of killing game…"and "The inhabitants of the several states shall have liberty to fowl and hunt in seasonable times…" Neither reference to hunting rights was ever subsequently debated regarding the drafting of the Second Amendment.[20] Does this mean we do not have a right to hunt, or was hunting already subordinate and implied in the right to bear arms? I'm not sure I have the answer for that specifically, but what we can conclude is that hunting is irrelevant to the Second Amendment right as evidenced by their choosing to ignore Whitehall's submissions for debate. On August 17th another version was read into the journal:

> A well regulated militia, composed of the body of the people, being the best security of a free State, the right of the people to keep and bear arms shall not be infringed; but no person religiously scrupulous shall be compelled to bear arms.[21]

On September 4 the Senate voted to remove the definition of militia and the conscientious objector clause.[22] Defining a militia could have made specific implications, such as forcing every citizen to be trained which Hamilton noted would be futile; the inclusion of a conscientious objector clause might have defined the amendment as a 'duty' instead of a 'right.' They declined to take either of those approaches. On September 9 the Senate proposed the words "for the common defence" be added after "bear arms" and was defeated.[23] Remember when Convention Parliament made the same decision to avoid only creating a collective right in the English Bill of Rights in 1689? Does this not suggest the intent of the Second Amendment was not solely to protect collective rights, such as the common defense, but also individual rights? Remember, the common defense was already addressed in Article I, Section 8 of the Constitution; the Second Amendment was intended to secure something else in order to get the Constitution ratified.

The Second Amendment was adopted on December 15, 1791 along with the rest of the Bill of Rights. The Second Amendment as passed by Congress states:

> A well regulated Militia, being necessary to the security of a free State, the right of the people to keep and bear Arms, shall not be infringed.[24]

There may very well be as many different interpretations of the final draft of the Second Amendment as there are regarding the meaning of life itself. We've seen how we arrived at this final drafting, and compromise often creates ambiguity. To conclude that there was 100 percent consensus among the Framers regarding all aspects of the Constitution, the Bill of Rights and specifically the Second Amendment would be incorrect, as there is substantial evidence that those issues were debated and the semantics were rewritten numerously both before the Constitution was drafted and during attempts at ratification when the Bill of Rights was drafted. The Semantics of the Second Amendment were specifically debated and refined as well. Over the years there seems to have developed some kind of belief that our founding fathers were all of one mind, standing around the floors of the newly formed Congress, holding hands and singing Kumbaya…and that just isn't so. Well, I can only say that with any level of confidence since Kumbaya wasn't written until the 1930's. They very well may have had 'High School Musical' type sing-along's in Congress in the 18th century, the men did wear wigs, I've just not found any reference to such musical interludes happening. Maybe *Schoolhouse Rock!* really has it right.

Regardless, this is most likely how the confusion has set in over the years. People tend to try to argue that "all Framers believed this or that" and it just isn't true. There were disagreements and compromise. Though Federalists and Anti-Federalists had different views on the degree of control of a federal government and the necessity for a federal army, all do seem to clearly reinforce an apprehension towards standing armies, a belief in the right and power of a militia of the people and that the right to bear arms was both an individual right and a collective right, not one or the other. I'm not saying that it absolutely doesn't exist, but I can find no argument made by any Framer of the Constitution or Bill of Rights that the people should be disarmed.

There are many questions left to ask. Was the omission of the words "by Congress" after "infringed" merely an oversight or inferred, or do you think that the intent was that the right shall not be infringed by anyone? Do you think the prefatory clause was intended to be restrictive on the right to keep and bear arms or were they merely protecting two unalienable rights that are distinct but partially correlated in one sentence? Does the conscious decision not to include "for the common defence" suggest there is an individual right here and not just a collective right? Does this either protect or restrict militia style arms specifically, and if so, do you think the Framers would have believed an "assault weapons" ban would be held to go no further than to restrain abuses of other citizen's rights, or a wanton and causeless restraint of the will of the subject? Do you think the Framers felt that a weak militia in any state would have affected the security of the Union overall, leaving the states allowed to circumvent not only their own safety but that of the Union by leaving the states to regulate the people who make up their militia to using only using sticks and stones in spite of the Second Amendment?

Having seen how the English Bill of Rights shaped the beliefs of the Framers of the Constitution and the Bill of

Rights and the subsequent interpretations being reflected in their own quotes, you should have a good foundation for answering these questions yourself, but we'll have to see how the Legislative, Executive and Judicial branches of government address these issues over time. One thing is for sure, the power struggle between the Federalists and the Anti-Federalists did not end with the ratification of the U.S. Constitution and the concessions the Anti-Federalists gained in the Bill of Rights would immediately start becoming eroded by Federalist ideologies and subsequent legislation.

Militia Act 1792 [25]

The Militia Act of 1792 was enacted after the U.S. Army, led by General Arthur St. Claire and now known as St. Claire's Defeat, got the shit kicked out of it by the Western Confederacy of American Indians during part of the Northwest Indian War.[26] I don't think I'm even taking any liberties here with the colloquialism, it is still held to be the greatest defeat of the U.S. Army by American Indians and the worst defeat the United States Army has ever suffered in relation to the proportion of total troops to losses, with just over 1,000 men going into battle and only 48 remaining unharmed. St. Claire had started with roughly 2,000 men including 600 Army regulars, 800 six month conscripts and 600 militia. Over a few days time, desertion and illness diminished this by half. Somewhat justifiably, due to the desertions, the Act provides for penalties imposed on militia members who do not obey orders.

More importantly, and you have to pay very close attention here to follow how this evolves over time, Section 1 of the Act gives the President the power to call in the militia against an invasion, or imminent danger of invasion, by a foreign nation or Indian tribe specifically. This stemmed from a fear that a recess of Congress would lead to a delay in mobilizing the state militias in times of imminent danger or rebellion. You also have to remember here that the perceived enemy of the time, American Indians, was an enemy already on United States soil and an imminent threat, as proven by St. Claire's Defeat. Section 1 also allows the President, in the event there is an insurrection against a state government, with specific approval from either that state's legislature (or executive power, if that state's legislature cannot be convened) to call forth another state's militia to suppress the insurrection. Section 2 gives the President the right to call in the militia if the laws of the United States shall be opposed or the execution thereof obstructed in any state only if an associate justice or district judge has notified the President that the power has not been controlled by ordinary measure. If that state's militia is not sufficient, and if the U.S. Congress is not in session, then the President is given the power to call in another state's militia for adequate suppression of the violation.

The President is not given broad powers over the militia here. He is given control in times of invasion, he's given limited power in state insurrections with that state's approval, he is given the power to use state militias to enforce violations of United States laws, again with that state's approval, and the power to use other state's militias for that purpose without the permission of Congress only if Congress is not in session. Less than a year after the Constitution is ratified, Congress already begins to break down the checks and balances built into the three tier system of the U.S. Government by ceding some of the power directly given to the Legislative branch in Article I Section 8 to the Executive branch. Here is the full text of Section 1 and 2 of the Act prior to its amendments in 1795, as the trend of change in these powers are relevant to our discussion.

Section 1. *Be it enacted by the Senate and House of Representatives of the United States of America in Congress assembled,* That whenever the United States shall be invaded, or be in imminent danger of invasion from any foreign nation or Indian tribe, it shall be lawful for the President of the United States, to call forth such number of the militia of the state or states most convenient to the place of danger or scene of action as he may judge necessary to repel such invasion, and to issue his orders for that purpose, to such officer or officers of the militia as he shall think proper; and in case of an insurrection in any state, against the government thereof, it shall be lawful for the President of the United States, on application of the legislature of such state, or of the executive (when the legislature cannot be convened) to call forth such number of the militia of any other state or states, as may be applied for, or as he may judge sufficient to suppress such insurrection.

Sec. 2. *And be it further enacted,* That whenever the laws of the United States shall be **opposed or the execution thereof obstructed**, in any state, by combinations too powerful to be suppressed by the ordinary course of judicial proceedings, or by the powers vested in the marshals by this act, the same being notified to the President of the United States, by an associate justice or the district judge, it shall be lawful for the President of the United States to call forth the militia of such state to **suppress** such combinations, and to cause the laws to be duly executed. And if the militia of a state, where such combinations may happen, **shall refuse**, or be insufficient to suppress the same, it shall be lawful for the President, if the legislature of the United States be not in session, to call forth and employ such numbers of the militia of any other state or states most convenient thereto, as may be necessary, and the use of militia, so to be called forth, may be continued, if necessary, until the expiration of thirty days after the commencement of the ensuing session.

The powers given to the President were to expire after 2 years, plus any remaining term of that session of Congress, from the time it was passed. Just before the 2 year expiration, President George Washington used this authority to call forth the militia to suppress the Whiskey rebellion in 1794.

Militia Act of 1795

The previous militia act being positively reinforced by successful use just as the two years was about to expire, Congress passed the Militia Act of 1795 making the provisions in the previous act permanent powers, amending a few and adding more.[27] It was actually passed on May 8, 1792 six days after the previous Act but was not approved until February 28, 1795 along with the previously mentioned amendments. It established the structure for the militia. It also went one step further and creates the first attempt at mandatory militia service. There is still no questioning of the right to keep and bear arms, in fact it is reinforced here by 'every free able-bodied white male citizen' being required to possess one.

I. Be it enacted by the Senate and House of Representatives of the United States of America, in Congress assembled, That each and every free able-bodied white male citizen of the respective States, resident therein, who is or shall be of age of eighteen years, and under the age of forty-five years (except as is herein after excepted) shall severally and respectively be enrolled in the militia, by the Captain or Commanding Officer of the company, within whose bounds such citizen shall reside, and that within twelve months after the passing of this Act. And it shall at all time hereafter be the duty of every such Captain or Commanding Officer of a company, to enroll every such citizen as aforesaid, and also those who shall, from time to time, arrive at the age of 18 years, or being at the age of 18 years, and under the age of 45 years (except as before excepted) shall come to reside within his bounds; and shall without delay notify such citizen of the said enrollment, by the proper non-commissioned Officer of the company, by whom such notice may be proved. That every citizen, so enrolled and notified, shall, within six months thereafter, provide himself with a good musket or firelock, a sufficient bayonet and belt, two spare flints, and a knapsack, a pouch, with a box therein, to contain not less than twenty four cartridges, suited to the bore of his musket or firelock, each cartridge to contain a proper quantity of powder and ball; or with a good rifle, knapsack, shot-pouch, and powder-horn, twenty balls suited to the bore of his rifle, and a quarter of a pound of powder; and shall appear so armed, accoutred and provided, when called out to exercise or into service, except, that when called out on company days to exercise only, he may appear without a knapsack. That the commissioned Officers

34

shall severally be armed with a sword or hanger, and espontoon; and that from and after five years from the passing of this Act, all muskets from arming the militia as is herein required, shall be of bores sufficient for balls of the eighteenth part of a pound; and every citizen so enrolled, and providing himself with the arms, ammunition and accoutrements, required as aforesaid, shall hold the same exempted from all suits, distresses, executions or sales, for debt or for the payment of taxes.

Section 2 was amended such that the President did not need confirmation from an associate justice or district judge that oppositions and obstructions to U.S. law were not being suppressed in order to call in that state's militia to attempt to suppress them, thus giving the President direct power over state militias at this point. Keep in mind that we are specifically talking about the militia here and not the Army or Navy. In fact, the Constitution didn't grant either the President or Congress the power to use the Army or Navy for domestic disorders and emergencies. We have, however, now vacated one ideology of the Bill of Rights in maintaining militias to keep the Federal Government in check. Should citizens of a state be opposed to a Federal action in opposition of state's rights, and resort to assembling its own state militia in defense, then the President can suggest the state itself is breaking Federal Law and seize control of the state militia for Federal purposes. Wasn't this one of the primary fears of the Anti-Federalists and basically the very thing both Hamilton and Madison believed would never happen under the Constitution...thus assuring the Anti-Federalists it could never happen?

It only took eight years (technically just four years from the actual adoption of the Bill of Rights in 1791) and a couple of uprisings to really knock the first chips out of the foundation of the U.S. Constitution by repurposing the state militias. This Act seems to confirm that the militia is in fact 'all the people' but that states, and even the U.S. Congress, only have a perceived power of control over them. The President now has autonomy over all state militias in times of invasion and insurrection, and over individual state militias if federal laws are being violated. Remember, the Constitution gave the President the power to be the militia's Commander in Chief only after they were called into actual service, the power of governing the militia was specifically given to Congress. Is this an amendment of the Article I Section 8 power given to Congress which says "To provide for the calling forth the Militia to execute the Laws of the Union, suppress Insurrections and repel Invasions" in violation of Article V requiring state ratification, or is ceding that power to the President merely an instance of the line before it "To make Rules for the Government and Regulation of the land and naval Forces" and nothing more, in spite of the definite shift in power between the branches?

The Constitutionality of this may be a tricky question to answer for certain, but you should still be aware that the question rightfully exists, as we've already seen historic evidence of a militia being used by a single person to oppress the people in England (which led to the English Bill of Rights.) James Madison, who is credited with drafting the first ten amendments to the Constitution, once said in a letter to Thomas Jefferson, "The constitution supposes, what the History of all [Governments] demonstrates, that the [Executive] is the branch of power most interested in war, & most prone to it. It has accordingly with studied care, vested the question of war in the [Legislative]."[28] Are the Militia Acts of 1792 and 1795 the first small steps towards circumventing that studied care? Either way, I think we can chalk one up for Federalist, former General and current President George Washington and the Federal Government overall.

Insurrection Act of 1807

Approved on the last day of the Ninth Congress on March 3, 1807:

> Be it enacted by the senate and house of representatives of the United States of America in congress assembled, That, in all cases of insurrection, or obstruction to the laws, either of the United States, or of any individual state or territory, where it is lawful for the President of the United States to call forth the militia for the purpose of suppressing such insurrection, or of causing the laws to be duly executed, it shall be lawful for him to employ, for the same purposes, such part of the land or naval force of the United States, as shall be judged necessary, having first observed all the pre-requisites of the law in that respect.[29]

The stimulus for the Act is relatively unknown, but some indicate it was in response to the Aaron Burr conspiracy.[30] With the passing of this act the President now has the power to call forth the Army and Navy in times of insurrection or obstruction of the laws in addition to calling forth the militia as allowed by the previous Militia Acts. Notice here that invasion is not mentioned, just insurrection and obstruction of the laws. Since militias would not be invading the country, it appears the new power given to the President to call forth the Army and Navy may be opening the door to suppress an apparent insurrection or obstruction of the laws by the militia itself should such an event arise, without requiring legislative approval. With this addition to the previous Militia Acts, the President now has autonomy over the militias directly in times of invasion, insurrection, and obstruction to the laws while also having autonomy over the Army and Navy in times of insurrection and obstruction to the laws. This effectively gives the President police powers over U.S. citizens under certain conditions. This continues the trend of Congress enacting legislation ceding emergency powers granted to it by the Constitution to the President. It also reinforces the concept that the militia and the federal armed forces are different entities.

We'll just note here that in 2006, Congress made some changes in the Act through the Defense Authorization Bill which broadened the scope of its use to "restore public order and enforce the laws of the United States when, as a result of a natural disaster, epidemic, or other serious public health emergency, terrorist attack or incident, or other condition..." Well, that's virtually any reason. This change was repealed in 2008 with a return to the previous wording.[31]

The War of 1812

Is it somewhat ironic that James Madison was the first President calling for a Declaration of War from Congress after the quote we just read? The reason we bring up the War of 1812 is due to the militia having been perceived as performing poorly in this war. Those subject to militia duty were not eager to volunteer, felt it was poor pay, objected to serving outside their home states and performed poorly when doing so and were not open to discipline.[32] The failure of New England to provide militia units or financial support was a serious blow as well.[33] The Navy, however, was seen as having been overall successful. Naval power on the Great Lakes became a contest of ship building, and a race towards increasing Naval power. A new theme we seem to have stuck with over the years. The British were successful with raids on the shores of the Chesapeake Bay though, resulting in the burning of the White House and Capitol. The government seeing the need for a strong Navy created a rapidly expanding program of building warships, passing into law an "Act for the gradual increase of the Navy" authorizing 9 ships of the line and 12 heavy frigates at a cost of $1,000,000 a year for eight years.[34] Yes, this is the Navy, but so much for the ideology of not maintaining standing armies due to their costs on society. A ship is not as easy to call up as a member of the militia though where time is of the essence. The War of 1812 leads us further away from the ideology that a militia is stronger than a standing army to some degree, in this case evidenced by the perceived success of the Navy and the perceived lack of success of the militia, and thus relevant to our discussion in that capacity. It appears this is where the "arms race" begins for the U.S.

Suppression of the Rebellion Act of 1861[35]

On the eve of the Civil War, Congress passed a direct amendment to the Militia Act of 1795. Section 1 of the Act amends sections 1 and 2 of the Militia Act of 1792 that were carried over in the 1795 act:

> Be it enacted by the Senate and House of Representatives of the United States of America in Congress assembled, That whenever, by reason of unlawful obstructions, combinations, or assemblages of persons, or rebellion against the authority of the Government of the United States, it shall become

Impracticable, in the judgment of the President of the United States, to enforce, by the ordinary course of judicial proceedings, the laws of the United States within any State or Territory of the United States, it shall be lawful for the President of the United States to call forth the militia of any or all the States of the Union, and to employ such parts of the land and naval forces of the United States as lie may deem necessary to enforce the faithful execution of the laws of the United States, or to suppress such rebellion in whatever State or Territory thereof the laws of the United States may be forcibly opposed, or the, execution thereof forcibly obstructed.

It now lies in the sole judgment of the President when it is impracticable to enforce the laws by traditional means and to call forth both the militia and the federal forces for that enforcement. The previous term insurrection is replaced by rebellion. Though both are often considered synonyms, an insurrection is a revolt (to renounce allegiance or subjection) against a civil authority or government while a rebellion can merely be an opposition to authority.[36-38] This power was previously related to acts which renounced the government, now it can be held to cover acts of those collectively trying to protect their civil rights from government abuse. The Constitution states that "The Privilege of the Writ of Habeas Corpus shall not be suspended, unless when in Cases of Rebellion or Invasion, the public Safety may require it."[39] The change in semantics in this act would bring those two concepts more in line and possibly provide the foundation for Martial Law. Sections 2, 3 and 4 of the 1795 Act were amended; Section 1 which created mandatory militia service for white able bodied citizens between a certain age and their required ownership of arms was left intact.

The Militia Act of 1862, passed by the U.S. (Union) Congress after the start of the Civil War, allowed African-Americans to serve in the militias. There were no other relevant changes regarding the militia overall, so we'll just note that specific legislation exists here before we head into the Civil War.[40]

The American Civil War (1861 -1865)

We've all heard about the 'War between the States.' I will try not to recap any more of it than necessary for our discussion. Nutshell version, we have our first official multi-state insurrection against the Federal Government…now what? It immediately brings to question the issue of state's rights. Were rights being conceded to the states in the Bill of Rights just to get states to ratify the Constitution in spite of their fears of federal power merely to strengthen the union, or was the overall sovereignty of the states really a major part of the goal? We had dealt with minor issues of insurrection before, but now that we have a multi-state and organized expression of it, we have to ask if the right, or even the concept, of insurrection had been built into the Constitution. We'll come back to insurrection in Chapter 4. It also brought up the concept of state's rights in regards to citizens. Some felt the rights they were afforded as a citizen of their state carried with them when they traveled to other states, while others felt that would be a violation of sovereignty of the state being visited. I don't think we need to get into a discussion on Dred Scott or slavery in general here to serve our purposes, just keep in mind the issue brought about a conundrum inherent in the Bill of Rights and vaguely addressed in the Constitution; where exactly do powers and rights reserved to the states end not only in regards to each other and in relation to federal powers, but in relation to the citizens independently? For instance, what happens when someone in a state that allows firearms drives to another state allowing firearms, but merely has to travel through a state that does not allow them? Which state's laws take precedent?

Before the war began the existing army was roughly only 16,000 troops, so we still didn't have a major standing army.[41]   After the attack on Fort Sumter, credited as the start of the actual war, Lincoln still had to call for the creation of a volunteer army from each state to attempt to retake it, roughly 75,000 troops.[42]   Volunteers became insufficient, and the U.S. military has its first conscription, or draft, into military service.[43] The invention of repeating firearms such as the Spencer Repeating Rifle (1860) and the Henry Repeating Rifle (1860) are credited as exacerbating the death toll and changing the nature of warfare.[44] The first machine gun (The Gatling Gun) followed a year later.[45] Keep this in mind for a later discussion; the repeating rifle only predates the machine gun by a single year. I guess I should also point out that we got our first Federal income tax statute out of this as well, in order to fund the war against the confederacy.[46] It seems there are those today who might argue that we didn't actually end slavery, we just effectively nationalized it more fairly by class instead of race with such a tax.

The states attempted insurrection by secession.   The insurrection was defeated by the United States. Many of those involved were held accountable (assuming they weren't already among the 750,000 plus dead) and prohibited from holding any type of office in the future and prohibited from seeking any recourse for the expense of their insurrection....and yet still the government goes to extra lengths to remove rights from the states directly, in a further attempt to strengthen the federal governments powers over the states.

The Fourteenth Amendment to the Constitution of the United States (Ratified 1868)

Nothing like a full scale multi-state insurrection against the Federal Government to bring about a resolution on state's rights. Though it is mostly about punishing the states for insurrection, part of the Fourteenth Amendment does protect the civil liberties of citizens against abuses by the states that occurred prior to the Civil War. As such, Section 1 is probably the only part necessary for our discussion.

> All persons born or naturalized in the United States, and subject to the jurisdiction thereof, are citizens of the United States and of the State wherein they reside. No State shall make or enforce any law which shall abridge the privileges or immunities of citizens of the United States; nor shall any State deprive any person of life, liberty, or property, without due process of law; nor deny to any person within its jurisdiction the equal protection of the laws.[47]

The Fourteenth Amendment defines citizenship, primarily being to the United States, and inconsequential to, secondarily being a citizen of the State in which you currently reside. This somewhat clarifies the state's rights conundrum. The definition of citizenship, with emphasis on the United States, does seem to strengthen the concept that the Constitution was intended to be a perpetual union, unable to be broken by the states regardless of any disagreement with the Federal government. While it does afford more protection to the citizens of the United States through the Bill of Rights, it definitely strengthens the role of the Federal government overall, and after nearly a century since concessions were made to appease both the Federalist and Anti-Federalist Framers of our Constitution, it appears the ideology of the Anti-Federalists was finally folded up and stuffed in the pockets of the beaten Confederates and told to take a long walk off a short pier. In reality, the states still retained a lot of rights, but any hope they had of restricting the federal government's power was effectively as dead as the 750,000 plus people who died in the Civil War.

The Fourteenth Amendment is important to our discussion due to a clarification of citizenship, along with the Privileges and Immunities and Due Process Clauses. For instance, does the Second Amendment now apply to the states as an overall civil liberty of American citizens, and would they have the right to take away a firearm that is your personal property without due process of law? Sorry, but you're going to have to wait more than a century to find out if the Fourteenth Amendment actually prohibits states from legislating away your Second Amendment rights...luckily that just means the next chapter.

Enforcement Act of 1871

The Enforcement Act of 1871 was passed as "An Act to enforce the Provisions of the Fourteenth Amendment to the Constitution of the United States, and for other Purposes."[48] It was most specifically for suppressing the Ku Klux Klan (it was also known as the Ku Klux Klan Act) at the time, and was deemed a success.[49] The President's power to call forth the militia and federal armed forces was expanded with the ability to resort to "other means", and the reasons for using the power were expanded from those given in the previous Militia, Insurrection and Rebellion Acts we've covered to include enforcement of civil rights conferred by the Act, the recently adopted Fourteenth Amendment and the Constitution in general. The most powerful provision in the

Act was in Section 4 which empowered the President to suspend the writ of habeas corpus under the circumstances enumerated above. The Act signifies a further move away from checks on Presidential authority and may very well create an Executive emergency power of martial law along with the ability to suspend habeas corpus. The President now has the autonomy to suppress any segment of the armed populace, or an entire state militia in general, if the President feels the civil rights of any of its citizens are being jeopardized by such a group, and it defines any acts by such a group as a rebellion against the government of the United States. The irony to me seems to be that this Act would also give the President autonomy to suppress any armed group or entire state militia who are attempting to defend civil rights they think were denied by the federal government through a circumvention of democracy without any legislative approval from the federal government or the states. I can't help but think that even Federalists Hamilton and Madison are rolling over in their graves right now. The slope seems to be getting more slippery.

United States v. Cruikshank, 92 U.S. 542 (1875)

After a tense gubernatorial election in November of 1872, a mob of white Democrats attacked a group of black Republican freedmen at a Louisiana courthouse, killing what was estimated to be somewhere around 200 of them. (No, I did not accidentally get the parties switched there.) Some of the attackers were convicted under the Enforcement Act of 1870 (there were 3 Enforcement Acts in1870-1871) and the Supreme Court overturned the conviction. In doing so, the court ruled that the Bill of Rights did not apply to the states, and more specifically to our discussion that the Second Amendment "has no other effect than to restrict the powers of the national government." Thus the ruling sets court precedent that the Second Amendment is only Federal in nature. In regards to the Fourteenth Amendment, it rules that the Due Process and Equal Protection clauses only "prohibits a State from depriving any person of life, liberty, or property, without due process of law; but this adds nothing to the rights of one citizen against another."

However, since this case has often been held to conclude that you have no right to bear arms at a state level, I would like to provide you with an expanded quote from the same paragraph regarding the Second Amendment from above, as it actually says something more:

> The right there specified is that of 'bearing arms for a lawful purpose.' This is not a right granted by the Constitution. Neither is it in any manner dependent upon that instrument for its existence. The second amendment declares that it shall not be infringed, but this, as has been seen, means no more than that it shall not be infringed by Congress. This is one of the amendments that has no other effect than to restrict the powers of the national government, leaving the people to look for their protection against any violation by their fellow citizens of the rights it recognizes, to what is called, in *The city of New York v Miln*, 11Pet. 139, the "powers which relate to merely municipal legislation, or what was, perhaps, more properly called internal police," "not surrendered or restrained" by the Constitution of the United States.

The court in Cruikshank quite clearly states you have a natural right to bear arms for a lawful purpose irrelevant of the Constitution or the Second Amendment, and they do not suggest that you do not have that right at a state level, in fact clearly explaining why you do. Cruikshank has somehow been repeated and cited through history as denying recognition of individual rights claims, not only in subsequent court precedent, but in arguments validating state regulation of firearms...yet right there in the court's own words they describe a natural right to bear arms for lawful purposes (which would have to include both individual and collective rights, as both are lawful.) This does not appear to be merely dicta, it is in the exact same paragraph as the one line that courts subsequently quote as precedent, prefatory to that statement, and is clearly pertinent to their decision and the context in which that line was written. Where you seek recourse for violations of that natural right is what they actually address here, in essence, you can only seek recourse through the federal courts for federal violations of rights (such as those granted in the Second Amendment if violated by Congress.)

Posse Comitatus Act 1878 (18 U.S.C. § 1385, original at 20 Stat. 152)

Merriam Webster defines Posse Comitatus as, "the entire body of the inhabitants who may be summoned by the sheriff to assist in preserving the public peace (as in a riot) or in executing a legal precept that is forcibly opposed including under the common law every male inhabitant who is above 15 years of age and not infirm."[50] It is the equivalent of summoning the militia to suppress civil disorder. The intent was to limit the powers of the federal government from using the Army to enforce state laws. The Act does not make it illegal to do so; it just states that the authority must exist in the Constitution or by an act of Congress. Here is the original act:

From and after the passage of this act it shall not be lawful to employ any part of the Army of the United States, as a posse comitatus, or otherwise, for the purpose of executing the laws, except in such cases and under such circumstances as such employment of said force may be expressly authorized by the Constitution or by act of Congress; and no money appropriated by this act shall be used to pay any of the expenses incurred in the employment of any troops in violation of this section and any person willfully violating the provisions of this section shall be deemed guilty of a misdemeanor and on conviction thereof shall be punished by fine not exceeding ten thousand dollars or imprisonment not exceeding two years or by both such fine and imprisonment.[51]

However, we've already seen the Acts of Congress that make the President exempt from the Posse Comitatus Act under many circumstances. In 1956 it is amended to this; "Whoever, except in cases and under circumstances expressly authorized by the Constitution or Act of Congress, willfully uses any part of the Army or the Air Force as a posse comitatus or otherwise to execute the laws shall be fined under this title or imprisoned not more than two years, or both." In addition to the Acts of Congress providing Presidential exceptions, the National Guard is exempt while under state authority as is the U.S. Coast Guard which operates under the Department of Homeland Security.[52] I include it because it appears we have not entirely lost the fear of a standing army being used against U.S. citizens. If the fear is still there, a desire to preserve the means to defend against it must still exist as well.

Herman Presser v. State of Illinois, 116 U.S. 252 (1886)

Herman Presser was a member of Lehr und Wehr Verein (Educational and Defense Society), an Illinois corporation and Chicago based socialist militia group. The organization trained for an anticipated confrontation between Capital and Labor, as some companies had been known to use services such as Pinkertons, who provided services ranging from security guards to private military contract work. In 1879, the Illinois legislature passed an act requiring all 'non state' militia to obtain a license from the Governor. Presser led a militia parade of roughly 40 men with rifles without a license and was indicted and found guilty. Presser claimed this violated his Second Amendment rights, the court ruling the Second Amendment does not apply to the states, only limiting the power of Congress.

The right to bear arms is never an issue in this case, and you will see that the court clearly disqualifies that from the ruling. Justice Woods actually quotes the full paragraph from Cruikshank above "is not a right granted by the Constitution. Neither is it in any manner dependent upon that instrument for its existence..." restating the natural right to bear arms, so obviously he did not think part of that paragraph was dicta. He follows it even further with a statement of his own:

> It is undoubtedly true that all citizens capable of bearing arms constitute the reserved military force or reserve militia of the United States as well as of the states, and, in view of this prerogative of the general government, as well as of its general powers, the states cannot, even laying the constitutional provision in question out of view, prohibit the people from keeping and bearing arms so as to deprive the United

States of their rightful resource for maintaining the public security, and disable the people from performing their duty to the general government.

Again, Justice Woods continues to confirm this is a natural right of the people irrelevant of the Constitution and clearly says the states cannot prohibit the people from keeping and bearing arms. Justice Woods' affirmation does, however, specifically point out the collective rights ideology in this case. The court does address the Fourteenth Amendment and concludes "A state may pass laws to regulate the privileges and immunities of its own citizens, provided that in so doing it does not abridge their privileges and immunities as citizens of the United States." However, and you can attempt to call this one dicta if you wish, Justice Woods had just clearly described in the quote above how states attempting to deprive citizens of the right to bear arms would do just that... abridge their privileges and immunities as citizens of the United States. State laws controlling the militia being the basis of this case, which would not deprive the people of a natural right or abridge other privileges or immunities, were clearly upheld.

How subsequent courts have been able to cherry pick a single sentence out of a decision, apparently throwing other relevant statements out as mere dicta and somehow continue to cite Cruikshank, and now Presser, as precedent that gives states the right to restrict the right of the people to bear arms is beyond me. It takes a perverse twisting of the facts to negate the conclusions the court makes in both cases regarding the natural rights of citizens to do just that. In these cases the Second Amendment does not apply to the states as it only restricts Congress, but both courts specifically say the people have a right to bear arms regardless of the Second Amendment which should not be prohibited and nothing the courts say in Cruikshank or Presser suggests the states have a right to control or regulate firearms, merely because that specific amendment doesn't prohibit them from doing so. Some acknowledge a restriction on firearm ownership the states can implement due to Justice Woods' statement, such that it cannot disarm people to the extent that there is no remaining militia. However, we've already seen that at this point in our timeline and since 1795 the militia is "each and every free able-bodied white male citizen" between 18 and 45, and since 1862 we can redact the adjective "white."

The Militia Act of 1903 [53]

The Militia Act of 1903 was also known as the Dick Act. No, not because of what the legislation said or what it did to state militias, but because it was sponsored by U.S. Senator Charles W.F. Dick, chair of the Committee on the Militia. [54] It was in response to two back to back wars; the Spanish American War of 1898 and the Philippine-American War (1899-1902). The details of each war aren't really pertinent to our discussion other than a couple of points. At the start of the Spanish-American war the regular army consisted of roughly 28,000 men; we still don't have a large standing army. The Army requested 50,000 new men and through volunteers and mobilization of state National Guards received over 220,000, so volunteers were not a problem this time. [55] Though the U.S. was deemed victorious in both cases, the conflicts seem to have again demonstrated a weakness in the militia and the U.S. military overall. This act was the result of that assessment. We bring it up in our analysis because it significantly redefines the nature of state militias even further.

The Dick Act extends the scope of militia constituents to include every able-bodied male of foreign birth who has declared his intention to become a citizen. I wonder how the illegals in our country, who claim to want to be made citizens, would feel about being called into militia service...maybe to defend the U.S. - Mexican border? It also splits the Militia into two distinct parts: the state National Guard - the regularly enlisted, organized and uniformed active militia; and the Reserve Militia - every able-bodied male citizen of appropriate age remaining, suggesting there is an element of the militia that is still all of the people.

The Dick Act provides for firearms to be provided to the National Guard, they are no longer required to bring their own arms. Any previous requirement for the regular militia to own firearms is dropped. It places the National Guard under the direct authority of the Army Reserve. This insures that the President can mobilize state military forces into the Federal armed forces at any time. It keeps Governors from using the state National Guard as "private armies" by superseding state power. At this point, the National Guards of the states officially become a tool of the Federal Government and its Army.

State militias; "You're in the Army now..."

Chapter III

Actually, It's More of a Guideline Than a Rule

"If cowardly and dishonorable men sometimes shoot unarmed men with army pistols or guns, the evil must be prevented by the penitentiary and gallows, and not by a general deprivation of constitutional privilege." - Hon. J. A. Williams, Circuit Judge [1]

The Sullivan Act (1911) [2]

The Sullivan Act is a gun control law enacted in 1911 in New York State. A murder suicide in what is now Gramercy Park prompted the local coroner George Petit le Brun to put political pressure on legislators to pass gun laws. Petit le Brun's main argument for banning guns seems to stem from his statement, "Within the last few years, since the sale of poisons has been regulated by law and they cannot be purchased as easily as they were some years ago, there has been a marked decrease in suicide by poison." Most of the statistics following his quote revolve around suicide and there is absolutely no data on gun-related homicides to support the article's title; Revolver Killings Fast Increasing. [3]

State Senator Tim Sullivan, a notoriously corrupt Tammany Hall politician, sponsored the law which was passed a few months later.[4] Some at the time argue Sullivan pushed the bill so that Tammany Hall could keep their gangster allies under control. In *"King of the Bowery: Big Tim Sullivan, Tammany Hall, and New York City from the Gilded Age to the Progressive Era,* Richard F. Welch writes, "Hoodlums who forgot who really ran things in the city could be easily arrested if found with a gun – or if one was slipped into their pocket."[5] According to the New York Times article published May 11, 1911, "The Sullivan bill makes the carrying of concealed weapons a felony, requires those using revolvers and small arms to obtain licenses from police Magistrates, and provides for the registration by dealers in firearms of all persons who buy revolvers or similar weapons."[6] From the same article, here are Sullivan's words in defense of the act, "A great big fellow driving a truck in one of the crowded streets of New York City only four days ago ran over a little Italian boy and killed him. The father in a burst of anger lost control of his temper and shot the poor truckman dead. Now there's that man's family, and he had a lot of children, and the man who did the shooting had a large number of children. That ought to be enough to pass this bill without any one getting up and saying a word against it." And that's just how quickly it can happen.

Though it has been amended over time this is one of the oldest standing gun control laws in the country and has served as a template for subsequent gun control legislation in the nation since; yet all accounts say it was sparked by two deaths (a murder / suicide), instigated by a coroner preoccupied with high local suicide rates and promoted by a State Senator likely to have ulterior and somewhat unethical political motives.[7] Over the years it has progressively been amended such that it is now a virtual ban on handguns in

New York.[8] Do you think this act reflects sensible law in restricting civil rights for the public good, or a 'wanton and causeless restraint of the will of the subject'?

World War I (1914-1918)

Then there is this skirmish called World War I, but there isn't much to say about firearm rights really as a result of that war. The first machine guns had been used in the Civil War, but the machine gun becomes one of the most effective tactical weapons used at the height of WWI.[9] By the end of WWI the United States had amassed an Army of roughly 3.5 million soldiers, when the General Staff called for the first peacetime assembly of an army in 1923, the Army had fewer than 400,000 troops.[10] It appears we still do not have a "standing army" mentality, but the number of peacetime troops has certainly grown. Historian James Huston noted that the United States "had revealed the greatest war-making capacity that the world had ever seen."[11] In other news, it appears that the "only Protestant subjects..." clan are fond of a right to bear arms and not so fond of a right to consume alcohol, and they lead a movement in the United States resulting in the Eighteenth Amendment to the Constitution.[12] They call it Prohibition. Prohibition leads us to major legislation regarding firearms.

The National Firearms Act 1934 ("NFA") [13]

Prohibition had just been repealed in 1933, and had been the cause of the rise of American gangsters such as Al Capone. "As organized crime syndicates grew throughout the Prohibition era, territorial disputes often transformed America's cities into violent battlegrounds. Homicides, burglaries, and assaults consequently increased significantly between 1920 and 1933."[14]   The NFA originally defined "firearm" as:

> A shotgun or rifle having a barrel of less than eighteen inches in length or any other weapon, other than a pistol or revolver, from which a shot is discharged by an explosive if such weapon is capable of being concealed on the person, or a machine gun, and includes a muffler or silencer for any firearm whether or not such a firearm is included in the foregoing definition.

The Act doesn't ban any weapons, it only requires registration and taxes certain weapons through what is at this time known as the Miscellaneous Tax Unit of the Bureau of Internal Revenue (yes, that IRS), control of which had just been returned to the U.S. Department of the Treasury after a brief stay at the Department of Justice under its moniker the Bureau of Prohibition.[15]   Remember Elliot Ness and The "Untouchables" from that HBO movie you watched?[16] Eventually this becomes the Bureau of Alcohol, Tobacco and Firearms so you may often hear ATF when speaking of the original NFA, though that title is not accurate until 1968. Explaining the history of the National Firearms Act, the Bureau of Alcohol, Tobacco, Firearms and Explosives (now BATFE) says:

> While the NFA was enacted by Congress as an exercise of its authority to tax, the NFA had an underlying purpose unrelated to revenue collection. As the legislative history of the law discloses, its underlying purpose was to curtail, if not prohibit, transactions in NFA firearms. Congress found these firearms to pose a significant crime problem because

of their frequent use in crime, particularly the gangland crimes of that era such as the St. Valentine's Day Massacre.[17]

Of course, they had already repealed the stimulus for the crimes themselves, but maybe taxing specific gangland weapons will stop future gangland violence? It should be noted that the homicide rate had peaked in 1933 and already began dropping after the repeal of Prohibition and before the passing of the NFA.[18]

United States v. Miller, 307 U.S. 174 (1939)

Jack Miller and Frank Layton were charged with violating the NFA by transporting an unregistered 'sawed off' double barreled shotgun across state lines. The District Court held that section eleven of the Act violates the Second Amendment and dismissed the indictment. The United States appealed. The Supreme Court reversed the decision and remanded the case back to the District court for further proceedings. Miller was murdered before the decision was ever rendered and Layton later made a plea bargain, so further proceedings never took place.[19] It should also be noted that neither the defendants nor their legal counsel were present at the appeal in front of the Supreme Court. In a unanimous opinion the Supreme Court stated "the objection that the Act usurps police power reserved to the States is plainly untenable." The court further sates:

> In the absence of any evidence tending to show that possession or use of a 'shotgun having a barrel of less than eighteen inches in length' at this time has some reasonable relationship to any preservation or efficiency of a well regulated militia, we cannot say

that the Second Amendment guarantees the right to keep and bear such an instrument. Certainly it is not within judicial notice that this weapon is any part of the ordinary military equipment or that its use could contribute to the common defense.

Some conclude the court states that "non-militia" arms can be regulated and taxed under NFA without violating the Second Amendment. The court rules that shotguns are not militia in nature, but that is factually incorrect.[20] Further, machine guns are listed under the original act as well. Can anyone possibly believe that the court was trying to argue that the NFA "overall" didn't violate Second Amendment rights because it only regulated "non-militia" firearms? WWI was 1914-1918 and the machine gun was one of the most common tactical weapons used in the height of that war.[21] Yes, even the National Guard, specifically a militia, was using machine guns prior to the *Miller* case in 1939.[22]

Some conclude it specifically guarantees Second Amendment rights to those arms of militia in nature. Maybe this is because the U.S. Government specifically argues this point as part of the foundation for their case; "The 'arms' referred to in the Second Amendment are, moreover, those which ordinarily are used for military or public defense purposes..."[23] Wow! You don't hear the government arguing that today, do you?

Some concluded that the court never considered the personal defense aspects of a shotgun, only its suitability for militia use, therefore there is no individual right to bear arms. Some conclude it deems NFA not in violation because it taxes firearms as a revenue measure only, doesn't ban them. Another of the arguments directly made by the U.S. Government during the hearings, "The NFA is intended as a revenue-collecting measure and therefore within the authority of the Department of the Treasury."[24] Of course, remember that quote earlier from BATFE? Here it is again, "While the NFA was enacted by Congress as an exercise of its authority to tax, the NFA had an underlying purpose unrelated to revenue collection. As the legislative history of the law discloses, its underlying purpose was to curtail, if not prohibit, transactions in NFA firearms. Congress found these firearms to pose a significant crime problem because of their frequent use in crime, particularly the gangland crimes of that era such as the St. Valentine's Day Massacre."[25] Hmmm...is the ATF accusing the U.S. Government of perjury in the *Miller* case suggesting the purpose was not merely to tax but actually to restrict these weapons?

Others conclude it sets precedent that the government can in fact regulate firearms, in spite of any interpretation by the courts of when or why. All that seems to be left is a "sense" that weapons can be regulated in spite of the Second Amendment. Ultimately, it appears this case didn't resolve any Second Amendment issues at all. However, remnants of these false conclusions have been used to establish subsequent legislation over the years. Does this court decision confirm a collective right, discount an individual right...or merely suggest that you have no rights when it comes to regulation falling under a division of what will eventually become the IRS? (Yes, that was meant in jest.) Things are starting to get a bit convoluted at this point regarding militias and gun rights, aren't they? But another World War ought to distract your attention for a while.

World War II (1939-1942)

At the end of World War II in 1942, the Army had 5.4 million troops, the cost of which was estimated to be about $68 billion to maintain. Three years after the war ends, the Army peaks at 8 million troops. President Roosevelt sets the maximum size of the Army to be 8.2 million.[26] This appears to be the first time we didn't immediately reduce the military dramatically after a conflict. Is this the first sign of an acceptance of a standing army? We definitely developed a euphoric admiration for the U.S. Army after WWII. It seems the fear of standing armies will be lost on a new generation. Well, maybe just until those same kids go to Vietnam. I can't find much in the way of changing ideologies specifically on gun rights after this war.

Israel Six-Day War 1967

I know this may seem obscure, but it ultimately has a dramatic effect on gun rights. The inclusion of the Six-Day War has not been included to denounce Judaism or Israel in any way, but the change in both political and societal ideologies in the United States as a result of the event is clearly relevant to our discussion. The Six-Day war was fought between Israel and the neighboring states of the United Arab Republic (Egypt), Jordan and Syria. At the end of the six days, Israel had taken control of the Gaza Strip and Sinai Peninsula from Egypt, the West Bank and East Jordan from Jordan and the Golan Heights from Syria. I'm sure none of this sounds familiar to you today. The details of the war itself aren't really important, but the drastic change in American sentiment immediately afterwards is. Prior to the Six-Day War, the United States had been the first to recognize the state of Israel. U.S. policy was to remain neutral and not become too closely allied with Israel, and we were selling weapons not only to Israel, but also Egypt and Jordan. The Middle Eastern views of the United States had gone from one of being the most popular western country in their eyes to subtle shifts toward an understanding that we were at least fair to deal with prior to the war. The United States government, however, began to feel the Arab states were drifting towards stronger allegiances with the Soviet Union. In 1968 President Lyndon B. Johnson authorized the sale of Phantom fighter jets to Israel, clearly providing an edge to the Israelis and setting precedent for U.S. support of the Israeli military.[27] As of the end of 2012, the United States provided 21 percent of the funds for Israel's military spending.[28] Though the initial agreement was scheduled to end in 2012, Israel currently receives roughly $3 billion annually in U.S. assistance through U.S. Foreign Military Financing (FMF). That is more than half of all FMF spending, and roughly 25 percent of Israel's military defense budget.[29] Seriously, let that sink in for a minute. We pay for roughly 25 percent of Israel's military and Americans wonder why groups of Muslims want to kill us.

The other change was that of American Jews. It is best summed up by Abraham H. Foxman, National Director of the Anti-Defamation League, in his article *The Six-Day War: 40 Years Later*:

> For American Jews, 1967 was transformative both for its impact on attitudes toward Israel and for Jewish self-perception. Zionism had been a controversial movement within the American Jewish community from the beginning of the century. American Jews took a long time to feel comfortable with the Zionist movement and after the creation of the state, there still were large numbers of American Jews who

> remained indifferent to the new state, and even some
> who made clear that that was not their state.
>
> The Six Day War made us all Zionists, if not literally
> than psychologically. The American Jewish
> connection to Israel was sealed. Even today, when
> one hears a lot about disaffection, the pride and depth
> of the continuing connection owe many of their roots
> to 1967.[30]

This change in ideology would reinforce government policy, and create a distinct change in both U.S.-Israel and U.S. Arab relations. The era of "Islamic extremist" terrorist attacks towards the United States seems to begin at this time as a result of that policy shift, and persists today. Unfortunately, I would have to concede that we chose our enemy; our enemy did not choose us. I can find no evidence of "Islamic extremist" terrorist attacks specifically directed at the United States prior to 1967. The first major event appears to be the Dawson's Field hijackings of 5 jet aircraft headed to New York by the Popular Front for the Liberation of Palestine, intending to trade U.S. hostages for PFLP prisoners held by Israel.[31] The eventual perception that terrorists are among us leads to extreme security measures and further restrictions on gun rights over time...of course to keep them out of the hands of the terrorists.

Gun Control Act of 1968 (Title I), NFA of 1968 (Title II) [32]

Well, it turns out that President Lyndon Johnson not only brought us an age of terrorism, he immediately signed legislation severely restricting civilian gun rights in the United States; the Gun Control Act of 1968 (Title I) and an amendment to the NFA renamed the National Firearms Act of 1968 (Title II.) This was brought about due to both legal and societal issues.

As far as legality, the original NFA had just been made impotent by the Supreme Court in *Haynes v. United States.*[33] Haynes was a convicted felon who was charged with possession of an NFA firearm without having registered it. Haynes effectively argued that his lack of registration was effectively "pleading the fifth" and would have been an admission of his guilt. The Supreme Court held that the original requirement of the NFA to register certain types of firearms did in fact violate the Fifth Amendment's self-incrimination clause.

Societal issues did help spur the passage of these Acts as well. John F. Kennedy had been assassinated with a bolt action rifle in 1963.[34] Malcolm X was assassinated with a double-barreled sawed-off shotgun in 1965, although the medical examiner said that two bullets of different calibers had also been removed from his body.[35] More convincing though, were two assassinations during the actual debate of the legislation in 1968; Robert F. Kennedy was shot with a .22 caliber revolver, and Martin Luther King Jr. was shot with a 30.06 rifle.[36,37] Of course I added the weapons specifically, as only one of these four men was shot with a firearm regulated under either version of the NFA. There are, however, conspiracy theories regarding every single one of these shootings regarding whether the documented weapon is really the one that killed the individual.

The Gun Control Act prohibits the selling of firearms to certain categories of individuals thought to be a threat to public safety. From 18 U.S.C Section 922(d):

It shall be unlawful for any person to sell or otherwise dispose of any firearm or ammunition to any person knowing or having reasonable cause to believe that such person - (1) is under indictment for, or has been convicted in any court of, a crime punishable by imprisonment for a term exceeding one year (2) is a fugitive from justice; (3) is an unlawful user of or addicted to any controlled substance (as defined in section 102 of the Controlled Substances Act (21 U.S.C. 802)); (4) has been adjudicated as a mental defective or has been committed to any mental institution; (5) who, being an alien - (A) is illegally or unlawfully in the United States; or (B) except as provided in subsection (y)(2), has been admitted to the United States under a nonimmigrant visa (as that term is defined in section 101(a)(26) of the Immigration and Nationality Act (8 U.S.C. 1101(a)(26))); (6) who has been discharged from the Armed Forces under dishonorable conditions; (7) who, having been a citizen of the United States, has renounced his citizenship; (8) is subject to a court order that restrains such person from harassing, stalking, or threatening an intimate partner of such person or child of such intimate partner or person, or engaging in other conduct that would place an intimate partner in reasonable fear of bodily injury to the partner or child, except that this paragraph shall only apply to a court order that - (A) was issued after a hearing of which such person received actual notice, and at which such person had the opportunity to participate; and (B)(i) includes a finding that such person represents a credible threat to the physical safety of such intimate partner or child; or (ii) by its terms explicitly prohibits the use, attempted use, or threatened use of physical force against such intimate partner or child that would reasonably be expected to cause bodily injury; or (9) has been convicted in any court of a misdemeanor crime of domestic violence.

The GCA also does a number of other things: It creates a Federal Firearms License System (FFL) for anyone in the business of buying or selling firearms; it creates a requirement for serial numbers on any newly-manufactured firearm produced by licensed manufacturers in the United States or imported into the United States; and it barred importation of handguns with specific features such as short barrel, small caliber and non-adjustable sights. I assume the very last restriction is an assumption that it is easier to conceal a handgun that does not have adjustable sights? The FFL and serial number restrictions seem relatively sound, but I can understand the concern that they lead to further restrictions.

That brings us to one last feature of the GCA, which creates a "sporting purposes" test in an attempt to ban imports of military surplus rifles, declaring that they must "be generally recognized as particularly suitable for or readily adaptable to sporting purposes." As interpreted by Bureau of Alcohol, Tobacco, Firearms and Explosives, "sporting purposes" includes only hunting and organized competitive target shooting, but does not include "plinking" or "practical shooting" nor does it allow for collection for historical or design interest.[38] As a result, foreign made assault rifles and machine guns such as the AK-47, the FN FAL or the Heckler & Koch MP5 could no longer be imported into the United States for civilian ownership (however, semi-automatic models of the same weapons were permitted until the definition of "sporting purpose" was further tightened in 1989.)[39] The trend towards "sporting purposes" being argued as the meaning of the Second Amendment by legislators really becomes abundantly clear now.

As a side note, and possibly comic relief, according to a letter from the ATF dated September 21, 2011 entitled "Open Letter to All Federal Firearms Licensees", holders of state-issued medical marijuana cards are automatically "prohibited persons" under 18 U.S.C 922(g)(3) and "shipping, transporting, receiving or possessing firearms or ammunition" by a medical marijuana card holder is a violation. Marijuana is a Schedule I controlled substance and the Federal Law makes no exceptions for medicinal purposes even if sanctioned by state law. Interesting.[40]

The revisions to the original NFA, now known as Title II, fixed the flaws pointed out in *Haynes* by making existing firearms impossible to register by civilians...not unnecessary, impossible. False information on an NFA form is allowed to be used as evidence against a person in criminal proceedings for violations of the law occurring after the filing of the registration form. The stripped down receiver of a machine gun is now a regulated firearm in and of itself, as are any unassembled individual internal parts that could be used to build a machine gun in most cases. A category listed as Destructive Devices is added to the act, which covers any firearm with a bore over 0.50 inches (exempting 12 gauge shotguns due to their "legitimate sporting use") and also covers grenades, bombs, explosive missiles, poison gas and related items.

There's that sporting use statement again in regards to the shotgun. What was it the U.S. Government argued in *United States v Miller* ...wasn't it that the Second Amendment protected military and public defense weapons exclusively? How did we suddenly end up allowing or restricting firearms to civilians through determinations of "sporting purposes?" The government sure changes its mind a lot to suit its purposes, doesn't it? Does anything we've covered so far indicate that the Second Amendment has ever been a "sporting" right prior to this legislation? If hunters in the United States had not been afforded some restrictions in the law, the people would never have obeyed it. You can always legislate away sporting and hunting rights later, as history has shown. This seems to set a clear precedent for further gun control.

The Vietnam War

The brevity of this paragraph is not meant to diminish the overall impact the Vietnam War had on overall sentiment in the United States regarding such matters, however, the war doesn't seem to have incited any gun regulations specifically. It was however the first televised war, leaving an impression that it gave the general public a distinct graphic image of firearms and armed combat.[41] It also trampled that euphoric admiration for the military we spoke of that arose after WWII. The U.S. people clearly did not embrace the soldiers returning from war.[42]

Firearms Owners' Protection Act (1986) [43]

In spite of the major point of contention in this act that gets repeated over time, the name of the act is really not a misnomer. Overall, it was intended to correct some abuses of the Gun Control Act. Allegations of abuse by the ATF led to Congressional review. The Senate Judiciary Subcommittee on the Constitution concludes:

> The conclusion is thus inescapable that the history, concept, and wording of the second amendment to the Constitution of the United States, as well as its interpretation by every major commentator and court in the first half century after its ratification, indicates that what is protected is an individual right of a private citizen to own and carry firearms in a peaceful manner.[44]

This act intended to correct some of the abuses thus implied to exist by the subcommittee. Under the act, interstate sales of long guns were once again allowed under certain circumstances, it legalized ammunition shipments through the U.S. Postal Service, it removed requirements for record keeping on non armor-piercing ammunition, and provided for a 'safe passage' provision for those possessing firearms while merely passing through states which might have stricter gun control laws than their home state. In contrast to this, it also extended the restrictions regarding certain categories of individuals thought to be a threat to public safety to private transactions.

FOPA effectively restricts the sale of newly manufactured machine guns to military and law enforcement only. Ownership and sales of previously manufactured machine guns are still legal under NFA terms. Prior to this there had been a number of drug murders in Miami that were making headlines. In *Targeting Guns*, Dr. Gary Kleck claims statistics on homicides during that period suggest that machine guns accounted for less than 1 percent of all homicides.[45] Trying not to rely on Kleck's evaluation exclusively, I have to admit I myself am having a hell of a time confirming more than one or two machine gun deaths in the United States since the end of Prohibition. In a 1981 Time Magazine article, James Kelly claims that 23 percent of

Miami murders in the previous year were from machine gun fire.[46] Many of the machine pistols claimed to be used in the Miami murders fire the same rounds as common handguns so I'm not sure how the coroner could conclude what type of weapon that round came from other than hearsay in many cases. Yet there is no denying that machine guns were at least used (though maybe not successfully) in Miami and that fact was heavily publicized by the media. Were machine guns a national problem at the passage of this act in 1986 justifying a ban? All available evidence suggests no.

Brady Handgun Violence Prevention Act of 1993 [47]

This act was named after former White House Press Secretary James Brady who was shot during an assassination attempt on President Ronald Reagan by John Hinckly, Jr. with a .22 caliber revolver and paralyzed.[48] The Brady Act requires background checks by FFLs established by the GCA on dealer sales through the National Instant Criminal Background Check System (NICS) maintained by the FBI. Private transfers of firearms do not require a background check. Curios and relics are also not covered by the Brady Bill. Section 922(g) prohibits the sending or receiving of firearms or ammunition by shipping or transport through interstate or foreign commerce transactions by the same group of prohibited people described by the GCA in Section 922(d) we quoted above. Section 922(n) places the same restrictions on anyone under indictment for a crime punishable by imprisonment for a term exceeding one year.

The Branch Dividians, Waco Texas (1993)

I swear I'm not trying to make this book about Protestants but I'm required to give credit where credit is due. The details behind the Waco siege, many of which seem still unresolved, are worthy of nothing short of a book of its own, but I'll try to keep this as brief as possible. Many of the details from both sides I can only explain as bizarre. The Branch Dividians are a deeply religious sect of Seventh Day Adventists, the latter being a sect of Protestantism. Members of the Dividians had a compound in Elk Texas, about nine miles northeast of Waco called Mount Carmel Center Ranch. Leading up to the time of the siege they were led by David Koresh. The Dividians also held the Seventh-day Adventist 'end of times' belief, and Koresh professed to be the second coming of Christ they awaited.[49] The ATF had been watching the place for roughly a year on reports of firearm deliveries, inert grenades and implications of receiving items used in making bombs, in addition to a few neighbors reporting machine gun fire. Though it appeared at the time that the AR-15s the ATF confirmed having been sent to the Dividians were legal, in the affidavit for the search warrant ATF agent Davy Aguilera states:

> I know based upon my training and experience that an AR-15 is a semi-automatic rifle practically identical to the M16 rifle carried by United States Armed Forces. The AR-15 rifle fires .223 caliber ammunition and, just like the M16, can carry magazines of ammunition ranging from 30 to 60 rounds of ammunition. I have been involved in many cases where defendants, following a relatively simple process, convert AR-15 semi-automatic rifles to fully automatic rifles of the nature of the M16. This conversion process can often be accomplished by an

individual purchasing certain parts which will quickly transform the rifle to fire fully automatic. Often times templates, milling machines, lathes and instruction guides are utilized by the converter.[50]

Aguilera also refers to Mount Carmel Center as a "religious cult commune" and how Koresh believed he was the messiah. Most of the gun related details in the affidavit appear to be hearsay; however the evidence that Branch Dividian had received all the components necessary to constitute a destructive device as defined by the NFA appeared to be confirmed, and thus a search deemed warranted. (We'll discuss a potential destructive device component issue in a little more detail in Chapter 7.) I bring this up because having read through the affidavit, I was shocked at how many assumptions were being made that legally acquired firearms were "most likely" being modified illegally in support of obtaining a search warrant. There was an overwhelming theme that Aguilera felt that Branch Dividian was guilty until proven innocent by a search. The implication is that anybody who owns an AR-15 should be subject to a search warrant merely because it is possible to convert the semi-automatic weapon to full auto with a number of modifications and therefore they must be suspect of doing so.

There are indications that the Dividians had learned of the coming raid on February 28, but ATF proceeded anyway, and they were accompanied by the media. Shots were fired as the ATF tried to serve the search warrant to initiate what was obviously intended as a raid, and a full scale gun fight followed. Four ATF agents and five Davidians were killed in the initial gunfight, and Koresh is reported to have been wounded in the wrist. There is still no determination as to who fired first, ATF or the Dividians. Stories appeared to waver. ATF initially said that someone in the compound fired on them first. One of the ATF agents later claimed that the first shots were fired by the ATF "dog team" sent to kill the dogs in the Davidians kennel.[51] Seriously, do you really need to shoot the dogs in a kennel for a search warrant? (If a pet is considered property under the law, does a search warrant constitute due process in order to deprive you of that property?) The whole event becomes a big media mess and ultimately ends violently 50 days later on April 19 during a second assault on the compound.

There is a controversy about the front door itself. One of the members inside the compound, Steve Schneider, told FBI agents during the siege that, "the evidence from the front door will clearly show how many bullets and what happened."[52] Houston attorney Dick DeGuerin had gone inside the compound during the siege and testified in court that only the right hand door panel had bullet holes in it and clearly showed that the bullet holes were made from incoming rounds. The right hand panel of the door mysteriously went missing before the trial. Texas Trooper Sgt. David Keys later testified that he saw something being loaded into a U-Haul by two men shortly after the seige ended which may have been the door, but was never confirmed.

There were also reports of child abuse on the compound. Other than Koresh himself saying he had fathered children with girls in their mid teens, and I'm not suggesting that isn't abuse, no other evidence of child abuse was ever found. In fact, during the siege the children on the compound didn't want to leave. Though the ATF referred to many of those in the compound as hostages, all accounts seem to suggest that nobody wanted to leave. Reports suggest that 21 children eventually left the compound during the siege. Attorney

General Janet Reno used child abuse and a fear of mass suicide to convince President Bill Clinton to approve the final raid, though neither of those issues appeared to be a threat. Reno did however specify no pyrotechnic devices be used in the assault.[53] She also noted the FBI was getting tired of waiting and the standoff was costing a million dollars a week. On April 19, the FBI punched holes in the walls of the compound with booms on their armored CEVs in order to pump tear gas into the compound to force out the inhabitants. It was later confirmed that the FBI did use pyrotechnic devices as well.[54] Three hours after the breach in the compound walls three fires broke out. It is still unclear how the fires began or which side was at fault. The fire engulfed the complex and 76 men, women and children died in the fire, including David Koresh. From the remains of the aftermath, the ATF claims that some weapons had been modified to full-auto fire.[55]

Many refer to the conflict as the Waco Massacre, and many details do still appear unresolved today. On one hand: It is not illegal to stockpile legal weapons for defense; the Branch Dividians were never accused of offensive crimes with the weapons prior to the siege and appear to have only intended them to be for defensive purposes of their compound, under a religious belief they held protected under the First Amendment; machine guns manufactured prior to 1986 were not illegal and thus machine gun fire is not necessarily a sign of criminal activity; possessing a weapon which could be modified to break the law does not violate the law until you modify the weapon, unless you have specific parts which break the law in and of themselves; did the confirmed evidence actually support a search warrant and full-scale raid on the compound accompanied by the media[?]; did they in fact deserve to die if they did not start the firefight? On the other hand: Evidence suggests they did alter some firearms illegally; does Freedom of Religion actually protect you from being judged delusional and a threat to society[?]; Koresh did admit to impregnating under-age girls; it is possible that they fired first when presented with the search warrant they had prior knowledge was coming. The whole thing played out on live TV. Time magazine conducted a poll in August of 1999 which indicated that roughly 61 percent of the people believed the Government started the fire.[56]

On the second anniversary of the burning of the Mount Carmel Complex, Timothy McVeigh and Terry Nichols set off a bomb at the Alfred P. Murrah Federal Building in Oklahoma City, now known as the Oklahoma City Bombing. McVeigh cited the mishandling of the Waco event by the federal government as the motivation for the bombing, thus choosing to set off the bomb on April 19. In fact, McVeigh has been confirmed to have been present in the crowd at the Waco Siege himself. In his own words McVeigh states:

> I chose to bomb a federal building because such an action served more purposes than other options. Foremost, the bombing was a retaliatory strike; a counter attack, for the cumulative raids (and subsequent violence and damage) that federal agents had participated in over the preceding years (including, but not limited to, Waco.) From the formation of such units as the FBI's "Hostage Rescue" and other assault teams amongst federal agencies during the '80's; culminating in the Waco incident, federal actions grew increasingly militaristic and violent, to the point where at Waco, our government - like the Chinese - was deploying tanks against its own citizens.[57]

I do not want to give the impression that I condone the actions of either the Branch Dividians or the subsequent actions of Timothy McVeigh in response to the Waco event. I cannot say having read through the affidavits and testimony I'm entirely in support of the ATF or FBI in regards to that specific event either. The event could have been handled better; it could have been handled worse. This event (and the subsequent Oklahoma City Bombing) I present here merely because it changed the perceptions of the overall public, legislators and law enforcement agencies dramatically. As a result, some fear government oppression more, others developing a greater fear of domestic terrorism. This results in a significant impact on the gun rights of average citizens.

Federal Assault Weapons Ban (AWB) (1994)

The Federal Assault Weapons Ban, also known as the Public Safety and Recreational Firearms Use Protection Act, was a subtitle of the Violent Crime Control and Law Enforcement Act of 1994 under Title XI, Subtitle A. The Stockton schoolyard shooting where Patrick Purdy killed 5 children and wounded 30 others in 1989, the subsequent Waco siege and the 101 California street shooting where Gian Luigi Ferri killed 8 people and himself in 1993 are often cited as events which created the major stimulus for the ban.[58,59] The Federal Assault Weapons Ban prohibited the manufacture, transfer or possession of semiautomatic 'assault weapons', as well as a prohibition on the transfer or possession of "large-capacity" ammunition feeding devices for civilian use for a period of ten years. Any assault weapons legally owned prior to the passing of the act were exempt. In addition to a long list of specifically named firearms, or any copies or duplicates of those firearms in any caliber, the act enumerates what

constitutes an "assault weapon" in regards to three classes of
firearms; semiautomatic rifles, semiautomatic pistols and
semiautomatic shotguns. The qualifications for making each
an assault weapon are listed below.[60]

A semiautomatic rifle that has an ability to accept a
detachable magazine and has at least two of the following
features:

- A folding or telescoping stock
- A pistol grip that protrudes beneath the action of the
weapon
- A bayonet mount
- A flash suppressor or threaded barrel
- A grenade launcher

A semiautomatic pistol that has an ability to accept a
detachable magazine and has at least two of the following:

- An ammunition magazine that attaches to the pistol
outside of the pistol grip
- A threaded barrel capable of attaching a barrel
extender, flash suppressor, handgrip or silencer
- A shroud around the barrel which can be used to hold
the firearm without being burned
- A manufactured weight of 50 ounces or more when
unloaded
- A semiautomatic version of an automatic firearm

A semiautomatic shotgun that has at least two of the
following features:

- A folding or telescoping stock
- A pistol grip that protrudes beneath the action of the
weapon

- A fixed magazine capacity in excess of 5 rounds
- An ability to accept a detachable magazine

Some pro-gun advocates argue that these are merely cosmetic features, but I would have to disagree in most cases. I know a lot of people are grumbling right now, but I'll address why. Many of these features do, in fact, deal with the stability of the weapon during fire. The bulk of restrictions around these weapons revolve around the ability to accept a detachable magazine which is not in the grip itself. As such, overall size of the weapon doesn't appear to be a major factor in regulating firearms in this act. A folding stock, however, is listed because of its ease of concealment and seems a silly addition since semiautomatic handguns with a magazine in the grip are easier to conceal and are not being banned, so I want to disqualify that one right now from being either functional or cosmetic. A telescoping stock, however, does provide a better fit for the shooter and thus more stability. A muzzle brake will help with recoil, a flash suppressor will help maintain your view of the target when dark and a suppressor will silence that weapon to some degree; so I would have to concede a threaded barrel is not merely cosmetic. A pistol grip or a forward grip on a rifle will provide more stability as well. A grenade launcher and a bayonet mount don't seem merely cosmetic either. It would be like arguing that a condom is merely a cosmetic feature for your penis, when in reality it does serve a non-aesthetic purpose.

However: First, the advantage of these features over a nearly identical firearm without as many of these features is most likely nominal in the big picture, the latter still firing the same caliber round at virtually the same speed between rounds with the same magazine capacity, possibly only less accurately (we'll revisit this topic in more detail later) in repetition; and second, excluding the grenade launcher and folding stock, if there is any edge in having these features on a weapon, they would provide the exact same advantage to a person trying to defend his life from one or more aggressors as would someone attempting to use the weapon for offensive purposes. You have to conclude that if any of these features are an offensive advantage in crime, those same features provide the same defensive advantage in self-defense scenarios, not merely in a militia or military defense capacity. Of course, that argument goes both ways.

The "large-capacity" magazine ban actually encompassed a substantially larger overall restriction, as many non "assault weapons" were designed with "large-capacity" magazines. The bulk of this law really lies in the restriction on "large-capacity" magazines, though it rarely gets the bulk of the attention with most people focusing on the weapon itself. In fact, if you look up "Federal Assault Weapons Ban" on Wikipedia, the "large-capacity" magazines barely even get a mention.[61] It may be because the restrictions are much easier to state than the "assault weapon" definitions. In regards to civilian use, you cannot transfer a magazine with a capacity higher than 10 rounds, and you cannot own one unless it was lawfully owned prior to this act. In the latter case regarding the ownership of pre-ban magazines, the government has the burden of proof regarding any accusations regarding violations of the law. This restriction on "large-capacity" magazines becomes extremely important when looking at statistics regarding this ban in the future. Later, we'll look at the newly labeled "assault weapons" and "large-capacity" magazines and the subsequent effect on crimes during the 10 year period under the Federal Assault Weapons Ban. In fact, the act itself required the Attorney General to investigate and study the effects of the subtitle on violent and drug trafficking crimes...that should be enlightening.

District of Columbia v. Heller, 554 U.S. 570 (2008)

District of Columbia v. Heller is a landmark Supreme Court case where the Second Amendment, quite literally, finally gets its day in court. It was decided on June 26, 2008. The District of Columbia had a layered set of laws that effectively prohibited handguns. It was a crime to carry an unregistered firearm and registration of firearms was prohibited. You could not carry a handgun without a license, and the chief of police may issue licenses for one year periods. Any lawfully owned firearms kept at home needed to be "unloaded and dissembled or bound by a trigger lock or similar device." The combined outcome was that you could not have a working firearm at home for self-defense purposes.

Dick Heller was a police officer who was authorized to carry a gun on duty and was denied a registration certificate for a handgun he wished to keep at home for self-defense. He filed a lawsuit in the Federal District Court claiming the ban violated Second Amendment rights, which was dismissed. The Court of Appeals held that the District of Columbia's effective total ban of handguns violated Second Amendment rights and reversed the decision. The Supreme Court was petitioned to hear the case. They affirmed the decision and held that the Second Amendment protects an individual's right to possess a firearm for traditionally lawful purposes. The decision in the District of Columbia, however, only applied federally and did not extend to the states. Justice Scalia delivered the opinion of the court, and noted that nothing in the previous cases of *Cruikshank*, *Presser* or

Miller forecloses their interpretation of the Second Amendment in this decision. As we previously noted, and Justice Scalia also confirms, the courts in the previous cases did in fact state that the right to bear arms was a natural and individual right. Though they state that nothing changes previous court decisions, it is a dramatic change in how many courts have interpreted the Second Amendment right to be a collective right only. The right to keep and bear arms is now officially an individual right supported by court precedent. The court also states that the handgun is the most common and lawful choice for self-defense, as such it is specifically protected under the Second Amendment.

In fact, Justice Scalia does an incredible job summing up an accurate history of the Second Amendment in dicta. However, I can't help but take note of a couple of questionable exceptions in subsequent logic which aren't necessarily important to the case decision but are important to present and future interpretations of the Second Amendment overall. Both deal with arms of military nature. First, again in dicta, Justice Scalia cites three prevailing definitions of arms in the 18th century; "weapons of offence, or armour of defence"; "any thing that a man wears for his defence, or takes into his hands, or useth in wrath to cast at or strike another"; and "instruments of offence generally made use of in war" with Justice Scalia noting that the latter source "stated that all firearms constituted "arms."" Yet Justice Scalia makes the comment, "The term [arms] was applied, then as now, to weapons that were not specifically designed for military use and were not employed in a military capacity." Granted, nothing in these definitions says that arms are specifically for military use, but where do any of these definitions imply that arms were never employed in a military capacity? Maybe 'not always employed in a military capacity' would have been more

80

appropriate. If all firearms constitute arms, and if no arms were employed in a military capacity, what does Justice Scalia believe 'was' employed in a military capacity...sticks and stones? In fact, one of the very definitions he provides states they were generally used in war. It gets more confusing, as he then states '"Keep arms" was simply a common way of referring to possessing arms, for militiamen and everyone else.' Militiamen, possessing those arms, are used in a military capacity. You don't have to know Latin to realize both words stem from the same root.[62] What exactly is he doing here? Is Justice Scalia specifically trying to deny that military weapons are protected under the Second Amendment, or is he just going too far out of his way to suggest that the Second Amendment right is not "only" a collective right held by members of a militia?

Justice Scalia specifies how modern firearms are still protected under the Second Amendment:

> Some have made the argument, bordering on the frivolous, that only those arms in existence in the 18th century are protected by the Second Amendment. We do not interpret constitutional rights that way. Just as the First Amendment protects modern forms of communications, e.g., Reno v. American Civil Liberties Union, 521 U.S. 844, 849 (1997), and the Fourth Amendment applies to modern forms of search, e.g., Kyllo v. United States, 533 U.S. 27, 35-36 (2001), the Second Amendment extends, prima facie, to all instruments that constitute bearable arms, even those that were not in existence at the time of the founding.

That appears to put "the Second Amendment only applied to single shot muskets crowd" in their place but what constitutes a modern weapon then; repeating rifles, semiautomatic pistols, machine guns? So based on his comment above these should be protected under the Second Amendment, right? Looking at his interpretation of Miller, he states, 'We therefore read Miller to say only that the Second Amendment does not protect those weapons not typically possessed by law-abiding citizens for lawful purposes..." Let's look at his further comments about machine guns to see how they align with this analysis of Miller:

> It may be objected that if weapons that are most useful in military service—M16 rifles and the like— may be banned, then the Second Amendment right is completely detached from the prefatory clause. But as we have said, the conception of the militia at the time of the Second Amendment's ratification was the body of all citizens capable of military service, who would bring the sorts of lawful weapons that they possessed at home to militia duty. It may well be true today that a militia, to be as effective as militias in the 18th century, would require sophisticated arms that are highly unusual in society at large. Indeed, it may be true that no amount of small arms could be useful against modern-day bombers and tanks. But the fact that modern developments have limited the degree of fit between the prefatory clause and the protected right cannot change our interpretation of the right.

I have read this paragraph well over 100 times now to try to decipher any bit of ambiguities I could be missing in its meaning...and I've contemplated a lot of them. The argument I finally believe Scalia is making here, also considering his analysis of the Miller decision, is that the banning of M16s does not detach the prefatory clause from the Second Amendment right since militia members at the time of the ratification would only bring weapons that were common and lawful at the time. The fact that those types of weapons would no longer be adequate for a present day militia due to modern technology being a moot point; an M16 is neither common nor lawful in present day society and thus not protected by the Second Amendment's prefatory clause. Yet we still have an individual right to keep and bear arms that are presently lawful regardless of the fit between the prefatory clause and the right itself and we must still acknowledge that right.

There appear to be some arguments that question Justice Scalia's conclusion here. He definitely doesn't address that ownership of very specific weapons and ammunition were almost immediately required through the subsequent Militia Acts, actually mandating what weapons the citizens comprising the militia must own. Scalia's suggestion that weapons most useful in military service - M16 rifles and the like - are not the sort of lawful weapons a citizen of society might bring to militia duty anyway, not being common and lawful in society at the time of the Heller decision, and therefore not protected by the Second Amendment fails to consider one fact: It is not necessarily "modern developments" that have limited the degree of fit between the prefatory clause of a militia and the protected right regarding firearms such as the M16, it is a series of regulations that have made the machine gun first "highly unusual in society at large" and finally unlawful, which may very well themselves be in violation of the Second Amendment.

Justice Scalia's argument creates this conundrum: If you ban all weapons in violation of the Second Amendment, then no weapons will continue to be common and lawful weapons in society at the time, and thus no weapons would be protected under the Second Amendment (and I guess the militia will not be bringing any weapons to the fight in spite of no detachment of the prefatory clause from the Second Amendment right being created). It is a circular argument. In 1934 the NFA taxed machine guns by requiring a registration. There is nothing to suggest that machine guns weren't common at the time; apparently they felt they were too common or else why seek to restrict them? They were certainly not uncommon in the military such as the court in Miller falsely concluded regarding the sawed off shotgun.[63] Machine guns were not banned until 1986 (with a grandfather clause.) At the time of Heller in 2008, of course machine guns were uncommon and unlawful in society; they had been restricted by the NFA of 1934 and subsequently banned by the Firearms Owners' Protection Act, which theoretically could be a violation of the Second Amendment depending on how specifically you want to apply Justice Scalia's interpretation of Miller to the Miller case itself in 1939. You know, when machine guns were lawful but recently taxed.

If a present argument were made that claims that the National Firearms Act of 1934 and the Firearms Owners' Protection Act of 1986 violated Second Amendment rights by regulating and then banning machine guns, a valid argument in rebuttal could not be made in this manner: The Second Amendment only secures rights to weapons that are 'common and lawful' in society at the time; machine guns are no longer 'common and lawful' in society due to the National Firearms Act of 1934 and the Firearms Owners' Protection Act of 1986 effectively restricting and banning their sale; therefore, the National Firearms Act of 1934 and the Firearms Owners' Protection Act of 1986 do not violate Second Amendment rights. Okay, one more time for any of you who just aren't quite seeing the problem yet: The government could confiscate all guns from society by any means, then attempting to cite Scalia's comments claim no guns are common or lawfully owned in society, and therefore no guns are protected by the Second Amendment. This ideology could ultimately be used to effectively defeat the very precedent set in this case; concluding that handguns are the most prevalent and lawful form of self-defense, therefore protected by the Second Amendment.

It appears to put the cart in front of the horse, by suggesting constitutionality is determined by restrictive legislation, and not that legislation is dictated and restrained by constitutionality. I honestly have no desire to ever own a fully automatic weapon or any personal reasons to argue for 'desiring' to own one specifically, as I think they effectively waste ammunition and create more of a disadvantage than advantage in most cases where someone isn't just handing you an endless supply of ammo for free. But if an M16 is banned through legislation based on a purely arbitrary decision and then that arbitrary decision becomes the reason it is no longer protected by the Second Amendment as Scalia's comments in this case suggest, then why would other firearms not follow suit as legislators try to repeat the tactic? Maybe something like another "assault weapons ban" for instance.

And yet further into the conundrum we go. It follows that by the very same argument, you could not constitutionally ban "assault weapons" based on Justice Scalia's comments because they are, in fact, highly common in society and currently lawfully owned. The prefatory clause not being detached from the Second Amendment, this is exactly the type of weapon a member of a modern day militia would bring! Is it not coincidentally amusing that the current argument is that "assault weapons" are "too common" in society? Wow, here we are again, with legislators attempting to regulate a firearm because it is perceived to be too common, though apparently protected by the Second Amendment for that very reason. Why are legislators, such as Diane Feinstein, continuing to do this in stark contrast to Justice Scalia's comments?[64] Is it because they realize the comments in the previous paragraph ring true? (On January 13, 2013 Diane Feinstein introduced the Assault Weapons Ban of 2013. The full title is: To regulate assault weapons, to ensure that the right to keep and bear arms is not unlimited, and for other purposes. It was defeated by Congress on April 17, 2013 by a vote of 40 to 60.)[65]

Further, I find it hard to accept Justice Scalia's implication that a machine gun is either a sophisticated arm of modern times or too dangerous and unusual, not sensible in the hands of the citizens that make up a militia nor something they would have possessed sans standing restrictions, suggesting it is in the ranks of modern-day bombers and tanks of which the militia should not possess. I can't imagine he's suggesting that the M16 won't work against bombers and tanks anyway; therefore you just can't have one? He's got to be suggesting it is too modern and sophisticated for the modern citizen, right?

In addition to the fact that he himself called such an argument frivolous, I think there are some other problems here. In fact, I might as well point out now that it is not illegal for civilians to own fighter jets or military tanks, so long as any weapons systems are deactivated.[66] That's right, contrary to what you might think Justice Scalia infers, you can have your very own fighter jet and your very own tank...just not an M16, that's too dangerous and unusual. The first notable machine gun in military service is considered to be the Gatling Gun and was invented in 1861 and used by General Benjamin Butler of the Union Army and tested by the United States Navy in 1862.[67,68] Yes, 19th century, 150 years ago. That is the middle of the American Civil War, where much of the fighting was done by - you guessed it - militias. Obviously, guys didn't bring these from home...but modern they are not. In all fairness to semantics, the first Gatling gun actually required a person to crank it to fire continuously; therefore it was considered a "machine gun" but was not a true automatic weapon. The first true "fully automatic weapon" was the Maxim gun, invented in 1884, which made use of the fired projectile's recoil force to reload the weapon...also used by militias.[69] This technology actually predates and inspires John Browning's M1911 handgun, which Justice Scalia just confirmed the Constitutional right to possess, and is thus an even more modern and sophisticated development than the machine gun that inspired it and due to its concealability and its .45 inch diameter projectile possibly more dangerous.[70]

The term 'machine gun' is about as vague as 'jet airplane.' Passing regulation on the general term with no distinction between an M16 and an M2 is like banning a Gulfwing because of an F-16. Maybe both should be banned independently on their own merits and flaws, but to ban them both because they are both "jets" would be a ludicrous misuse of semantics. Maybe we need more refinement in the semantics we use regarding automatic weapons and machine guns, segregating what are heavy artillery machine guns from small handheld machine guns. Let me ask you, do you think there is a distinct difference between someone with a full auto .223 (5.56) submachine gun in their hand and someone with a .50 caliber heavy artillery machine gun mounted in a turret on the roof of their house? (I'm sure this is just a reminder for you; increasing the diameter of a circle times 2, such as the diameter of the cross section of a bullet, increases the area times 4.) Would it even be fair to reference them both with the same general term "machine gun?" Would you find one to be more dangerous and unusual than the other?

A change in technology from a single shot rifle or musket to a weapon that fires multiple rounds without reload is not a change that is a 'modern development', but a weapon that fires those same rounds with a single pull of the trigger is? A six shot revolver was deemed more dangerous at its invention in comparison to a single shot musket just as an M16 might now be deemed dangerous in comparison to a six shot revolver. Remember, the repeating rifle only predated the machine gun by a single year as well.[71] Dangerous is not only a matter of subjective perception, it is often a matter of a modern invention in the hands of an as of yet untrained individual, and thus a matter of acclimation to technology. Automobiles were once considered dangerous and unusual. Where exactly do you justify drawing the line between what is modern and sophisticated, and what is dangerous?

On the surface, it appears that Justice Scalia did not think through his arms not used in a military capacity or M16 comments logically at all. In reality, he was probably doing the best he could to balance a new court precedent that confirms a Constitutional individual right to keep and bear arms as addressed in this specific case, while not entirely dismantling every single piece of legislation regarding the militia or firearms in the past 100 years which is merely implicated at violating Second Amendment rights in this decision with no other considerations as to that specific legislation's merit. None of this was to attack Justice Scalia in any way, but seeing the juggling he had to do in regards to militia and machine guns should at least make you ask if much of the prior standing legislation up until now isn't just a house of cards that ultimately crumbles around confirmation of an individual right to keep and bear arms. Hopefully it doesn't crumble around the paradox Justice Scalia may have created.

It should be clear to you by now that the Supreme Court just brought us back in line with the historical meaning of the Second Amendment in regards to individual rights, though this case does appear to diminish the collective rights ideology somewhat. Whether you choose to personally possess firearms or not is irrelevant, you've just had a civil liberty restored either way. Unless of course you get called into militia service and only have a handgun to bring to the fight, I guess.

McDonald v. Chicago, 561 U.S. 742 (2010) [72]

McDonald v. Chicago is another landmark decision by the Supreme Court which held that the Second Amendment is incorporated by the Due Process Clause of the Fourteenth Amendment, and thus extends the *Heller* decision to apply to the states. Much like the District of Columbia, the City of Chicago had required that all firearms in the city be registered while also refusing to register handguns after a 1982 ban, effectively making handguns illegal. Otis McDonald was an elderly man who had bought a house nearly 40 years ago and had watched the neighborhood decline drastically in that time. Though McDonald did own shotguns, he felt that a handgun was more appropriate for home self-defense, and along with three others filed lawsuits. The District Court dismissed the suits. The Court of Appeals for the Seventh Circuit affirmed.

The Supreme Court reversed the decision in a 5-4 vote. The majority held that the Due Process clause of the Fourteenth Amendment incorporates the Second Amendment rights in *Heller*. Justice Clarence Thomas disagreed with the Due Process claim and felt the Second Amendment was better incorporated through the Privileges and Immunities Clause, which would have effectively overturned the Slaughterhouse Cases and applied the entire Bill of Rights to the states. Justice Breyer, joined by Justices Ginsburg and Sotomayor, dissented in the opinion and argued that there is nothing in the Second Amendment's "text, history, or underlying rationale" that characterizes it as a "fundamental right" which would warrant incorporation of the Second Amendment to the states through the Fourteenth Amendment. I know these are Supreme Court Justices, but after the history we have covered so far, I'm beginning to wonder if these three can even read. I mean seriously, nothing in history suggesting that the right to keep and bear arms is a fundamental right? Nearly everything we've seen in history, including the courts in *Cruikshank* and *Presser*, say the right to keep and bear arms is a fundamental and natural right of man. It's like suggesting there is no evidence that the sun, from the perception of those in the United States, rises in the East. Do you think these three Justices really believe this, or are they trying to take a political stand through a body of government that is supposed to remain apolitical and unbiased?

Moore v. Madigan (USDC 11-CV-405-WDS, 11-CV-03134; 7th Cir. 12-1269, 12-1788) (2013)

Moore v. Madigan was actually one in a set of two cases in appeal, consolidated together by the court for oral argument, which challenged an Illinois law which banned the carrying of firearms in public (outside of a few exceptions). Appellants felt the Illinois law violated Second Amendment rights as interpreted in both *District of Columbia v. Heller* and *McDonald v. City of Chicago*. However, neither of these cases specifically addressed that right outside of the home. Judge Richard Posner in writing the opinion of the court stated, "To confine the right to be armed to the home is to divorce the Second Amendment from the right of self-defense described in *Heller* and *McDonald*" later adding "The Supreme Court has decided that the amendment confers a right to bear arms for self-defense, which is as important outside the home as inside." Judge Posner also seems to warn legislators about initiating permit systems that only favor certain groups of individuals while effectively removing the rights of the average citizen to obtain a permit. As we've seen, this is not an uncommon practice in an attempt to restrict gun rights. The court stayed the mandate for 180 days to allow Illinois legislature the opportunity to draft new legislation. They were given a final 30 day extension to draft a law by July 9, 2013, and though defendants were considering an appeal to the United States Supreme Court, the Illinois legislature passed a "shall issue" concealed carry law in July making further appeal a moot point. In the end, the legislature overrode a veto of the governor and approved Illinois concealed carry to begin January 2014, at the latest.[73-76]

Sandy Hook Elementary School Shooting (2012)

The Sandy Hook Elementary School Shooting took place on December 14, 2012 at a kindergarten through fourth grade school in Newtown Connecticut. It was the second deadliest U.S. "mass shooting" after the Virginia Tech shootings in 2007. Adam Lanza was a 20-year-old male who shot and killed his mother at their home, then proceeded to the school where he killed 20 children and 6 adult staff members before killing himself. He shot his mother with a bolt action .22 rifle, the fatalities at the school were with a Bushmaster SM15-E2S which is an AR-15 semi-automatic rifle clone with one military style feature (pistol grip below the action), and he shot himself with a handgun. Note: Adam Lanza's Bushmaster was not, by definition, an "assault weapon" at the time of the shooting as it only possessed the one military style feature. All of the weapons were registered and legally owned by his mother, Nancy Lanza. Since the event immediately brought up renewed debates about magazine capacity, it seems prudent to mention that it was noted that during the shooting Adam Lanza often made tactical reloads (changing out a magazine before it is empty), sometimes shooting as few as 15 shots from a 30 round magazine.[77]

I point a couple of things out here because I'm finding it present in lots of distorted media stories and statistics. I found so many articles that referred to Lanza's Bushmaster as an "assault weapon" that I got tired of counting, yet at the time it was neither illegal nor by any standing definition an "assault weapon." I also consistently find "large-capacity" magazines mentioned in statistics, but rarely if ever any reference to how many rounds were actually fired from each magazine. I applaud that reporting in this case. A 30 round magazine with only 10 rounds fired out of it in an event gives no valid logical argument that the "large-capacity" magazine in question had any relation to the outcome due merely to its capacity if the larger capacity never came into play. It's like mentioning that a suspect was driving a Chevy with a 427 when talking about the suspect running a stop sign. The 427 may have had no impact on the running of the stop sign, but the reference certainly gives the impression that they ran the stop sign at 100 miles an hour. They may have run the stop sign at 2 miles an hour, the 427 being irrelevant to the breaking of the law. That may be fine, and the mentioning of the 427 merely factual...until the media or legislature uses that instance in a data set to then argue that high displacement engines are responsible for the illegal running of stop signs. At that point statistical errors are created by confusing cause and effect, which distort the facts and ultimately distorts the perceptions of the people. The murder of 20 children is certainly horrible enough, but the media did a lot of distorting people's perceptions as well and part of society demanded an immediate response by the government to the perceived "school shooting epidemic."

The New York Secure Ammunition and Firearms Enforcement [SAFE] Act (2013)

The NY SAFE Act is a series of firearm related laws, mostly amending other pre-existing laws, passed in the state of New York by the New York State Legislature and signed into law by Governor Andrew M. Cuomo on January 15, 2013. The law was passed primarily in response to the shooting which happened at Sandy Hook Elementary School in Newtown Connecticut a month earlier.[78] Since some people claim the bill's passage was basically forced without proper consideration, it seems fair to point out that the bill was passed in the middle of the night under a "message of necessity" which bypassed the state's required 3 day review period. Governor Andrew Cuomo signed the bill into law the following morning after it passed the legislature.[79]

Here are the key points of the NY SAFE Act:

- The law redefined the term "assault weapon" as any semi-automatic gun with a detachable magazine, from requiring two features commonly associated with military weapons previously adopted from the definition from the expired Federal Assault Weapons Ban, to requiring only one feature to be an "assault weapon." [A folding or telescoping stock; a pistol grip that protrudes conspicuously beneath the action of the weapon; a thumbhole stock; a second handgrip or a protruding grip that can be held by the non-trigger hand; a bayonet mount; a flash suppressor, muzzle break, muzzle compensator, or threaded barrel designed to accommodate a flash suppressor, muzzle break, or muzzle compensator; or a grenade launcher.] The sale or transfer of the newly defined "assault weapon" is banned within the state. Out of state sales are still permitted. Any New Yorker who already owns a weapon falling under the new ban must register that weapon with the state within one year.

- Establishes a statewide gun license and record database.

- All firearm purchases must be done though a licensed firearm dealer (FFL.) Transfers between family members are exempt.

- Background checks are required on all firearm sales, including private sellers. Transfers between family members are exempt.

- Anyone who owns a handgun or pre-ban "assault rifle" will have to recertify their permit every five years through their county of residence.

- Bans possession of any "large-capacity magazines" with a maximum capacity over 10 rounds. A 10 round magazine may be loaded with no more than 7 rounds. Any pre-ban 30 round magazine which was exempt prior, must be sold within one year to an out of state resident or surrendered to local authorities.

- An ammunition dealer is required to be registered with the superintendent of the State Police, to conduct a background check through a state-created database on all ammunition sales and is required to allow access of all sales and amounts to the state. Internet sales of ammunition are allowed, but the ammunition must be shipped to a licensed dealer within the state of NY for pickup. As of this writing, the electronic background check has not yet been implemented as an adequate system has yet to be designed.

- Any mental health professional who believes a patient made a credible threat to harm others must report such threat to a mental health director, who would have to report the threat to the state Department of Criminal Justice Services. Those patients will be checked on the new state database to see if they possess firearms, and that patient can then have any firearm licenses or permits revoked and firearms confiscated by law enforcement.

- All stolen guns must be reported within 24 hours, failure to do so can result in a misdemeanor.

- Creates safe storage requirements from any household member who may be a prohibited person under the law. Unsafe storage of an "assault weapon" is a misdemeanor.

- Enhanced criminal penalties on gun crimes; taking a gun on school property is now a felony; penalties for participation in gang activity that results in the commission of a violent crime; Amends aggravated murder Law to increase penalties for murdering a first responder.

- Protects state registered handgun owners from being identified publicly "if" they choose to opt in to being protected from disclosure by filing a form within 120 days of the law's enactment.

- When a judge issues a protection order and finds a substantial risk that the individual subjected to the order will use a gun against the person protected by the order, the judge is required to order the surrender of the weapon.

Here is a quote from the New York State Senate website in their "Statement of Support" section regarding the Act: "Some weapons are so dangerous and some ammunition devices so lethal that we simply cannot afford to continue selling them in our state. Assault weapons that have military-style features unnecessary for hunting and sporting purposes are this kind of weapon. The test adopted in this legislation is intended to bring a simplicity of definition focusing on the lethality of the weapon, amplified by the particular features. Given the difficulty of maintaining a list of guns that keeps pace with changes in weapon design, the one-feature test is a more comprehensive means for addressing these dangerous weapons."[80] There's that peculiar "hunting and sporting purposes" clause again.

I'm not sure I can agree that redefining the term "assault weapon" to be different than that presented by the Federal

Government is really "intended to bring a simplicity of definition" to the situation. It actually seems to distort the meaning of the definition, at least currently accepted as consistent in the debate, though arguably inaccurate to begin with. Can we really allow multiple entities to recreate definitions on their own whim? Does this not further confuse any debate about the topic? As I sit here staring at this quote, I can't help but think that "some ammunition devices are so lethal" is not unlike arguing that the size of the box the pizza comes in is the reason for obesity. How long does it really take to open up that second box of pizza and grab the next slice? Adam Lanza wasn't lethal because he had 30 round magazines. Again, news reports said that he changed magazines before they were empty. He was lethal because he knew how to manage his ammo, learned how to change magazines effectively and learned how to manage tactical reloads to his advantage. More importantly, witnesses pointed out he took specific aim at specific targets while shooting. At this point in my research, I'm struggling to find any sound logic that an "ammunition device", in and of itself, can be more or less lethal...but we'll get back to that later.

We've seen recent court decisions that reaffirm your Second Amendment right to keep and bear arms and your right to do so in public which has been extended to a state level. The NY SAFE Act covers a pretty broad area in regards to different aspects of different laws. Some of these appear sound, others questionable. The Courts have not determined that the Second Amendment should be entirely unregulated. The NY Legislature feels that their definition of "assault weapons" also meets the Court's definition of "dangerous and unusual" weapons, thus arguing that their "assault weapon" ban is constitutional. At present, an AR-15 is far from unusual and would actually be the weapon most likely for a member of a militia of the people to bring into service if required to do so. So the question then becomes: Does New York have a constitutional right to redefine classes of firearms as they see fit and an unrestrained right to restrict them, or does restricting one of the most common rifles held by American citizens merely represent "a wanton and causeless restraint of the will of the subject" in regards to the most recent Supreme Court decisions? You knew this was going to get challenged, right...so let's see where that stands at present.

New York State Rifle & Pistol Ass'n, Inc., et al. v. Cuomo, et al.
Connecticut Citizens' Defense League, et al. v. Malloy, et al.
(2015)[81]
14-36-cv(Lead); 14-319-cv (XAP)

The United States Court of Appeals for the Second Circuit consolidated two similar appeals, one (specifically regarding The SAFE Act) from the U.S. District Court for the Western District of New York, and a similar case (regarding Connecticut's subsequent and similar law) from the U.S. District Court for the District of Connecticut. They were quite similar in regards to the core of the complaints, so we'll just discuss this case from the perspective of The SAFE Act as the decision ultimately applied to both. The District Court case was filed December 31, 2013. The appeal was decided October 19, 2015.

The Plaintiffs originally challenged a number of changes made under The Safe Act which included the constitutionality of the amended "assault weapons" category, the ban on "large-capacity" magazines, challenged a number of the provisions as being constitutionally vague and challenged a provision that required ammunition purchases be made in person. The District Court found that the requirement that all ammunition sales be conducted in person did not unduly burden interstate commerce, as an out of state company was not prohibited from making a "brick and mortar" presence in the state to sell ammunition to New Yorkers. This issue does not appear to have gone to appeal. Three provisions were struck down as vague by the lower District Court, but they all got overturned later in appeal (and honestly there wasn't really anything there all that critical.) So let's look at the logic of the Court regarding the remaining issues that were challenged in appeal and affirmed by the Appellate Court.

The Court's logic is interesting to follow. The Heller decision had defined Second Amendment rights regarding a number of issues, but at the same time left open and ambiguous the level of scrutiny they had applied and thus what regulation was outside the scope of Second Amendment protection. The Court used a 3 tier evaluation process. If the prohibition would be protected under the Second Amendment at a tier, then it would be evaluated at the next tier. If the prohibition would not be protected at a tier, the prohibition would be deemed constitutional at that point with no further review necessary.

The first tier being evaluated was "Common Use." The District Court deferred mostly to the Heller decision and followed the conclusion that "common use" defined in common use at the present time and not at the time of the writing of the Amendment. The Courts found that both "assault weapons" and "large-capacity" magazines are in common use at the present time, though they found empirical evidence showing they are commonly possessed "for lawful purposes" to be "elusive." Assuming the "lawful purposes" use to be true by the Court, both categories were protected under the Second Amendment at this tier of evaluation.

The second tier in the evaluation process was "Substantial Burden." If the average law-abiding citizen were required by a prohibition to break the law in order to exercise their Second Amendment rights then the prohibition would be unconstitutional. The Court stated "Further, because the SAFE Act renders acquisition of these weapons illegal under most circumstances, this Court finds that the restrictions at issue more than "minimally affect" Plaintiffs' ability to acquire and use the firearms, and they therefore impose a substantial burden on Plaintiffs' Second Amendment rights." Again, the Court felt the same regarding "large-capacity" magazines under the substantial burden tier. Both categories are protected under the Second Amendment at this tier of evaluation as well.

The third tier of evaluation would be the level of scrutiny that would be applied. The Second Circuit felt that Intermediate Scrutiny, and not Strict Scrutiny, was the appropriate level of scrutiny to apply in this situation for three reasons: 1) The courts have historically taken an Intermediate Scrutiny approach to laws which substantially burden Second Amendment rights; 2) The Court felt that Strict Scrutiny would be inconsistent with the rulings in *Heller* and *McDonald* since the Court recognized some restrictions (such as laws creating restrictions on felons, mentally ill and on school property) as being outside the scope of Second Amendment protections; and 3) The Court refers to several standards of scrutiny being appropriate in regards to First Amendment issues, depending upon the nature of the law in question. The reason they ultimately chose Intermediate Scrutiny is because the nature of the law only banned a subset of firearms with certain features and did not ban an entire class of firearms. Because there are alternative options to the weapons being banned, only Intermediate Scrutiny should apply.

When applying Intermediate Scrutiny, the Court must ask whether the challenged restrictions are "substantially related to the achievement of an important governmental interest." The Court felt that the evidence being presented supported the argument that the laws would achieve that governmental interest. Plaintiffs argued that military type features do not make the firearm more lethal but only make the firearm easier to use, yet when Defendants pointed out those features add utility to a criminal shooter, Plaintiffs argued that those features also increased the utility for self-defense. The Courts felt the latter was the Plaintiffs admitting that the features increase lethality. The Court stated "There thus can be no serious dispute that the very features that increase a weapon's utility for self-defense also increase its dangerousness to the public at large."

Well, I think I can make a serious dispute about that right now. The features make the firearm easier to use, but lethality depends upon a bullet striking an intended target in a specific way. The ability to make a firearm easier to use does not necessarily relate to lethality, what it relates to is accuracy and precision in repeated shooting. Now, in regards to the "public at large" that can be viewed two ways. A properly trained person taking determined aim with a more accurate and precise weapon may therefore make more accurate shots and thus be more lethal having the ability to maximize the benefits of such features. However, a less accurate/precise gun with reduced features in the hands of the same shooter can also lead to that shooter hitting unintended targets...thus being more lethal to innocent people due to a lower level of accuracy obtainable by a gun without named features and thus also more dangerous to the public at large. Look, these are all "good for the goose, good for the gander" circular arguments at their core which constantly get repeated from both sides. Whatever benefits a criminal receives from the features of a weapon, a person using the same weapon for self-defense receives the same benefit, and vice versa. You can argue the counter argument all day long back and forth. More lethal for self-defense, then it is more lethal for a criminal. More effective for a criminal, more effective for self-defense. Both sides in Second Amendment debates do it to support their cause because it is true, all the benefits are exactly the same to shooters on both sides of the law...assuming all shooters have the same level of training.

All other things being equal, if we are seriously going to debate this from an Economic perspective of utility, who would have the greatest utility from the features: A criminal intent on shooting multiple people until (s)he is shot, captured, commits suicide or escapes; or the person who desperately needs that weapon to save their own life? Having a background in Economics, I think I would argue the civilian trying to save his/her life would get the greatest utility from that specific firearm setup.

What the Legislature and Court are really arguing here is that they want everyone to have less accurate and precise semi-automatic firearms, and that result will somehow achieve an important governmental interest. Stop and think about that for a second.

In regards to "large-capacity" magazines, the Court felt that the fulfillment of the state's interest regarding public safety was arguably even stronger for the magazines than the "assault weapons" themselves. Evidence submitted to the

Court reflected that "large-capacity" magazines were used in half the mass shootings since 1982 and that more people die when a "large-capacity" magazine is used. Though I will address both of those claims more specifically later, I can find nothing distinguishing specific round counts fired from each magazine to determine if the large capacity was implemented and had a true causal effect on the outcome or is merely circumstantial because large-capacity magazines are statistically more prominent than lower capacity magazines and possibly that experienced shooters (accounting for the more accurate shooting and fatalities) may merely be more likely to have "large-capacity" magazines on hand.

What appears to be a stronger argument is that "large-capacity" magazines are also used in weapons that are not deemed "assault weapons" thus effectively restricting how a much larger class of weapons can be implemented. Though I'm still finding most of the "large-capacity" arguments flawed due to ignorance of the devices themselves, the latter argument may at least be sound in regards to being more highly correlated to the achievement of an "important governmental interest" than the others. At least this is an across the board approach which does not merely rely on making the weapon less accurate or precise, exacerbating the lack of training many people have with the weapon. The magazine capacity restrictions on all weapons may in fact slow the shooting from an untrained shooter under a greater set of circumstances. It will do little to slow the shooting of a trained shooter. The overall outcome here may still be more of a benefit to society than a burden to Second Amendment rights. The burden, in this case, can mostly be overcome by training.

The District Court, however, concluded that the 7 round limit was unconstitutional. "It stretches the bounds of this Court's deference to the predictive judgments of the legislature to suppose that those intent on doing harm (whom, of course, the Act is aimed to stop) will load their weapon with only the permitted seven rounds. In this sense, the provision is not "substantially related" to the important government interest in public safety and crime prevention." The court felt that provision could ultimately leave law-abiding citizens defending themselves from a criminal with a fully loaded magazine.

Here the courts found that the law would disproportionately disadvantage the law abiding citizens as compared to the criminal. Plaintiffs argued this regarding all aspects of the law, but the Court felt it only applied here because criminals could still buy 10 round magazines, which are still legal to own. Here is where I find another problem with the perceptions of either the Legislature or the Courts. The same exact Logic they are using to argue that the 7 round limit is unconstitutional does in fact apply to an AR-15, and here is why: When defining what an "assault weapon" is, the greatest defining factor is the number of military type "features" that the weapon has. The fallacy in the argument comes into play in the Legislature's and Court's lack of understanding that an AR-15 is a "modular" weapons platform. I've seen references of options to registering grandfathered "assault weapons", I've seen references to options to sell them to dealers or out of state...but I've not seen any reference that an owner can "remove" any number of features to be in compliance, as if the Courts and Legislature have no clue that it is possible with many of these modular weapons platforms. They seem to be of the belief that an AR-15 on the shelf in a gun store will not or cannot change its number of features. This is absolute ignorance.

The number of military style features which define an "assault weapon" can change, all of the features are modular items which are still legally sold and can be interchanged among any of a number of AR-15 (and clones) platforms. Most of the common features are still legal and easy to buy, just like 10 round magazines are still legal to buy, and therefore a person intent on making a criminal act can easily buy a version with no features, legally buy as many of the features they want, and in many cases without requiring any experience in gunsmithing add and remove any number of those features at will. The features concept, being modular in nature, is the exact same Logic as the 7 rounds of ammo in a 10 round magazine scenario. A criminal, with little effort, can circumvent the law while the law-abiding citizen cannot.

You don't think ammunition is modular? Each round is an individual component, and I can choose to load a 10 round magazine with 3 Full Metal Jacket rounds, 3 Armor Piercing rounds, 2 Open Tip Match rounds and 2 Soft Point rounds...each type of round serving a different purpose, all in the same magazine. Same thing with an automatic shotgun; you could load birdshot, buckshot, slugs or even less than lethal rubber rounds in any order or combination you want. Ammunition is a modular component.

The Court repeatedly points out that under Intermediate Scrutiny the Court must give "substantial deference to the predictive judgments of the legislature as it is much better equipped to evaluate the policy judgments regarding firearms." From the perspective of Intermediate Scrutiny, I would have to conclude the Court's decision is sound here. The things I have addressed to the contrary, I sincerely believe have become ingrained flaws in the Second Amendment debate, but I do not know that they would change the decision of the Court applying this level of scrutiny. This will obviously go to the Supreme Court, and I believe the outcome will be decided based upon the level of Scrutiny the Supreme Court feels is appropriate to apply. I'm certain many pro Second Amendment supporters now go to bed every night praying for Justice Scalia's continued health.

Note: As this book goes to print, the passing of Justice Antonin Scalia has already... well, come to pass. There is currently a battle regarding a new Supreme Court appointment and whether the current or subsequent administration should get to make it, but the full ramifications of his death in regards to the Second Amendment have yet to be determined. As such, I've left the comments I've made in this book regarding Justice Scalia, including any which now appear to foreshadow his death, as I had previously written them.

Part II

But Things are Different This Time

Chapter IV

The Insurrection: Restoration of Rights or Armed Pity Party?

"Everything that happens once can never happen again. But everything that happens twice will surely happen a third time." - *Paulo Coelho* [1]

We've seen how the fear of insurrection and attempts at insurrection have affected firearm and militia related legislation over time. We have not yet fully addressed discussions about a perceived right of insurrection existing and if such a right exists when expressing that right is justified. We have seen how past concerns led us to the Posse Comitatus Act but we have not looked at any recent non firearm related legislation or events which might warrant the people to embrace an ideology of insurrection at the present time. I don't think an historic account of the Second Amendment would really be complete until we more fully address the concept of insurrection, and whether such a concept was implied in the right to keep and bear arms.

Is insurrection ever justified? Can a system of government allow for its own demise by violent overthrow, if it understands that governments can be corrupted and the people oppressed by them? Jefferson's words in the Declaration of Independence address this directly. I don't mean to sound biased, but seriously, just read the document and it is clear as day. The Declaration of Independence itself is an act of insurrection and explains quite clearly "why" they have the unalienable right to do so under "specific" circumstances:

> We hold these truths to be self-evident, that all men are created equal, that they are endowed by their Creator with certain unalienable Rights, that among these are Life, Liberty and the pursuit of Happiness.-- That to secure these rights, Governments are instituted among Men, deriving their just powers from the consent of the governed, --That whenever any Form of Government becomes destructive of these ends, it is the Right of the People to alter or to abolish it, and to institute new Government, laying its foundation on such principles and organizing its powers in such form, as to them shall seem most likely to effect their Safety and Happiness. Prudence, indeed, will dictate that Governments long established should not be changed for light and transient causes; and accordingly all experience hath shewn, that mankind are more disposed to suffer, while evils are sufferable, than to right themselves by abolishing the forms to which they are accustomed. But when a long train of abuses and usurpations, pursuing invariably the same Object evinces a design to reduce them under absolute Despotism, it is their right, it is their duty, to throw off such Government, and to provide new Guards for their future security.--

Such has been the patient sufferance of these Colonies; and such is now the necessity which constrains them to alter their former Systems of Government. The history of the present King of Great Britain is a history of repeated injuries and usurpations, all having in direct object the establishment of an absolute Tyranny over these States. To prove this, let Facts be submitted to a candid world.[2]

Any American who would argue that the Founding Fathers did not believe in a right of insurrection, or that a need for insurrection can never one day arise, is either a hypocrite at best or delusional at worst. Our present government was formed through insurrection. Were any Framers of the Constitution Loyalists during the Revolutionary War? It appears not. Aside from the claim that Jared Ingersoll abstained from politics during the Revolutionary War, out of respect for his father who was deemed a Loyalist having been appointed Stamp Master by the British Crown for collecting Stamp Act revenue, which has been cited as the stimulus for American insurrection towards Britain, but then openly sided with the revolution after the colonies declared their independence, I can find no references to suggest that a single signer of the Constitution had been a Loyalist during the American Revolutionary War.[3-5]

If all signers were on the side of insurrection, they would have to concede insurrection is a viable option when the concept of Democracy (or in this instance displayed by taxation without representation) has failed. I have found no instances where any Framer has said something along the lines of "we tried insurrection against the British crown, and even though we were successful we realize it was wrong, we have therefore created a U.S. Constitution and attached a

Bill of Rights to make sure people do not make the same mistake in the future." Though some have argued the Second Amendment was intended to secure the rights to the states to oppose the federal government, history clearly shows that right was ultimately given to the people and one of those reasons was to defend themselves against a tyrannical and oppressive government should it arise. The colonies had just fought for their freedom from what they perceived as an oppressive government.

Did this give anybody the right to attempt insurrection against the government for any reason? Of course not, and it would be ludicrous to argue the Framers intended an unquestionable right of insurrection for any reason. In fact, the fear of unjustified insurrections was already shown in many of the events we covered. Evidence we've seen, however, shows they were definitely preserving for themselves and their offspring the ability to take such actions should the Republic fail.

The concept of insurrection against an oppressive government is a slippery slope. There is a grey area of uncertainty and deception about whether the government's intent is really trending towards oppression or just a moderate misunderstanding and abuse of laws over the citizens, yet confirmation often comes too late to take any further action if the oppressed have delayed. Should we not also ask if other amendments protecting rights regarding trials somehow relate to the right to take action in regards to this grey area, while also having the right to be judged fairly on its validity by your peers?

Colonel Charles J. Dunlap, Jr USAF tries to address insurrections in his essay *Revolt of the Masses: Armed Civilians and the Insurrectionary Theory of the Second*

Amendment.[6]   Colonel Dunlap concludes, "No system of government can allow for its own demise by violent overthrow" but confirms the right exists when the Constitution's system has failed.   If the right is acknowledged to exist in such circumstances, why couldn't a system of government that was created by the people have a built in mechanism to also protect the people themselves from tyranny and oppression if that worst case scenario should arise? Maybe a right of the people to keep and bear arms shall not be infringed clause? It is like arguing that you can't adopt a prenuptial agreement as part of the terms of marriage because a marriage can't allow for its own demise through divorce. Colonel Dunlap goes on to say:

> Possession of small arms, including assault-type weapons, does not meaningfully check the combat power of advanced military establishments like those of the United States.   To suggest that civilians equipped with Second Amendment-type weapons are any match for modern security forces invites murderous confrontations that armed civilians will inevitably lose.

Well, first off, "advanced military establishments like those of the United States" sounds a hell of a lot like a standing army, the very thing the Framers feared.   Second, the existence of any perceived right of insurrection has no correlation with the success of such an insurrection. Even in modern movies, the good guys don't always win.   Third, modern day computer hackers can wreak havoc on your advanced military establishments, since much of it is electronics based, so a lack in "advanced" projectile weaponry doesn't necessarily mean a militia of the people lack other "advanced" non projectile weapons with which to even the odds against a modern standing army. Without judging the merits of their actions, you have to concede that groups like Anonymous do ultimately wield some destructive power.

At the time of Colonel Dunlap's essay there was still a general understanding that previous court precedent held only a collective right in the Second Amendment with some feeling that was therefore only granted to the National Guard. Even still, in an argument regarding a theory of a right of insurrection the success of the insurrection is irrelevant. And though Colonel Dunlap doesn't think a militia of the people would have any chance against the U.S. military today, the Framers of the Constitution clearly felt otherwise. Just because Colonel Dunlap argues that the Framers ultimately may have been wrong in their belief, doesn't mean they didn't hold the belief.

Another error Colonel Dunlap seems to make is the false conclusion that any member of a possible standing army would not subsequently hold the same beliefs as those attempting insurrection and fight for the people instead of the government. In fact, the restrictions on a right to bear arms don't seem to sit well with many members of the military, as many have spoken up. In a letter to Diane Feinstein, who was proposing another assault weapons ban, Former Marine Joshua Boston had this to say:

> I will not register my weapons should this bill be passed, as I do not believe it is the government's right to know what I own. Nor do I think it prudent to tell you what I own so that it may be taken from me by a group of people who enjoy armed protection yet decry me having the same a crime. You ma'am have overstepped a line that is not your domain. I am a Marine Corps Veteran of 8 years, and I will not have

some woman who proclaims the evil of an inanimate object, yet carries one, tell me I may not have one.

I am not your subject. I am the man who keeps you free. I am not your servant. I am the person whom you serve. I am not your peasant. I am the flesh and blood of America.

I am the man who fought for my country. I am the man who learned. I am an American. You will not tell me that I must register my semi-automatic AR-15 because of the actions of some evil man.

I will not be disarmed to suit the fear that has been established by the media and your misinformation campaign against the American public.[7]

In response to the letter, Diane Feinstein assured people "The legislation will be carefully focused to protect the rights of existing gun owners by exempting hundreds of weapons used for hunting and sporting purposes."[8] There we are with that hunting and sporting interpretation again. What does that have anything to do with the Second Amendment or recent court decisions protecting Second Amendment rights for self-defense, other than point out the exact method those rights were once circumvented by an oppressive monarch in England?

Since the time of Colonel Dunlap's essay, we have seen that the courts have confirmed an individual right to keep and bear arms, independent of militia membership, which discounts many of his arguments. It also seems clear from the essay that Colonel Dunlap's perspective is one of a paid Colonel in the United States Air Force, which now appears to be a subset of the equivalent of a standing army, while suggesting that the defending of any government usurpation of power "does not require civilians keeping and bearing arms." I can't help but feel Colonel Dunlap actually strengthens the fear of a standing army and desire for the right to defend yourself against a tyrannical and oppressive government, due to the very conclusion he makes that the people could never overcome the existing military and a USAF Colonel's opinion that the people need not be armed. Federalists Alexander Hamilton and James Madison argued it could never happen, but maybe they were wrong.

If arguing the validity of insurrection rights, we must look for present signs in today's society, if any, that the U.S. government might intend to restrict citizen's rights in defiance of Democracy. If such conditions don't exist, any right of insurrection may be moot to begin with. I don't want this to turn into a "conspiracy theory" book, but you still have to discuss existing facts objectively. I know some of these topics are hotbeds for conspiracy theorists, but they exist nonetheless, so we must look for any trends.

Remember when President George H. W. Bush talked about a New World Order in his speech of September 11, 1990, "Out of these troubled times, our fifth objective -- a new world order -- can emerge: a new era -- freer from the threat of terror, stronger in the pursuit of justice, and more secure in the quest for peace."[9] Though he continued to talk about the United Nations in the speech, the comment wasn't exactly clear as to what he really meant. On January 16, 1991 he was more specific:

> We have before us the opportunity to forge for ourselves and for future generations a new world order -- a world where the rule of law, not the law of the jungle, governs the conduct of nations. When we

are successful -- and we will be -- we have a real chance at this new world order, an order in which a credible United Nations can use its peacekeeping role to fulfill the promise and vision of the U.N.'s founders.[10]

What is the United Nations exactly? From the United Nations website [www.un.org], "The United Nations is an international organization founded in 1945 after the Second World War by 51 countries committed to maintaining international peace and security, developing friendly relations among nations and promoting social progress, better living standards and human rights."[11] That sounds honorable and at the same time creates reasons for concern. It really depends on how you define an international organization using resources for peace and security. Is this concept that of sovereign nations working together for peace, or is this concept nations giving up sovereignty for an international rule of law as President Bush implied? Does the concept of a United Nations threaten the sovereignty of a nation?

In the case of Libya in 2011 it sure as hell did, as the U.N. authorized the strike.[12] Was the attack necessary for the security and sovereignty of the United States or merely a use of the U.S. military to enforce global humanitarian causes? At the end of the day, the American people may just never have enough information to answer that question. If the will of the people is to support any international conflicts the United Nations brings the United States into, then I assume there is no problem. If it circumvents the will of American citizens who would vote not to put American lives at risk unless the sovereignty of our nation is at risk, then this may truly be a shift away from American Democracy. There are lots of shades of grey here, ultimately depending on how much power the United States cedes to international organizations such as the United Nations.

References to the strike on Libya bring us to the North American Treaty Organization (NATO). Unlike the United Nations, NATO is an intergovernmental military alliance of 28 countries headquartered in Brussels, Belgium where its members agree to mutual defense in response to an attack by any external party.[13] Article 5 of the Washington Treaty states:

> The Parties agree that an armed attack against one or more of them in Europe or North America shall be considered an attack against them all and consequently they agree that, if such an armed attack occurs, each of them, in exercise of the right of individual or collective self-defence recognised by Article 51 of the Charter of the United Nations, will assist the Party or Parties so attacked by taking forthwith, individually and in concert with the other Parties, such action as it deems necessary, including the use of armed force, to restore and maintain the security of the North Atlantic area.
>
> Any such armed attack and all measures taken as a result thereof shall immediately be reported to the Security Council. Such measures shall be terminated when the Security Council has taken the measures necessary to restore and maintain international peace and security.

So Libya attacked a member NATO country and NATO was required to respond? Not at all. The Libyan Civil War was an armed rebellion in 2011 in the large Libyan city of Benghazi that intended to overthrow Libyan rule by

Muammar Gaddafi.[14]   The details of their civil war aren't really necessary to the discussion. Since no external country was targeted in the conflict the uprising didn't attack or threaten the sovereignty of any other nation. So why did NATO ultimately strike Libya? On the NATO website, they say this:

> It is crucial to promote stability in regions where tensions pose security threats. This is why NATO takes an active role in crisis management operations, most of them under a UN Security Council mandate.[15]

Well, there you have it. NATO also acts as the military arm of the United Nations Security Council. I'm all for world peace if it is possible, but how did we go from a fear of standing armies to having a standing army that often serves the will of an international organization? Who decides the appropriate outcome for a specific regional crisis? For example, what if the United Nations decides that the United States Supreme Court's rulings that firearms are an individual right and the subsequent possession of firearms by citizens of the United States poses a threat to the peace and security of the United Nations members overall? Article VI of the Constitution does make treaties the "supreme law of the land" if they were made "under the authority of the United States."

Okay, I can hear some of you suddenly trying to do your best Horshack impression from here. You want to tell me about the Arms Trade Treaty and how UN resolution 2117 point #11 calls for the disarming of all UN countries, huh? That's really just false propaganda...at least for the moment. Here is point #11 unedited, "11. *Calls for Member States* to support weapons collection, disarmament, demobilization and reintegration of ex-combatants, as well as physical security and stockpile management programmes by United Nations peacekeeping operations where so mandated." It is specifically referencing ex-combatants, such as rebels and militant groups, and not members of the civilian population. In fact, in speaking on behalf of the U.S. as United States Ambassador to the United Nations, Samantha Powers explicitly expressed that it was important to recognize the right of countries to defend themselves and to use small arms and light weapons for legitimate purposes and emphasized an opposition to any effort that might be aimed at constraining the constitutional right of United States citizens to bear arms.[16]

However, #3 does appear to call for "implementing national weapons marking programmes in accordance with the International Tracing Instrument." This does, in fact, appear to call for what would not only be an accurate international marking mechanism but also a national registration of small arms and light weapons in the United States in order to comply, "For the purposes of this instrument, 'tracing' is the systematic tracking of illicit small arms and light weapons found or seized on the territory of a State from the point of manufacture or the point of importation through the lines of supply to the point at which they became illicit." Though it says the "methods for record-keeping is a national prerogative"; it may prove difficult to track something "through the lines of supply" from point A to point Z, as opposed to merely tracking it at point A and then later at point Z, without a registration upon purchase and each subsequent sale.[17] I'm finding that one to be a little more ambiguous. I do offer a possible solution to this in chapter 8.

I can see the benefits of organizations like the UN and NATO, but I can also see the extreme potential for abuse by such organizations to suppress the will of sovereign nations. I can't say I was a fan of Muammar Gaddafi by any means, but the UN and NATO certainly decided that the overthrow of the Libyan government was not only the proper avenue to resolve the regional crises but well within their mandated power to do so. Do you as a citizen of the United States feel the United States military should be used to decide the fate of a foreign nation's civil war?

France did help us fight for our independence from Britain. Should we help the French attack Syria after the recent orchestrated attacks in Paris on November 13, 2015? They could have cited article 5 of the Treaty in order to force us to do so.[18] But was France attacked by Syria? No, not exactly. It appears the Paris attack was done by supporters of the Islamic State (ISIL, ISIS), though it is unclear if the Islamic State itself actually orchestrated the attack or merely a few followers of the ideology. The Islamic State's "Muslim extremism" is an ideology that is spread across regions of the globe, and only has a perceived central area of control located in Syria. It is not the actions of Syria overall. To get even more convoluted, the current reports of the event suggest that at least half of the suspected "terrorists" involved were actually French nationals.[19] I'm not suggesting action isn't in order, but action towards exactly "who" specifically is quite ambiguous. Yet it was possible the United States could have been called upon to defend the French from the (cough) Syrians. If we should take such measures, should the decision be made by the United States to do so or by a conglomerate of foreign nations with different sovereign interests? My wife and I have fewer arguments if we don't interject ourselves into other couple's marital disputes. It might be argued that there would be more world peace if the UN and NATO would not turn every regional conflict into a world conflict.

The Homeland Security Act of 2002 was introduced after the September 11 terrorist attacks in 2001. It created the United States Department of Homeland Security under which a number of other agencies are consolidated, some of which are U.S. Customs and Border Protection, U.S. Immigration and Customs Enforcement, Federal Emergency Management Agency (FEMA), Office of Cybersecurity and Communications, U.S. Coast Guard and the U.S. Secret Service. Many of these organizations are used to exercise the power of the USA PATRIOT Act. The Patriot Act had been signed into law on October 26, 2001 prior to the Homeland Security Act. The title of the act is a ten letter backronym (USA PATRIOT) that stands for Uniting (and) Strengthening America (by) Providing Appropriate Tools Required (to) Intercept (and) Obstruct Terrorism Act of 2001. The stated purpose of the Act is "To deter and punish terrorist acts in the United States and around the world, to enhance law enforcement investigatory tools, and for other purposes."[20] Don't you just love those vague "and for other purposes" clauses?

Some argue the Homeland Security Act reduces privacy, increases government secrecy and strengthens government protection of special interests.[21] The scope of the Patriot Act is very broad under 10 different titles and a thorough coverage of the Act would require a book on its own so I'll only touch on a few points. It expands the definition of terrorism to include that of "domestic terrorism" enlarging the scope of the Act overall. Section 412 allows for the indefinite detention of immigrants. As a curiosity, do any of you know the exact status at this moment of the clause in the National Defense Authorization Act (NDAA) which addresses the indefinite detention of American citizens? I'll let you look that up yourselves. The Patriot Act also covers restrictions on the movement of money and the reporting of financial transactions regarding all citizens. If you take more than $10,000 in cash into or out of the United States you are subject to up to 5 years in prison, forcing many international transactions to be electronic. Any domestic transactions over $10,000 are required to be reported as well.

It expands the scope of allowable surveillance through wiretaps and voicemail stored with electronic service providers. One of the concerns is the National Security Letters which have been used to demand financial, credit and employment records of citizens, their library records and in some cases receiving health records. Some elements of the Act have already been ruled unconstitutional by the Supreme Court, such as tracking devices used without a warrant in *United States v. Antoine Jones* and "sneak and peek" searches without a search order.[22] The question is really one of whether we are strictly monitoring the activities of already known terrorists through violating their privacy, or are we violating the privacy of all the citizens of the United States in order to find out who the potential or "suspected" terrorists are?

Thanks to Edward Snowden, it appears we can answer that question. For those that have been living in a cave, Snowden is a former CIA employee and former government contractor that leaked classified information from the United States National Security Agency (NSA) to the world in 2013. I'm not going to give much back-story on it, mostly because two years later both sides are still attempting to discredit virtually everything the other side says leading up to the leak, and Snowden's act itself really isn't the point. I'm not going to pass judgment one way or another on Snowden's actions. I'll leave that up to you personally. Though there seems to be documentation suggesting an extreme amount of

NSA spying on individuals, I don't even want to get into the validity of those claims.[23]

What we do now know, beyond question, is that NSA has a program called PRISM which collects stored internet communications from companies such as Google which match certain search terms and collected digitally stored telecommunications data from telecom companies.[24] The initial information that was leaked evidenced the ordering of a subsidiary of Verizon Wireless to turn over logs of all their customers' telephone calls to the U.S. Foreign Intelligence Surveillance Court which supervises PRISM...answering the above question. The NSA was collecting data on everyone, not just "suspected" terrorists. On May 7, 2015 the United States Court of Appeals ruled that section 215 of the Patriot Act did not give the NSA the authority to collect bulk data on all citizens.[25] On November 29, 2015 the bulk collection of phone data officially ended.[26] That should be sufficient evidence to at least show that a problem with the government spying on U.S. citizens exists. I urge you to take the time to look into the overall scope of that problem on your own and make your own decisions.

If you feel that potentially unconstitutional measures should be taken to protect against potential terrorism and that you'll never somehow be accused of being or supporting a terrorist or committing acts of domestic terror, then maybe you don't think the Patriot Act is a cause for concern. You've got nothing to hide, right? If you feel that depriving citizens of constitutional rights to prevent acts that have yet to occur is a sign of an oppressive government, you're probably terrified more of your government than any potential "terrorists" that dislike your government. In Michael Moore's movie *Fahrenheit 9/11*, Congressman Jim McDermott alleged that no Senator had even read the [USA PATRIOT Act] bill.[27]

How can you approve, let alone know the constitutionality of, something you haven't read? I haven't signed a contract without reading it since before I was 18 years old. I learned that in High School. Since some provisions of the Act have already been used against U.S. citizens and struck down as being unconstitutional, we would have to at least concede there is a justifiable fear of continued misuse of this Act in the future.

Another situation to address is one best described by Rachel Maddow in her book *Drift: The Unmooring of American Military Power.*[28] In spite of an undeniable political skew for one party over another, Maddow seems to present a fairly accurate accounting of events that have not only moved the U.S. further towards a standing army over time, entirely against the ideologies of the Framers of the Constitution, but how past Presidents have found ways to circumvent the Constitution and effectively create wars without Congressional approval and without a whole lot of residual recourse from having done so. President Reagan appears to have begun the trend by invading Granada with no Congressional approval. Maddow sums up the trend in power shift stating, "By the time Bill Clinton left office in 2001, an Operation Other Than War, as the Pentagon forces called them, could go on indefinitely... without real political costs or consequences, or much civilian notice. We'd gotten used to it. By 2001, the ability of a president to start and wage military operations without (or even in spite of) Congress was established." She concludes that by the time of the 9/11 attacks, "the war-making authority in the United States had become, for all intents and purposes, uncontested and unilateral: one man's decision to make." So one man not only has autonomy over the militia and federal military in regards to events on our soil, but recent Presidents have also figured out how to circumvent Congress to have autonomy over committing the nation to war. Sorry... of course I mean a military "operation other than war." Is this not at least evidence that preserving the right of defense against a powerful military, recently often shown to be controlled by the will of one man, isn't at least a valid concern?

I have one last question for you to ponder in this Chapter: When the New Orleans Police and Louisiana National Guard disarmed the citizens by gunpoint after Hurricane Katrina, do you feel the action was in the best interests of the people overall as being defended by arguments that it prohibited racial violence from getting out of hand in the aftermath, or do you feel it was depriving those citizens of their Second Amendment rights to bear arms for their defense when they may have needed them most?[29]

Chapter V

One Nation, Under Canada, With Liberty and Justice for...

a.k.a. Why God Doesn't Belong in 2nd Amendment Debates

"maybe it's time for some school boards and administrators to say look, we don't care. The lives of our children are just too important to us, we are going to pray in our schools at the beginning of the day, we are going to pray for protection, and I don't care what the Supreme Court says." - Bryan Fischer, American Family Association [1]

As I mentioned before, this is not a book about the First Amendment. However, we've seen how the struggle against religious oppression played an instrumental role in the evolution of the Second Amendment. Religion was the primary reason why gun rights were restricted in England. Even when gun rights were restored to one oppressed religion, when they gained control from the other they immediately turned around and denied members of the other religion the same rights.

I don't want to get into arguments favoring one religion over another or even any regarding validation of organized religions as a whole. I do want to look at one argument that is being made in the gun control debate. A general synopsis of that argument would be "the problem is not with guns; the problem is that we (the United States) need to return to being a Christian nation and bring God back into our Government."[2] Is this a sound argument for Second Amendment rights, or does it present false premises?

First, I think we need to look at the premises in the argument itself. Was our government founded on a specific religious belief, such as Christianity, or did our Founding Fathers specifically try to promote Religious Freedom? Let's look at the First Amendment:

> Congress shall make no law respecting an establishment of religion, or prohibiting the free exercise thereof; or abridging the freedom of speech, or of the press; or the right of the people peaceably to assemble, and to petition the Government for a redress of grievances.

Read that a hundred times if you need to, it will not change. (Well, not unless you actually push to have it amended and are successful.) These are the words of the men who founded our nation. The answer is the United States was not constructed to be a religious nation; it was not founded as a Christian nation, it was not founded as a Muslim nation, it was not founded as a Luciferian nation. More importantly, it protects the rights of the people to believe in any one of those religions, any other religion or even no religion as they see fit without the persecutions readily experienced in England and prohibits the United States Government from making laws or taking oppressive actions based on religion. The United

States was founded upon a belief in a right to Religious Freedom.[3]

That not enough proof for you? How about Article VI of the U.S. Constitution itself, before the Bill of Rights was even added, "The Senators and Representatives before mentioned, and the members of the several state legislatures, and all executive and judicial officers, both of the United States and of the several states, shall be bound by oath or affirmation, to support this Constitution; but no religious test shall ever be required as a qualification to any office or public trust under the United States."[4] Honestly, there's not much left to debate about the construction of our government regarding religious intent. Some, however, continue to point out that many were Freemasons as a counter argument.

Many of the Founding Fathers were Freemasons, but does that mean Christian? I'm not a Freemason, but my understanding is that it is not a religion itself and the requirement in that regard be that you believe in a monotheistic deity (a Supreme Being) and not multiple deities.[5] Therefore you can be Muslim and a Freemason, Christian and a Freemason, I think you can even be Catholic and worship a hundred "Saints" so long as you don't call any of the saints you worship gods and still be a Freemason. You can worship "Lucifer" if you believe he is the only one true "God" and still be a Freemason. (No, I am not making the long existing claim that Masons specifically worship Lucifer.) It appears you can even believe that "God" is an "It" and not an anthropomorphized he or she, leaving open the interpretation that the Great Architect of the Universe itself is a single power and still meet the qualifications to be a Freemason. Note: There are a few forms of Freemasonry across the planet which do have stricter requirements regarding beliefs than typically held of Freemasons in the United States.

As one of the counter arguments to "religious freedom," supporters of a Christian nation ideology often cite the use of the term "God" in historic writings. Upon inspection of those accounts, they tend to reflect the Freemason's interpretation of the concept of "God" and not exclusively a Christian God. The phrase "In God We Trust" has been of great controversy over the past roughly 60 years as many use that to argue that we were intended to be a Christian nation. The motto was originally used on coins as early as 1864, and as the U.S. Treasury explains, "The motto IN GOD WE TRUST was placed on United States coins largely because of the increased religious sentiment existing during the Civil War."[6] It was not adopted as the motto of the United States until 1956, roughly 60 years ago at the time of this writing. Much like the adoption of the phrase on coins after the Civil War, it seems coincidental it became our national motto after two virtually consecutive world wars and the Korean War ending in 1953. For the first 180 years of this nation's existence, "E Pluribus Unum" (One from many) was used as our *de facto* motto.

Though the new motto has become a source of great debate in and of itself, and I myself do admit to finding it somewhat religiously oppressive overall, the real truth is it does not define a specific "God" and does at least leave the subject open to the same monotheistic interpretations as Freemasonry, of which many of our Founding Fathers were members. What this does not represent, in any capacity, is evidence that the United States is currently or ever was a "Christian" nation. What it does suggest is that the United States government has taken a more prominent, let's call it spiritual tone, in the most recent 60 years than it did during the first 180 years after the government was founded. When the country does take on a religious sentiment, it appears to come from a sense of mortality immediately following major wars. Debating whether inclusions such as these violate First Amendment rights is unnecessary for our current discussion, other than noting that debate exists. However, the United States government appears to have more religion in it presently than the first 180 years of its existence.

If you look at history, you will see that England was not the only place where religion was controversial at the time. The world was at the tail end of what was effectively 800 years of Christian (Roman Catholic) Inquisitions which did not end until after our nation was founded.[7] Our Founding Fathers lived in an era where specific religious beliefs were still being forced upon people with fear of death and torture for non compliance. I would be willing to wager this had some bearing on the creation of the Freemasons in 1717 as a "secret" society.

It has been noted that "religious freedom" was the leading stimulus for immigration to the American colonies.[8] Historically, religious freedom in this case would have been freedom "from" Christian Inquisitions. You may sometimes hear an invalid argument that no separation of church and state was intended because the exact words "Separation of Church and State" were never used in the Constitution, so it doesn't exist.[9] The First Amendment quite clearly confirms the intent to keep both the religious beliefs of the people out of our government and our government out of the religious beliefs of the people.

I believe the Founding Fathers thought the First Amendment issues were important, which may even be why they put them first. In fact, religious freedom is the absolute first thing addressed in the Bill of Rights. Okay, technically it was proposed as Article Three, but the first two articles didn't get ratified at the time.[10]

Here is where we run into the conundrums with the "God" argument. The Second Amendment, as we have seen from history, would be the tool for society to protect itself from violations of First Amendment rights (meaning government violations where both Legislative and Judicial branches were involved.) Does it then make any sense to violate the rights of the First Amendment (the underlying concepts) in order to validate the Second Amendment right (the tools to defend the concepts)? Can one argue to abandon the Constitution in order to defend the Constitution? If you argue that the First Amendment is in error and needs to be amended, you're conceding the same exact argument can be made regarding the Second Amendment! Normally, it would be logically incorrect to suggest the validity of one amendment has a bearing on the validity of another amendment in general, but in this particular case the Second Amendment has a very high correlation to the existence and defense of the First Amendment.

The second issue is the God argument alienates you from other defenders of the Second Amendment, as many supporters of the Second Amendment do so because they fear people will try to force the United States into being a religious nation, and attempt to do away with the Establishment Clause in the First Amendment. I will be absolutely honest and tell you that one of the primary reasons I chose to be a firearms owner is the increasing religious debate between Christian and Muslim, though I am neither and view both as equal potential risks to my Freedoms. Inquisition mentality appears to quickly be on the rise once again; therefore I embrace my Second

Amendment rights to preserve my First Amendment rights. I read the "God" argument for the Second Amendment, and quickly understand that you are potentially my adversary and not my ally. I support your First Amendment rights to believe what you want to believe, I do not support your attempt to make our government a religious institution. The bigger fear here for you is that you are successful in your Second Amendment argument by amending the First Amendment, and then the very religion you fear actually becomes the dominant and oppressive religion of the government.

In what I can only say is a bizarre irony, Supreme Court Justice Antonin Scalia, who expressed the opinions of the Court in the *Heller* decision while specifically protecting handguns under the Second Amendment, has become a prime example of this conundrum. While speaking to a Catholic high school in New Orleans, Justice Scalia told students that while the government can't favor one religion over another, there is nothing that restrains the government from forcing religion over non-religion saying "To tell you the truth there is no place for that in our constitutional tradition." Justice Scalia goes on to credit "God" with America's success, "God has been very good to us. That we won the revolution was extraordinary. The Battle of Midway was extraordinary. I think one of the reasons God has been good to us is that we have done him honor. Unlike the other countries of the world that do not even invoke his name we do him honor. In presidential addresses, in Thanksgiving proclamations and in many other ways." We have a standing Supreme Court justice suggesting that the right to be non-religious is not constitutionally protected. It may very well prove a hard correlation to break between the religious and their guns.[11]

From the perspective of United States citizens, it may appear that the bulk of "terrorism" around the world is from "Islamic extremists." That may even be a sound statement. The problem is with the false logical conclusion that often follows; all Muslim are terrorists. Even if all the people in the data set "terrorists" are a subset of the data set "Islamic" it does not then logically follow that all people in the data set "Islamic" are in the data set "terrorists." If you believe that, you've actually become part of the problem because you too can now be classified under the term "extremist" due to your extreme conclusions resulting from your misinterpretation of logic. It is hard to successfully argue that all Muslim are terrorists, but it would be substantially easier to argue that anyone who takes extreme actions is an "extremist." Even then, all extremists may not go so far as to take "extremist" actions.

From the perspective of a Syrian citizen being bombed because they are in the proximity of a few people that promote a certain ideology, the United States might be viewed as taking "extremist" actions in bombing what may be mostly innocent victims who are not "Islamic extremists." It is easy to see how those people might ultimately later adopt extremist ideologies in response to what they believe to be extremist actions taken against them. It perpetuates and expands the perceived problem, from both side's perspectives, without actually addressing the real problem. It is a self fulfilling prophecy, creating more and more extremism. Muslim blames Christian, Christian blames Muslim. As "perceived" attacks are responded to with "perceived" counter attacks upon the other, more people of each category move their ideologies to the extremes and more people who were initially neutral take sides.

The religious extremist ideology is certainly an issue that needs to be addressed and a cycle that needs to end. Religion is not the result of a gun problem nor is it the solution to a gun problem. An argument in favor of a specific religious belief therefore does not belong in the Second Amendment debate. The corollary though, that Second Amendment rights belong in the Religious extremist debate, is sound as that right is required to defend oneself from potential oppression by religious extremists who might come into power.

Chapter VI

Don't Believe Everything You Make Up

"Meanwhile, it is to be feared the crabbed satirist was partly right, as things go: 'A judicious man,' says he, 'looks at Statistics, not to get knowledge, but to save himself from having ignorance foisted on him.'" -Thomas Carlyle [1]

Let's talk about the problems with statistics and semantic manipulation inherent in the Second Amendment debate. To begin, let me point out that statistics really address nothing about the Second Amendment right itself. As we have seen, it is held to be an unalienable right. Where statistical analysis becomes important is in making decisions as to how much of that unalienable right we are willing to set aside for the benefit of society overall. If you are worried about violations of ethics and morality more than unalienable rights, that is why laws exist to break people's resolve to commit them with punishment for any subsequent violations. If you also have an overwhelming fear (baa) that someone "might" break one of those laws anyway merely because they have access to certain resources, we design laws for that too. However, we do need to make sure the laws we pass are based on sound logical principles and not on emotional over-reaction if we want them to achieve the intended effect while not placing unwarranted restrictions on the rights of the people overall. This is where sound statistical analysis can be of assistance. Yet it is here we come across another problem.

I'm not going to go into great detail regarding specific statistics pertaining to the issue as there are reliable sources for such info already available. Some are listed as references throughout this book. What I want to address is the inherent problem with unsound statistical analysis, and the misinterpretation of semantics which leads to confusion.

Many might argue that we don't collect enough gun statistics, or delineate enough factors in gun statistics to truly make an informed decision on certain specific issues. That might be a sound argument, and it certainly couldn't hurt to have more delineated data to evaluate. However, some conclusions can be drawn from existing statistical data, sometimes cross references with other sets of data. Unfortunately many people seem to think the statistic itself is sufficient and sound evaluation of that statistic unnecessary. This can lead to wild distortions in conclusions if you don't understand what data sets you are actually using, or what those data sets actually represent. Especially when the writer of the conclusions believes the reader doesn't understand those things.

One of the biggest problems I find with current statistics being presented is that those supplying the data interchange words that are not synonymous. For instance, someone will pull up a report that gives a figure on overall gun homicides at maybe 10,000 in one period, and then report that 10,000 people were "murdered" by guns in that period. Well, that would be false because a homicide and a murder are not the same. I see this one repeated endlessly in the media. Here is the legal definition of homicide from Nolo's online legal encyclopedia:

> Homicide is a legal term for any killing of a human being by another human being. Homicide itself is not necessarily a crime—some homicides are legal, such as a justifiable killing of a suspect by the police or a killing in self-defense—but unlawful homicides are classified as crimes like murder and manslaughter.[2]

A homicide can be a murder, it could be the police upholding the law, or it could actually be someone embracing their Second Amendment rights and legally defending their life with a firearm. If 5,000 of those statistics were self-defense shootings and another 3,000 justified police shootings, how does that affect the gun murder numbers as a percentage of the overall gun homicide statistics? Now, I'm not saying these are accurate numbers or percentages, just showing how the numbers often get misrepresented as meaning something that they don't. All 10,000 homicides could even be self-defense shootings without a single murder among them, yet still be fallaciously reported as "murder" statistics, or "gun violence" statistics when they were not. Sometimes the mistake appears to sincerely be nothing other than ignorance but, as we'll see later, in other cases it appears to be done clearly to manipulate the perceptions of the people.

That leads to another issue I commonly encountered which involves the use of the term "gun crime." A gun crime initially gives the impression of an armed robbery or maybe a murder; in other words a violent gun crime. The truth is, some gun crimes are merely the violation of gun laws themselves, and not the use of a gun in what would otherwise still be a crime. For instance, a person may be carrying a concealed handgun without a permit, when a permit in their state or county is required. That is the committing of a "gun crime." The problem with presenting all "gun crimes" instead of "crimes using a gun" or "violent gun crimes" as a need for more gun legislation then becomes somewhat obvious. Crimes using guns could be on a steep decline, while violations of gun laws themselves be on the rise due to an increase in the number of gun laws. Merely giving "gun crime" numbers becomes deceiving to the public and makes people believe that crimes using guns are on the rise. Further, as we've seen in our historical analysis and recent court decisions, many of those gun laws could turn out to be violations of your Second Amendment rights to begin with.

The reason this often happens brings up another issue revolving around statistics. Many people don't care about the facts, only their beliefs, so they disregard the statistics entirely or distort the statistics as above when they cannot disregard them. I read an article posted on Facebook recently titled "More Americans killed by guns since 1968 than in all U.S. wars." It was basically an amended version of Richard Hofstadter's previous premise we'll look at briefly regarding the term "gun culture" in chapter 7. It was pointed out that the individual statistics were relatively accurate in a very broad and general sense, in and of themselves, however how the statistics were dissected and evaluated didn't exactly address the premise of the title's argument and the conclusions which were "implied" to be made were relatively fallacious and misleading. For just a couple of examples: "killed by guns" includes suicides; the military suicides falls under the first categories data set and not the second related to war; the second data set was actually "killed by guns in all U.S. wars" and did not account for deaths by bomb, IED, disease or (again) PTSD suicide due to war. Furthermore, the comparison itself has virtually no correlation to, and is irrelevant in, a gun control debate. It sincerely is a version of comparing apples to oranges...in this case intentionally throwing a few apples in with the oranges and vice versa just to confuse the matter. This is an actual quote in response from someone in Atlanta GA, which I will leave as anonymous: "i think i would like to live in this America with no guns. (dont really know or f'ing care about facts) thats kind of like a dream right. Ive lived in a country almost like america but it had no guns - it was nice but it feels like it wasnt as nice as an america with no guns. i like my dreams."[sic] Wow. The reason the United States is a Democratic Republic is such that the narcissistic desires of one person doesn't supersede the desires of the majority of society as a whole.

Each side of the debate needs to stop throwing out fallacious propaganda merely to suit their desires. There is a portion of people on both sides who clearly just want what they want because they want it, in spite of the facts. They try to spin the facts to support their beliefs, instead of altering and constructing their beliefs based on the facts. It does nothing but confuse the voting public and circumvents the true meaning of Democracy. A person cannot accurately vote for that which is in their best interests, or the best interests of society, if they are deceived as to the facts of the issue at hand.

What this leads to is a propaganda war and how to misrepresent data merely in order to support someone's personal desire for what they "wish" things were in spite of the facts or the consequences. Every action creates a chain of events. Your "wish" may create a positive chain of events or a negative chain of events for society. To not consider this when merely wanting something to be a certain way, for no other logical reason than that is what you "wish" it were in the present, with no regard for the facts or future consequence, is really narcissistic selfishness; even if it appears to be under the guise of empathy for victims of gun violence or the guise of Second Amendment Constitutional Rights. Everytown for Gun Safety is such a prime example of this problem, let's talk about their organization and analyze some of the information they spread.

Everytown for Gun Safety

According to Michael Bloomberg, Everytown for Gun Safety was founded to match the National Rifle Association in political influence. Everytown is a consolidation of other gun control groups Bloomberg was already funding; Mayors Against Illegal Guns and Moms Demand Action for Gun Sense in America.[3] I went through their entire website, and I honestly found it disturbing. In some cases all aspects of the argument have been manipulated or fabricated. In others, the statistics themselves actually seem to be credible, but then they play semantic "bait and switch" games with their conclusions to give false impressions. I picked just a few of the quotes from their website to discuss below.

"Since 2013, there have been at least 160 school shootings in America — an average of nearly one a week." –October 3, 2015[4]

First off, keep in mind that it is already a crime to have a loaded firearm on school property other than a few very distinct exceptions.[5] (It is left to the states to determine how to regulate carry permit holders on school property.

Although New York strengthened their law to be a felony in the NY SAFE Act, many states have recently become more lenient in allowing licensed permit holders to carry on school property.) Below this heading and subsequent article is the listing of each individual "school shooting" they cite. It is interesting to look at the individual events creating the data set to see what they feel is a "school shooting." Before I go on, take a second and think of what the phrase "school shooting" means to you. Here is the breakdown from the 160 events: 98 are listed as "Attack on other persons(s) resulting in injury or death" [typo is theirs, not mine]; 18 are listed as "Attempted or completed suicide, with no intent to injure other person"; 31 listed as "Gun fired but no one injured"; and 13 are listed as "Gun fired unintentionally resulting in injury or death."

They segregate "Attack on other persons(s) resulting in injury or death" but no distinction in numbers between injury or death. Does injured mean shot and not killed, or tripped over a desk? There is also nothing to distinguish if this was an intended mass murder or some other scenario. Maybe the shooting could have even been self-defense. I'm willing to go out on a limb here and suggest that when most people hear "school shooting" these days they think mass shooting at a school. At least this category does suggest someone intended to attack someone else at a school, regardless of specific circumstances.

Of the 160 events, 18 are intended suicides with no threat to others. It may be another semantics issue, but do you think that an attempted suicide on school property with a gun is the same thing as a "school shooting" as the phrase has come to be understood? I'm not suggesting suicides aren't an issue, but is this a suicide or a "school shooting" merely because someone shot themselves on school property? The distinction is quite important. The location may be irrelevant, yet it is being presented as a defining factor.

Those two categories are relatively clear, but the next two are extremely ambiguous. There are 31 events that are listed as "Gun fired but no one injured." I'm unsure if these are events where a gun was intentionally fired at someone and missed or merely unintentional discharges of a weapon that didn't injure anyone. Another 13 are listed as "Gun fired unintentionally resulting in injury or death" which I guess could also be labeled as "unintentional" shootings on school property.

To confuse matters more, I decided to randomly look up some of the events to see what actually was reported. On August 22, 2013 there is an event listed as "gun fired but no one injured" where a 5-year-old had a gun in their backpack that discharged while they were in the cafeteria.[6] A 5-year-old with a gun in their backpack disturbing? Absolutely! And there is definitely a problem here, but is this really a "school shooting" or an example of a gun illegally on school property that accidentally discharged? And why does a 5-year-old have a gun...because of school issues? I highly doubt that.

Next, I picked the previous event listed as a "school shooting" on August 20, 2013 at Discovery Learning Academy in Decatur, GA. This one actually does appear to be a 20-year-old male who fired multiple shots at police at an elementary school. It is also listed as "gun fired but no one injured" and not as an attack on other people because no one was injured.[7] At least this appears to have intended to be a possible "school shooting" as the phrase implies, but where is the consistency in the data sets here? Intent does not seem to be a distinguishing factor in their interpretations of the media reports.

I pulled another random event: January 20, 2014 at Widener University in Chester, PA. A student was shot sitting in their car in the parking lot of Widener University's athletic center. The university spokesman said that "all indications are this was not a random act of violence."[8] So what we appear to have here is a targeted shooting on a specific individual which just happened to take place on University property as opposed to a shooter targeting schools to shoot up. Once again, a sad situation but is this really a "school shooting" as the people understand it?

I chose these three events at random. Only one would I say honestly meets the requirements of being a "school shooting" as the event appears to be perceived by the general public and even then no one was actually shot. For a moment, I honestly felt I wasn't giving Everytown a fair enough shake so I picked one more at random. (I swear I'm not making this up. I picked them all randomly in this order.) I clicked on an event on April 24, 2014, which was listed as a suicide and already unrepresentative of an actual "shooting", so I clicked on the event next to it on the same day listed as an attack on other persons. This event was listed as taking place at St. Mary Catholic School in Griffith, IN. Ironically, it took a minute or two to find an article that didn't actually preface the story by listing its place in Everytown's already existing running statistic on "school shootings" that we're trying to evaluate here. I finally found an article that did not open with such a bias from Channel 5, NBC Chicago titled "Man Shoots Estranged Wife in School Parking Lot."

Turns out, it was exactly what the title suggests. Remanard Castro was estranged from his wife Nina Castro and already had a history of domestic violence with a handgun. School was technically out of session for the Easter holiday, but Nina Castro was picking up her 14 year old son from an after school program when her estranged husband shot her in the parking lot of the school and then fled on motorcycle. He later committed suicide at home when confronted by police.[9] It is hard for me to logically conclude this is a "school shooting" merely because it happened to take place in a school parking lot, as the school location appears entirely circumstantial here.

Honestly, I did try one more after this as I did initially hope to at least provide one unarguable "school shooting" where someone was injured. I picked May 21, 2014. A 10-year-old girl caught in crossfire between two other people shooting at each other across the Clarke Street School Playground. Took place at 7:15pm in the evening.[10] Horrible story, but again the location seems entirely circumstantial in this event. I fear this pattern could go on all day. I'll look through all the rest later, but please go to the link (http://everytownresearch.org/school-shootings/) and check the events individually for yourself, which is the real point here.

These are what Everytown is presenting to the people as "school shootings."   What do you think, is it an accurate description of the problem inherent specifically with schools when considering gun laws? Or are they abusing the use of the word "school" to create the false perception that the "school shooting" problem is greater than it really is just to give an extra tug on those heartstrings? To me it appears very clearly to be the latter. Remember, it's already illegal to have a loaded weapon on school property in many cases.

It is not that the events didn't happen. It isn't that the events aren't a problem. The problem is that at least a portion of their data is being intentionally misrepresented to reflect a distinct type of event that the public has come to be aware of, that being attempted mass murders at schools now known as a "school shooting", with the intent of distorting the frequency with which those events are perceived by the general public to occur. Their data set is extremely ambiguous and the semantics which they ultimately use to express their conclusions are incredibly deceiving. What they are expressing is 160 cases where laws that already exist were most likely broken. What this is not are 160 cases where someone intended to shoot people on school property, yet that is how it is presented.

Let me quickly address something about Gun Free Zones as well since we're on the topic of schools. There are arguments being made both for and against the issue. One of the arguments against them is that potential shooters target them specifically due to a lack of resistance by armed defenders. The contradictory evidence in favor of Gun Free Zones does suggest that they only represent a small portion of the locations where mass murders are attempted with guns. Though both arguments have elements of being right and wrong, I think both are kind of missing the real point. The problem is not about whether they are specifically targeted or not. Yes, maybe a few people target Gun Free Zones specifically because they are "gun free" but the biggest problem with Gun Free Zones is not in their being perceived as easy targets to begin with. The problem lies in their lack of ability to dissuade a potential shooter from following through with their plan after considering it as a target for some other reason. It's not about if a location is specifically targeted for attack, it's about whether a location targeted for attack has enough risk or threat of defense to have the ability to break the resolve of those initially planning to do so. A Gun Free Zone lacks the ability to break that resolve in those few who have specifically targeted those areas regardless of the initial reason. Many criminals might originally think to target a Brinks truck for their theft; there's a reason they end up robbing the liquor store instead.

"Currently, federal law requires licensed gun dealers to conduct background checks for all gun sales, but in most states, background checks are not required for person-to-person sales by an unlicensed seller. Many of these sales take place between anonymous strangers who meet online, where a vast digital marketplace for guns has emerged. Today, hundreds of thousands of guns are available for sale from unlicensed online sellers at the click of a mouse, no questions asked and no background check required." [11]

Anyone who is selling anything other than items from their own personal firearms collection is required to register as an FFL, that's already law. You can't buy guns privately, repair or restore them, and then sell them privately from your "collection", repeatedly, without being required to register as an FFL. You can't legally buy guns from an FFL to merely sell them through a private party sale at a high price markup without a background check. This is not a loophole for unlicensed repeat sellers to do so while avoiding background checks merely by being on the internet. What they are referring to as an online seller is actually an online forum that allows both private parties and FFLs to post listings for weapons they want to sell...they can merely post those sales online as opposed to a print publication. Yes, FFLs also list items for sale on the forums and still require background checks on every sale.

The entire sale isn't exactly at the click of a mouse except in limited cases. It is true there are some allowances to mailing firearms for private parties. Private parties can mail firearms to FFLs in any state. Private parties can mail rifles and shotguns to each other within the same state only.[12] There arguably is a hint of ambiguity in the law that suggests private parties might legally be able to mail handguns (possibly through common or contract carriers. It is quite specifically prohibited through USPS), to other private parties within the same state exclusively. However, it is typically understood by the major carriers to be prohibited. USPS and DHL will only ship handguns between FFLs (includes licensees and state and federal government officials) exclusively and UPS and FedEx will only ship handguns between FFLs, from an individual to an FFL, or from an FFL returning a handgun to the lawful individual owner.[13-16] Federal law requires that you notify the carrier the shipment contains a firearm, so you legally can't just lie to the carrier about shipping a handgun either.[17] Even if the ambiguity in the law were to favor the private parties, good luck trying to legally ship that handgun in a private party sale. If a state requires background checks on private party transactions (most likely through an FFL) then that must still be done. The only time a sale might really be entirely online is during intrastate sales of rifles and shotguns in states that do not otherwise restrict private party sales. Of course, that is exactly the same for guns sold from print publications. In most cases, the subsequent sale does not happen entirely online or digitally...and certainly not in the way Everytown implies.

They call out one sales forum directly, "Research by Everytown has shown that just one online gun marketplace — Armslist.com — transfers an estimated 25,000 guns to criminals each year." However a thorough visit to Armslist.com clearly suggests they were designed for local interactions and have no direct involvement with the transaction between the parties. It does not appear as though Armslist.com transfers "any" firearms to "anyone", the same way Craigslist does not transfer any privately listed items sold to any buyers. On another section of Everytown's website the wording for the actual report they had previously conducted is a little different, "Mayors Against Illegal Guns' investigation of illegal online gun sales examined online gun listings on the website Armslist.com, and found that this single website could potentially transfer more than 25,000 guns to individuals with criminal records just this year."[18] Amazing how it went from "could potentially transfer" to "transfers" isn't it? I'm also finding nothing to suggest Armslist.com conducts any "illegal" online sales.

It appears even worse when you understand what their investigation actually entailed. "The investigation reached these conclusions by analyzing a unique data set: the contact information prospective gun buyers voluntarily provided in 'want-to-buy' ads they placed on Armslist in search of gun sellers. We examined 13,000 listings posted between February and May 2013, matched contact information to criminal records, and found that at least 1 in 30 would-be gun-buyers had felony or domestic abuse records that barred them from purchasing or possessing guns." They used contact information listed for prospective buyers, only listed on want-to-buy ads mind you, and cross referenced that contact information with some criminal records database somewhere to somehow conclude those specific people were the same ones prohibited from buying firearms, and then drew their conclusions regarding sales to prohibited people based upon transactions that never actually took place other than in theory.

This isn't 1 in 30 of all potential buyers either. This is 1 in 30 people who posted want-to-buy ads. Not all buyers post want-to-buy ads. Honestly, in my roughly 30 years experience of buying and selling things through publications, I'd guess it to be a pretty low percentage of buyers who actually do unless they are looking for something specific that isn't regularly listed for sale or are otherwise having problems buying the item to begin with. You cannot then extrapolate that 1 in 30 of all sales that take place are to prohibited people from the want-to-buy postings. The whole process is extremely flawed. More so, I have admired the attractiveness of many women walking by in the past 10 years, but you cannot assume that makes me an adulterer merely because I was looking at the merchandise. In other words, not everyone who posts a want-to-buy ad actually has the capacity to buy.

Everytown is posing this as an internet problem that allows people dealing in firearms to sell them in bulk over the internet without a license and without a background check. It just isn't the case, unless they are already breaking other existing laws. At its core this is a private party background check argument, but presented in a way as to exacerbate the ideology that there is some enormous loophole, when really private party background checks are not required by federal law. At which point you realize that none of the numbers they cite, or subsequent arguments they make, actually mean anything and are merely restatements of the fact that 40 percent of all legal gun sales are done in private party transactions presented in a distorted and emotionally charged context. The sad thing is, I agree with extending the background checks to private party transactions, as you'll later see why the evidence suggests I must. But when I see Everytown's approach to the issue, I grow substantially more sympathetic with the NRA's fear mongering tactics.

"Every day, 88 Americans are killed with guns. That's why Everytown for Gun Safety Support Fund seeks to improve our understanding of the causes of gun violence and the means to reduce it." [19]

They start their analysis with "killed." It is true that on average 88 people are killed by guns every day. It is also true that "killed" could reference murders, unintentional shootings, suicides, or possibly even justifiable homicides such as self-defense by civilians to save their own lives. And on their website in another location where they actually reference the CDC statistics, it verifies that to be just the case: 35 percent homicide (11,294 avg.), 62 percent suicide (19,992 avg.), 3 percent unintentional or undetermined (815 avg.), though it does not segregate the homicides by murder and justifiable homicide.[20] Their subsequent statement then switches to "gun violence" as though the two things are the same. They are not. Killed does not mean murdered, and a justifiable homicide is not "gun violence." It is clearly designed to deceive you into believing 88 people are murdered each day in "gun violence", which is a fallacy. In the FBI's 2014 Uniform Crime Reports under "violent crimes" it lists 8,124 murders from all firearms in the year 2014.[21] That breaks down to 22 people killed by gun violence daily. Not good; but certainly not 88. It is only 25 percent of the number they implied were from gun violence.

"Everytown's research has shown that expanding the areas where guns can be carried and the circumstances in which they can be used is only associated with greater harm. So-called Stand Your Ground laws, which encourage the use of deadly force outside the home, are associated with significantly higher justifiable -homicide rates. After Georgia passed its Stand Your Ground law, the number of justifiable

homicides in the states increased by 83 percent. In Florida, it tripled. This push towards allowing easy access to guns in a growing variety of public places has only resulted in a greater risk of gun violence, often justified by increasingly permissive laws." [22]

See how this starts out as suggesting that expanding the areas where you can carry and use a gun is associated with "greater harm?" It then gives evidence of how justifiable homicides have increased by 83 percent in Georgia and 200 percent in Florida due to the Stand Your Ground Laws to support their argument. Justifiable homicides means these people legally used a gun to save a life in a potentially life threatening scenario. That is called "self-defense." Sure, that certainly is "greater harm" to those threatening others. Now look at the spin here. Suddenly the conclusion is made in the semantics of "gun violence" and yet the examples presented were legally "self-defense" shootings. They have suddenly framed The Stand Your Ground Laws as merely increasingly permissive laws that apparently allow "gun violence" to be justified, and kind of seems to suggest that the laws were actually passed *in order* to justify "gun violence." They have to spin it this way because the numbers actually reflect a benefit for "self-defense" scenarios; the very thing they don't want you to think exists. Notice how they omit the change in actual "gun violence" statistics in GA and FL from the argument entirely? Those are the numbers they should actually be presenting to support their "gun violence" conclusion to expanded use and circumstance.

The Stand Your Ground Laws clearly increased the opportunities for people to defend themselves but did violent crimes actually increase or decrease? I found some statistics on violent crime rates (not specifically violent gun crime) per capita in Florida between 2000 and 2010. After 2000 total violent crimes already appeared to be decreasing slightly. In 2005 they increased mildly and continued to rise a bit through 2007, they then returned to their decline until the end of our data in 2010. The report suggests that violent crimes were down 12 percent between 2000 and 2005, and then were down 23 percent between 2005 and 2010, so the rate of decline, on average, about doubled after passing the Stand Your Ground Laws.[23] I might be lenient and conclude that the Stand Your Ground Laws were an overall wash in regards to "violent crime" without more data. You'd even have to concede the possibility that some were able to abuse the Stand Your Ground Laws for their benefit. But can you conclude that they resulted in a greater risk of "gun violence?" There's just no evidence to support that argument, but violent crimes overall did drop. I don't know about you, but all other things being equal, I'll accept the outcome of a "self-defense" shooting over the murder of an innocent victim every time.

"There's been a lot of tough talk in Congress lately about keeping America safe. But here's one thing you won't hear discussed: America currently allows gun sales to suspected terrorists." [24]

This one is gaining traction lately, so you actually hear it discussed all the time. And you know what; it's actually TRUE. You know what else is true: The Fifth Amendment of the U.S. Constitution says that no person shall be deprived of life, liberty, or property, without Due Process of law. That would specifically apply to the portion of American citizens and lawful permanent residents who can currently buy firearms in the United States. Our nation is not at War, and these people are not War criminals under that exclusion nor would they meet the definition of "alien unlawful enemy combatant" under the Military Commissions Act of 2006.[25] These are merely American citizens and lawful permanent residents on a "secret" government list "suspected" of possibly being terrorists. Therefore I don't believe their chosen semantics for the problem, "The Terror Gap," is quite accurate and is, for the most part, fear mongering.

The problem is obviously with the word "suspected" here. You're probably also suddenly recalling Chapter 4 right now and realizing there may also be a problem with the word "terrorist" and what that actually defines these days. Is Everytown really suggesting we set aside the Due Process clause of the Fifth Amendment and punish people who have not been convicted of a crime but are merely "suspected" of something? It appears so. And that's a "Terror Gap?" Should we prohibit "suspected" pedophiles from frequenting schools and Catholic churches? How about "suspected" drug users from working at hospitals and pharmacies? How about prohibiting "suspected" religious fanatics from buying Kool-Aid? To make matters worse, "suspected" here is only established by a "secret" government list. The ideology that people are innocent until proven guilty is one of the cornerstones of the Nation all this is intended to protect. If we abandon the Constitution and its Fifth Amendment, what exactly are we fighting for?

I'll admit, on face value it initially sends a chill down your spine when you read the suggestion that terrorists can legally buy guns in the United States. But again, these are "suspected" terrorists and not convicted terrorists. We are also not merely talking about suspected "foreign" terrorists here either; we're talking about U.S. citizens as well.

You merely have to read some of Everytown's Twitter posts

to see how they attempt to manipulate the perceptions of the people, such as arbitrarily dropping the word "suspected" when it suits their purposes: "NRA extremists think terrorists have Second Amendment rights. Most Americans—including NRA members—disagree." Of course most people don't think terrorists should have Second Amendment rights, and I doubt the NRA actually does either. But people merely "suspected" of something clearly have rights in this country. I'm envisioning Bloomberg right now muttering to himself in his best Lada Gaga voice: "You know that I'll be your, Propa-propaganda."

It is true that some non citizens can legally purchase weapons, but being lawful permanent residents they are also entitled to Fifth Amendment protection. According to the FBI there are roughly 420,000 people on the Terrorist Watch List administered by the FBI's Terrorist Screening Center. Of those, only 2 percent are American citizens or lawful permanent residents legally able to buy a gun.[26] What we're really talking about is roughly 8,400 people on the list. Of that number it is unclear how many may already be prohibited from buying firearms for other reasons. Even if we conclude all would pass a background check, that is still a smaller number than the 10,000 Syrian refugees we have committed to admitting into the United States as of this writing.[27] I'm not passing judgment on the refugees or their situation, but it seems a hard story to swallow that we have an extreme fear of terrorists when selling firearms to Americans and lawful permanent residents and yet not have an extreme fear of terrorists when allowing Syrian refugees into the country. The truth is that it's probably an extremely small percentage of either group who pose a real threat to American citizens, if any at all.

Ever since I first typed in "How to get off Terrorist Watch List" on Google this morning, my 200 Mbps high speed internet has slowed to a crawl. I hope I don't end up on the list merely for Googling how to get off of it. I'm only half kidding. That is really the biggest problem with abandoning Fifth Amendment rights though; who decides you're on the list, who tells you that you're on the list, who tells you "why" you are on the list and more importantly how the hell do you get off of the list? Apparently, if you find out (on your own, because they aren't going to tell you) that you might be on the Terrorist Watch List, such as finding you are on the no-fly list, you can file a complaint with the Department of Homeland Security's Traveler Redress Inquiry Program (DHS TRIP). Apparently that review "is not subject to oversight by any court or entity outside the counter-terrorism community." They don't even have to inform you of any subsequently updated status.[28] Read: You have no Fifth Amendment Rights if you end up on the Terrorist Watch List. Basically you are guilty until proven innocent, and at present there is no way to prove you are innocent.

In regards to the no-fly list itself, a federal judge in 2014 did rule that the no-fly lists denied people their constitutional rights to Due Process because the government's procedures to challenge your inclusion on the list were "wholly ineffective."[29] On April 13, 2015 the U.S. filed notice regarding new redress procedures regarding the DHS TRIP with the U.S. District Court in *Mohamed v. Holder.*[30] The new redress procedures will now provide confirmation if someone is on the no-fly list, give limited explanation as to why, and provide for an opportunity to send in a written appeal where one can provide evidence. Of course, the irony in the last point seems to be that they most likely already have any information you could ever provide to attempt to prove you're "not" a terrorist before they put you on the list, thus making the last point seem kind of moot. Either way, that is still guilty until proven innocent. There is still no real path to have a hearing for due process through the U.S. judicial system, and the ACLU currently trying to pave one says "Unfortunately, the government's new redress process still falls far short of constitutional requirements."[31] A U.S. Appellate Court, however, has recently ruled that they have subject-matter jurisdiction to hear challenges to inclusion on the list.[32] That particular Appellate Court case also suggests evidence that the they are still not providing people on the no-fly list with a reason for their inclusion.[33] Hopefully the problem will soon be resolved, but at present I find it a hard argument to abandon the Fifth Amendment because a few people are worried about the intentions of 8,400 people who can currently buy firearms. Now, it is certainly possible to have slightly different and stricter background checks for lawful permanent residents than U.S. citizens in hopes of prohibiting a few "foreign suspected" terrorists from buying weapons, but I don't hear anybody proposing that solution here.

Everytown for Gun Safety also funds other websites through their Everytown for Gun Safety Support Fund, who then spread the same information such as TheTrace.com. "The Trace is organized as a nonprofit corporation and is in the process of applying for tax-exempt status with the IRS. Our seed funding was provided by the Everytown for Gun Safety Support Fund and the Joyce Foundation; individual donors include Ken Lerer and Nick Hanauer."

The most heartbreaking part of looking at Everytown for Gun Safety is that, with the amount of money Michael Bloomberg is throwing at this, he could have made a real difference in the education of the people regarding the issue at hand instead of just trying to mind-fu©k them with propaganda in order to get what he wants. Instead he just seems to want to prove he has a bigger swinging dick than the NRA. In reference to his work on gun safety, obesity and smoking cessation, Bloomberg stated "I am telling you if there is a God, when I get to heaven I'm not stopping to be interviewed. I am heading straight in. I have earned my place in heaven. It's not even close."[34] I don't know, maybe he really does think he has more power than "God." For that matter, I guess if you're really willing to drop that much money strictly for your ego, maybe he did buy a larger penis? Either way, his organization is clearly part of the problem and not part of the solution.

I'll reference one last quote from Everytown for Gun Safety's website as it leads us back into our discussion on semantics, "Everytown for Gun Safety is a movement of Americans fighting for common-sense reforms to reduce gun violence." This is another one of those misused phrases: common sense. You see this phrase thrown around a lot lately by one side in the debate as though merely suggesting the phrase supports their side of the argument. Isn't the entire debate about "what exactly are" sensible solutions? Even the tone of this book addresses how the biases lead us away from "common-sense."

So what are "common-sense" reforms? Unfortunately, in most cases in this debate it is merely another semantics trick. It is typically used in either one of two ways: To give the impression that your argument is inherently sound when you can't make an otherwise sound argument; or, as a general rebuttal to the oppositions argument, thrown out as though it is an answer to the problem when really no argument is subsequently provided to evidence a solution that actually is "common-sense." It is very deceptive to the people. The chant "we need common sense gun regulation" gets repeated over and over...and often without providing any further clarification, as though the statement in and of itself suggests a valid solution to the problem. It really means nothing.

You often hear some groups making versions of a statement along the lines of; X% of Americans – including NRA members – want "common-sense" gun control.[35] (I pulled up references to support this: turns out the first one was mikebloomberg.com. Seeing a pattern here?) That may even be a distorted interpretation of a valid survey done by someone to address some specific regulation, yet it gets repeated in that ambiguous manner. If "common-sense" isn't specifically defined then what exactly are you suggesting people want but aren't getting? If I ask you "do you favor common-sense gun regulations" what would you answer? I'm surprised they don't list the percentage as 100 percent...but then again, that would obviously point out the ambiguity.

It is basically a false premise in an argument. It does not mean the people support the proposed gun reforms of the group making the statistical statement unless the question was posed as supporting a specific issue. If that is the case, then the presenter is again the one determining that issue is thus "common sense." As we've seen above, Everytown's arguments clearly are not "common sense" but often fallacious propaganda. The phrase "common sense" isn't offering an actual solution. People need to stop presenting it as though it does. Sure, I want common-sense gun regulations, but based on my research that would actually mean removing many existing laws, and adding a few moderate laws more precisely targeted to the intended goals.

We've seen how the Second Amendment itself is really "common sense" in protecting a natural right of self-defense and a collective right against oppression, tyranny and attack. How does suggesting we negate common sense with common sense make any damn sense at all? The average (median) IQ is only 100, so sense may not be that common.[36] Just because someone "says" something is common sense does not mean that it is. What's worse, apparently sense is not as common as propaganda... because there's also Mass Shooting Tracker.

Mass Shooting Tracker

A more recent attempt at skewing the public's perception, much like what appears to have happened with the term "assault weapon" is currently unfolding with the term "mass shooting." There is no real consistent definition for mass shooting, so there can be no clear definition of the data set being provided in statistics for their occurrence. Much like the term "assault weapon" attempting to give the impression that semi automatic weapons are full auto military weapons, the term "mass shooting" appears to be casually interchanged with mass murder to give the public the impression they are one in the same...when they are not. The FBI historically defined mass murder as four or more people killed during an event with no "cooling-off period" between the murders. Nation of Change states this about the term "Mass Shooting": "Broadly speaking, the term refers to an incident involving multiple victims of gun violence, but there is no official set of criteria or definition for a mass shooting, according to criminology experts and FBI officials. Generally, there are three terms you'll see to describe a perpetrator of this type of gun violence: mass murderer, spree killer, or serial killer. The primary distinction between a mass murderer and a spree killer is that the latter strikes in multiple locations. A serial killer is distinguished by striking over a longer time frame."[37]

Well, that seems relatively sound to me taken as a whole. The combined definition still gives intent to a specific perpetrator(s), choosing to do harm to multiple members of the general public. Although, it is still vague in its definition of how many victims are required to create a "mass" thus prohibiting accurate statistical analysis. I would have to concur that there needs to be criteria for distinguishing a mass murder from a mass shooting which was "intended" to be a mass murder while not ignoring the latter statistically. Success or failure of accuracy should not change the intent of the shooter in statistical analysis regarding gun violence. There should be a category which includes "attempted gun mass murders," and I believe the definition above serves that purpose if the number of victims were defined.

However, the problem with the current ambiguity is that websites like Mass Shooting Tracker are created (www.shootingtracker.com) and distort that ambiguity to suit their political agenda. To compound the problem, Mass Shooting Tracker is now getting credit by media news agencies as representing actual credible statistics on gun violence. As you'll later notice, Mass Shooting Tracker actually gets their statistics from the media itself. The question then becomes, what "exactly" are they providing statistics on? So I thought I'd take a look at their website and see how they defined "mass shooting."

Taken from the Mass Shooting Tracker website: "The only requirement is that four or more people are shot in a spree or setting, likely without a cooling off period. This may include the gunman himself (because they often suicide by cop or use a gun to kill themselves to escape punishment), or police shootings of civilians around the gunman. The reasoning behind the latter being that if the shooter is arrested, he will often be charged with injuring people the police actually shot, as that is a foreseeable result of a shooting spree."

Foreseeable result that cops will shoot civilians? Um...seriously? Think about that for a minute. If a guy fires a gun in the air and shoots absolutely no one (maybe is just wielding what merely looks like a gun), possibly having no intention of actually shooting anyone, and then cops mistakenly shoot 3 bystanders and then the gunman ...that is listed as a "mass shooting" EVEN THOUGH THE SUSPECTED GUNMAN DIDN'T SHOOT ANYONE. That is still four or more people shot in a spree or setting.

Three armed intruders break into my home and one shoots me in the leg; I then shoot all three of them in self-defense. That meets their requirements for a "mass shooting"....when really it is a home invasion. Four armed masked robbers walk into a bank and shoot off a couple rounds to scare the bank personnel, undercover cop shoots all four..."mass shooting", not a foiled bank robbery. Do you see the problem?

Now MST might come back with a rebuttal and say those scenarios wouldn't qualify as "mass shootings", even though they fit their definition for one. If they were to argue that the home intrusion scenario would not be counted as a "mass shooting", I'd have to ask where the definition is that consistently excludes it from the data set. I cannot find one. Four people, when including the gunmen, were shot in a spree or setting. If it were to be excluded, how is that decided; undisclosed definition, vote, general gut feeling by one person at MST?

Here is the disclaimer on their website: "Suspects harvested from news reports are not assumed to be guilty, merely identified as suspects. Information in the list is gleaned from journalistic sources and can not attempt to be an exhaustive listing, merely a listing of all known incidents." As I pointed out before, they get their information from the media. The media chooses which stories to report and how to spin them, thus the media itself creates the statistic; though, as they disclose, suspects might not even be guilty of a crime. The media then reports the "mass shooting" statistic as coming from a credible outside source.

Looking through the individual articles referenced as constituting their data set, I found a lot of discrepancies that didn't even meet their own broad definition for "mass shooting." A number of the news articles cited only referenced injuries and not whether those injured were actually gunshots.[38-41] Others clearly fall short of four or more people actually being shot.[42,43] Many appear to start as group fights with multiple perpetrators shooting each other.[44,45] In a number of cases where police responded to a report of gunfire there weren't even 4 shooting victims on the scene, sometimes no shooting victims at all, but victims were later assumed to be attributed to those events after calling local hospitals to inquire if they had any recent gunshot victims.[46,47] Some of the referenced links point to non-existent news stories, or stories that have been removed by the news source.[48,49] This leads to the number of "mass shootings" getting extremely overstated. Where exactly are the checks and balances on the data set before presenting credible statistics to the public?

The "About Mass Shooting Tracker" page is also full of semantics tricks to deceive the reader. I specifically liked this section:

Here is how they [FBI] define mass *murder*, and *not* mass shootings, these are direct quotes:

Old Definition:

• "Generally, mass *murder* was described as a number of *murders* (four or more) occurring during the same incident, with no distinctive time period between the murders."

New Generally Accepted Definition:
• "The general definition of spree *murder* is two or more *murders* committed by an offender or offenders, without a cooling-off period."

http://www.fbi.gov/stats-services/publications/serial-murder/serial-murder-1#two

Let's summarize and keep it simple by giving an *accurate* and *precise* definition of a mass shooting:

A mass shooting is when four or more people are shot in an event, or related series of events, likely without a cooling off period.

The italicized words are as their website shows them. Notice how they highlight the word "murder" and "not" with the stars, and then italicize only the word murder in the following definitions. They're basically telling you the information they are about to provide has no relation to "mass shootings" and is related to murders specifically. But further it attempts to mask the fact that they then proceed to give you the definition for mass murder as some "old definition" as if it is an erroneous definition for mass shooting, replaced it with the definition for spree murder which is defining an entirely different category of murder and making you think it is an amended definition for mass murder or mass shooting by calling it the "New Generally Accepted Definition" continuing to highlight only the word "murder", and then follow up by giving you their "*accurate and precise*" definition for "mass shooting" as though they are correcting the FBI's definition by showing that it doesn't require a "murder."

They want you to believe that the FBI is defining "mass shooting" incorrectly, when they have not. They have just not defined "mass shooting", they have defined mass murder and spree murder. Further, "mass murder "and "spree murder" include murders that were committed with tools other than guns. In continuing to make the correlation between murder statistics and mass shootings, MST is trying to give you the false impression that mass murders and spree murders are all committed with guns and should therefore all be labeled as "shootings", further suggesting people who merely get shot are incorrectly omitted (from murder statistics, which they are not), and that the FBI is intentionally deceiving you in not reporting those under murder statistics. As I said before, there is validity in tracking attempted mass killings that were unsuccessful for statistical purposes regarding gun violence but as we have seen MST's definition is not really accurate or precise in defining such an event.

I loved this subtle semantics trick in their "imagine this" scenario:

> A reporter goes up to a victim who has been shot and asks "What's happened here?" The victim replies "There has been a mass shooting, that gun owner just

shot four of us." The reporter replies "Sorry, that wasn't a mass shooting."

Did you catch the neuro-linguistic programming (NLP) there? That "gun owner" just shot four of us. Not gunman, not shooter, not criminal, not man, not woman..."gun owner." What do you think? Are they specifically targeting potential criminals...or all gun owners here? The other deception here is the last line. What it should say is "Sorry, that wasn't a mass murder." Nobody ever claimed this scenario isn't a "mass shooting" as their imagination implies. They are intentionally trying to program you to think that mass murder, spree murder and mass shooting are the same thing and that any of their statistics for "mass shooting" are statistics for attempted mass murder.

Mass Shooting Tracker is an anti-gun propaganda site...period. They have made up their own definition for mass shooting which incredibly overstates the number of real mass shooting events. The only way to make a logically sound decision as to how to further reduce gun violence is to evaluate the real facts in the matter. Either side making things up and presenting fallacious and distorted data doesn't do any of us any good.

I guess one could argue that Mass Murders are caused by (at least temporarily) mentally disturbed people who (theoretically) don't care about laws who intend to kill people. Mass Shooting, as being presented by MST, is an ambiguous term that is so indefinable as to original intent, or who or how many shooters there were, or even which side of the law the shooters and victims were on, as to be virtually meaningless in analysis. As mentioned above, it appears this is a new semantics trick that is designed to confuse you into assuming that all "Mass Shootings" and their statistics are events that were intended to be Mass Murders...which is a huge fallacy.

I've seen evidence to suggest it is already working. I saw a pro-gun meme that stated that "Mass Shootings are caused by mentally disturbed people who don't care about laws who intend to kill people." At first glance, the problem here may go unnoticed by most, but I'm guessing having read this far you already see the problem. Obviously, the meme's response is in relation to the motivation for an attempted mass murder, not necessarily what ultimately played out as a mass shooting, at least not by MST's definition. The argument to follow then becomes a rebuttal to this meme; not all "mass shootings" are due to mentally disturbed people. Well, that's an accurate rebuttal to that argument, although it wasn't the argument the pro-gun supporter thought they were making because a key word was switched in their mind without real comprehension...murder to shooting.

It does appear we're subtly being trained to believe that mass murder and mass shooting are synonyms...and interchangeable. What that does is discreetly remove the "intent" of any shooting from the equation by making even justified shootings appear to be the societal problem in question, suddenly suggesting any gun use is the problem and not "gun violence." The conclusion could fallaciously be made that, with no intent necessary to create a mass shooting, the shooting itself must be due to the availability of the gun and not the intent of any specific shooter. Mass Shooting Tracker removes "intent" from the equation and places the blame on any gun involved, no matter who shot who or what the circumstances were.

I know it is a cliché, but we need to stop anthropomorphizing tools as though they have thoughts and intent. Even the way the cliché is written is deceivingly phrased to leave some ambiguity in the thought. You know the cliché; "Guns don't kill people, people kill people." The reality is guns do kill people, so the debate ensues. The reality is also that the phrase, in its true sense, is meant to be "Guns don't choose to kill people, people choose to kill people"...the prior is merely a semantics construct of language where the reader is supposed to assume the gun "chooses" to do something or someone "chooses" to do something with the gun, without being explicitly stated. It's like the statement "the window was broken." The person is to know the window was broken by something or someone, at some time, without the remaining details necessarily having to be qualified. If you want to evaluate "how to stop windows from being broken," you have to then clarify those factors in the breaking of the window. Those factors become crucial to the analysis.

The ambiguity in that particular gun statement is now gone, and there is nothing left for people to debate about the argument. Guns do not choose to kill people, people choose to kill people. Arguing against this is anthropomorphizing an inanimate object.

As this book was going to print, I read that Gun Violence Archive recently absorbed or merged with Mass Shooting Tracker at the start of 2016. I began to look through some of their data to see how they compared to Mass Shooting Tracker. At first glance, it appeared they fixed a few of the notorious discrepancies that I have previously highlighted in the definition of "mass shooting," which I thought might diminish some of the false data that was being pitched to the public. A large portion of this chapter addresses Mass Shooting Tracker's propaganda specifically, so I wanted to try to update the book accordingly before print...possibly even reporting the problem had been resolved. I first sent the following (albeit probably snarky) email to Gun Violence Archive but received no response:

Hi,

I just noticed your "merger" of sorts. Hopefully these statistics will now be more credible as your newly acquired partner was horribly exacerbating the problem. Of course now I'll have to edit out the half of a chapter entirely discrediting everything on their entire site before publication, but I'd rather the people be more accurately informed than continue to be fed propaganda which I then have to discredit. For too long the propaganda from both sides has been confusing this debate and Mass Shooting Tracker became a primary source of fear mongering and distorted data.

So far, reading your General Methodology page, I'm somewhat optimistic your new partnership will be providing substantially more accurate data. I see that a lot of the problems with MST appear to be gone, but I can't clearly distinguish what your position is on including police officers accidentally shooting bystanders when calculating the injured in mass shootings; are you counting those to determine the required quantity of 4 shot or do those fall exclusively under "officer involved shootings?" In other places, it does appear you're focusing more on intent of an actual shooter(s) than merely blaming any gun involved but there is a bit of ambiguity.

I'm sincerely trying to find at least one organization in this mess I can actually support...maybe you will finally be it. Although I did immediately pull up an article under 2016 mass shootings (http://abc13.com/news/four-wounded-by-gunfire-after-new-years-party/1143166/) that only has 3 confirmed victims (honestly, it doesn't even confirm the injuries were gunshots, but I won't split hairs on that one) and regarding the fourth states, "They are investigating the possibility that another person discovered wounded nearby on Antoine could also be related to the same scene." That is NOT 4 confirmed people shot at the event...it's 3 people and a "guess" that a 4th "might" have been related to the shooting. That's just bad data! A single piece of bad data and your credibility entirely falls apart. The fact that you like Bloomberg funded The Trace.com on Facebook squelches my optimism some as well, as they just regurgitate the anti-gun propaganda without evaluation while trying to pitch themselves as unbiased.

Best Regards,

Doug Hawk

I didn't get any response. I later saw a post on their Facebook page showing two "mass shootings" already for 2016, the event I previously referenced was one of the two claimed on their website represented on this list. I then had an interesting exchange with them. I asked some questions about their process and pointed out that the specific mass shooting claimed to have occurred in 2016 didn't appear to fit their own definition, citing alternate news sources. Apparently they didn't like my questions or comments because they deleted them and felt compelled to go so far as to block me from their Facebook page. Here is a copy of the full exchange on the thread before they deleted the comments, and then shows their comment after deletion. I think the action speaks volumes about the intent of their organization...but you be the judge:

Gun Violence Archive:

GVA Summary Ledger January 1 – January 6

For always up to the hour summaries, full details of all incidents and our fully searchable database, go to gunviolencearchive.org

I appreciate your visits and propagating our data. We strive to make it right and it is always 100% provable. Thanks

[there was an image here claiming there were 2 mass shootings so far in 2016]

Doug Hawk:

If they are 100% provable, could you please do me a favor and prove the claimed mass shooting cited above from January 1, 2016 at 6500 block of TC Jester had four victims, because the article you cite suggests 3 people were shot and is merely "guessing" that a fourth injury from another location "might" be related to this shooting. Have you confirmed the fourth person is from the same shooting, making this fit your definition for a mass shooting, or is the fourth victim still questionable?

This article suggests that only 2 people were hit by gunfire at that location. Any other injuries in the general area have not been linked. In this report, even

in all locations, only 3 people appear to have been shot.
http://www.fox26houston.com/news/67560754-story

A third basically says 4 people were shot in northwest Houston and police do not know if they are connected:
http://www.click2houston.com/news/police-investigate-double-shooting-in-northwest-houston

How are you deciding which news report is correct?

Gun Violence Archive:

When there is conflict in numbers [which is seldom] we may look at a dozen or more sources to determine what happened, to whom and where. We then have a conversation between several researchers and log a conclusion based on the best available data.

As time passes we have the opportunity to see other data [sometimes weeks later] that either corroborates or questions our original decisions. At those points we either keep the classification or remove it.

Last year there was an incident where five were listed as wounded in a shooting at a hotel lobby. All sources used pretty much the same verbiage. Later, when we got the police report we saw that 2 were shot, two were cut by marble shrapnel and one ran through a glass door getting away. We removed three victims from the incident report and changed the designation.

Shorter answer...we have processes in place to address this sort of thing.

Doug Hawk:

When it comes to preserving the integrity of credible data, would it not be best to confirm the data first and then report it after confirmation...as opposed to reporting speculative information to the public prematurely and then having to redact the information sometimes weeks later? That clearly skews the bias towards more mass shootings on a running basis and confuses the public.

If you truly want to provide credible statistics and not merely try to present as many mass shootings as possible as quickly as possible creating a biased perspective, that would be the appropriate path. This particular case clearly does not appear to be a mass shooting, yet there it is telling the public there was one.

In this particular case, how then did you decide specifically that this event was a mass shooting and 4 people were shot under the scope of the same event in spite of the news reports? If you are "guessing" at data, it ceases to be credible regardless of how many researchers are "guessing" that 4 people were shot. Even the police directly investigating the shootings, with complete details of the cases not known by the media, have not concluded they are related...what do your researchers know that the police don't? Your process should not be a secret, if we are to evaluate the credibility of the data set.

I'm sincerely not trying to be antagonistic, but you claim these are 100% provable...and yet your own response suggests a method that clearly states they are not proven. Your conversation between several researchers describes evaluations of probability and not evaluations of proof. Opinions and facts are two different things. It is a good thing our legal system does not work that way.

I've also gone through a number of your events at this point, and cross referenced them with other news reports. Some are clearly unquestionable mass shootings by your definition, but saying that conflicts in the media reports are "seldom" appears to be more puffery than accurate.

I do appreciate your reply though; I think I have a better understanding of both the intent and accuracy of your organization's data.

At this point they deleted my comments and blocked me from their page, posting the following:

Gun Violence Archive:

Some comments removed because someone didn't like our process...so it goes.

What do you think? Should this be the response of an organization who is providing statistics on life and death scenarios regarding gun violence to the general public? Statistics which are used to create legislation and now to support Executive Orders? Should we not be allowed to question the methodology they use in creating their data or validating their data set? I asked a few valid questions and made a few valid statements, and the response was to delete my comments and block me from their Facebook page. How is that not representative of clear intent to provide biased data with no checks and balances? If they truly wanted to provide accurate and unbiased data to the public, my comments should have been highly welcomed, and not hidden from public view while banning me from ever commenting on their page. Isn't the "what do you have to hide?" argument the same one the anti-gun lobby makes in regards to people who do not want gun control measures? I think it is too soon to know if they are going to conduct business after the merger/acquisition any differently than Mass Shooting Tracker did on their own. So far, it appears nothing but the name has changed.

We'll cover more examples like Everytown and Mass Shooting Tracker later; I merely bring these up here to bring about awareness of the problem. Look not only at the statistics being presented but their source, the delineation of the data set, and whether it is semantically being misrepresented as something it is not. If everyone who bought a ShamWow were accurately put on a list, it may be a Sham list...but it doesn't mean the list is a sham. Let's look at how some of these misperceptions have affected public opinion and how laws have been applied and possibly misapplied as a result.

Chapter VII

We the Media of the United States, in Order to Form a Political Union

"Well, I'm not a doctor, although I play one on TV" – Robert Young [1]

Danny Glover

"I'm not really the President; I just played one on TV." In the spirit of Robert Young (a.k.a. Marcus Welby, M.D.) in 1974 Sanka ads, actor Danny Glover should have made such a disclosure before telling a group of students at Texas A&M that the reason for the Second Amendment was to protect slavery:

> I don't know if people know the genesis of the right to bear arms. The Second Amendment comes from the right to protect, to protect themselves from the slave revolts and from the uprisings from Native Americans. A revolt from people who were stolen from their land or revolt from people whose land was

stolen from, that's what the genesis of the Second Amendment is."[2]

This is how we end up with misinterpretations of facts and law through emotional and irrational responses. The people then vote with these misrepresentations and fallacies in mind. It becomes clear from the remainder of Glover's statements that his comment above was intended to evidence racism regarding blacks in general. In 1787 there were blacks in the United States who were "'freemen" and not slaves. I'm not condoning slavery and I'm certainly not denying that racism existed at the time, but nothing in Section I Article 8 of the Constitution defines "who" constitutes the militia and nothing in the Constitution actually prohibited free blacks from the right to bear arms, and state laws or any racist societal norms against blacks bearing arms are irrelevant to the meaning of the Second Amendment itself. This concept appears to stem from a 1998 study by Carl T. Bogus called *The Hidden History of the Second Amendment* where Bogus argues that the intent of drafting the Second Amendment was to preserve the militia in order to enforce slavery, as evidenced by a comment made by Patrick Henry at the Richmond Convention and the fact that George Mason owned slaves. Though it was never stated by Henry or Mason, Bogus argues that those in the crowd would have "known" that these two men really meant to "protect slavery" while fighting to preserve the militia and a right to bear arms. Might this have been the concern of a few people brought up in debate who were unwilling to ratify the Constitution as it stood? Possibly, but to suggest it is the entire reason for the existence of the Second Amendment is clearly just...well, "bogus."[3]

The Militia Act of 1792 does designate the militia to be "white" but that is independent of the right to bear arms in the Second Amendment as well, and is a restriction after the fact solely on the nature of the militia. We've already seen that the Framers intended both an individual right and a collective right in the Second Amendment. Glover could also ignorantly be addressing the subsequent Militia Act legislation that restricts the militia from including blacks and cedes power from Congress to the President to more easily fight Native American uprisings without Congressional approval, but again this is not the "genesis" of the Second Amendment and is merely post Bill of Rights legislation. Racist and oppressive to blacks and Native Americans at the time, absolutely, but the genesis of the right to bear arms established over the previous millennium, hardly. Yet how many people are going to spread famous actor Danny Glover's words about the meaning of the Second Amendment as fact, merely because they like his acting and "want" to believe what he is saying? Based on the positive comments under the online article; plenty.

It is possible that bad decisions have been made by the courts themselves due to the current situation at the time of the decision, and thus setting improper precedent in the judicial system. Since we are on the subject of how laws have been applied or misapplied over time, we really should bring up something about *Dred Scott v. Sandford* at this point to show that societal bias can infiltrate even the Supreme Court. In delivering the opinion of the court, Chief Justice Roger Tany held that Blacks could not be citizens, here is his explanation:

> It would give to persons of the negro race, who were recognized as citizens in any one State of the Union, the right to enter every other State whenever they pleased, singly or in companies, without pass or passport, and without obstruction, to sojourn there as

long as they pleased, to go where they pleased at every hour of the day or night without molestation, unless they committed some violation of law for which a white man would be punished; and it would give them the full liberty of speech in public and in private upon all subjects upon which its own citizens might speak; to hold public meetings upon political affairs, and to keep and carry arms wherever they went. And all of this would be done in the face of the subject race of the same color, both free and slaves, and inevitably producing discontent and insubordination among them, and endangering the peace and safety of the State.[4]

Blacks can't be citizens because it would give them the right to keep and carry arms wherever they want? That's a pretty messed up interpretation of the law right there, though it only superficially cites the Second Amendment. Does it evidence how even the Supreme Court can make biased rulings based on personal prejudice of a majority of its members? Absolutely. At the same time though, our obviously racist Supreme Court judge also implies that every citizen has the right to keep and carry arms wherever he wants. Again, this case might lead to the fallacious conclusions of Danny Glover, but this interpretation of citizenship citing the Second Amendment has no bearing on its genesis.

Society often appears to be misled by celebrities who become politically involved, those "professionals" claiming to be "authorities on the subject" while using substandard and manipulated data and by media propaganda in general. Comparing the sound statistical data with the subsequent laws seems to suggest that these manipulations do lead people towards adopting illogical laws, often applied in ignorance due to emotional overreaction after a recent event, and promoted through semantics tricks like "assault weapon" and "Saturday night special."

Reports of mass murders and assassinations of public figures appear to skew the people's opinion towards gun control most dramatically. We've covered some of the weapons used in the assassinations of a few public figures and how those were not typically weapons restricted by gun control legislation, so we'll focus on mass murder / killings for a moment to see how they have effected public perception and legislation. As mentioned earlier, the FBI historically defined mass murder as four or more people killed during an event with no "cooling-off period" between the murders.

The Spin Doctors

Over the years, the media has played a pivotal role in shaping the opinions of the public regarding gun control. As overall crimes go, those occurring the least frequently are often those that tend to get the most media attention. Since mass killings have been shown to be statistically anomalous events, they appear to be embraced as entertaining news and ratings boosters by news media and more likely to be reported thus skewing the public's perception of their frequency and threat to society. As Grant Duwe states in the conclusion of his essay *A Circle of Distortion: The Social Construction of Mass Murder in the United States*:

> The growing incidence of these [mass public shooting] cases—which are the most newsworthy and, thus, highly visible mass killings—shaped perceptions about the prevalence and patterns of mass murder

and helped produce three "spinoff" problems—assault weapons, workplace violence, and school shootings...

Those making claims about mass murder, however, have not demonstrated an awareness of the ways in which the celebrated cases are biased as a sample of mass murder in general. Therefore, by uncritically using the atypical high-profile cases, claimsmakers have made a number of questionable assertions, which have, in turn, led to policy proposals that have targeted rare aspects of mass murder such as assault weapon use and workplace and school violence. And the news media have been the chief means through which these claims have been promulgated, thus completing the circle of distortion.[5]

It appears the media has not merely played a passive role in this by presenting the most anomalous events as entertaining news. In many instances they have favored the gun-control side of the argument intentionally and misrepresented facts in order to manipulate public perception.

On an episode titled *Massacre!* of the A&E program *20th Century with Mike Wallace*, Wallace claims; "In the late twentieth century a new phenomenon appeared: attacks, without warning, by men intent on killing as many people as they could." Virtually every aspect of this comment has been discredited by Grant Duwe in *Mass Murder in the United States: A History*. First, mass murder is not a new phenomenon to the late 20th century and has been shown to have been as prevalent in the 1920's and 1930's, though the rate of occurrence did drop off significantly through the mid part of the century.[6] Second, evidence suggests that many people who commit mass murder do in fact give some indication they intend to do so.[7] Third, most cases of mass murder are either familicides or murders of specific groups of acquaintances for which the killer holds some type of resentment, and not merely murders of strangers to rack up body counts for the record books.[8] Wallace goes on to say; "There can be no doubt that in the latter decades of the twentieth century, the senseless and appalling crime of mass murder has occurred more frequently than ever before in history, and that is a grim legacy that America will take in the next century. Part of what has made that possible is the easy availability of guns." In explaining why the media and those like Wallace have had poor results in pushing mass murder as a real problem, Duwe points out that mass killings are still rare and that they have "limited their chances for success by framing mass murder as a gun problem."[9]

In the 1989 New York Times article *Mass Murderers Prefer Semiautomatic Rifles*, Robert .M. Ackerman, Dickinson School of Law professor, seems to make a leap well beyond the definition of poetic license for the title.[10] The last place we should accept the use of poetic license is during a conversation actually regarding the facts themselves. The whole article revolves around an event on September 25, 1982 where George Banks went on a shooting spree killing 13 people with an AR-15. This was predominantly a familicide, with a couple of non family victims, not a random mass murder of strangers. In the article, Ackerman was describing how he had brought suit against Colt Industries, Sugarman Drug that sold Regina Clemens the firearm that her common law husband Banks used in the murders and against Banks himself through negligence and product liability law regarding the AR-15. He concedes the court had not found any defect in the AR-15. In the middle of the article about his previous court defeat, Ackerman slips in this statement; "What the recent school tragedy in Stockton, Calif., bears out is that semiautomatic assault rifles like the AR-15 and AK-47 are the weapons of choice of mass murderers." This was in response to the Patrick Purdy shooting in 1989, roughly a month before this article was written, where Purdy used an AK-47 rifle to kill 5 Asian-American children and wound 30 other people. Ackerman spends the bulk of the article talking about a familicide committed by Banks in 1982 with an AR-15 and then concludes that because Purdy used an AK-47 rifle seven years later, semiautomatic rifles are the weapons of choice for mass murderers. The title of this article has no basis in any fact supported by evidence in the article, but the title skews public perception nonetheless. Do you think this type of manipulation of public perception provided any acceptance by the people for the Federal Assault Weapons Ban of 1994, in spite of any factual statistics regarding those weapons at the time?

In some cases, news reporters have actually admitted to decidedly manipulating the public perception in an attempt to lobby for gun control. In *Armed: New Perspectives on Gun Control*, Gary Kleck cites a congressional Research Service Report where KABC-TV news commentator Bill Press, while testifying in front of the U.S. Senate, talks about the network intentionally deciding to manipulate viewers, "We are working every day with the Los Angeles Police Department. Every time there is an incident using a semiautomatic rifle in the city of Los Angeles, we report it on the news and we ask people to write to the State legislature to ban these weapons."[11] If the news media itself has declared war on an issue, how do you think it will effect public perception by those viewing the news?

In the late 80s and early 90s it was not uncommon for the media to confuse a semiautomatic rifle such as a civilian model AR-15 with a full auto rifle such as an M16 after which it was modeled. (Technically, the AR-15 came first; the M16 for the military was modeled after the AR-15. The confusion lies in the fact that Colt, after buying the rights from Armalite, released a "civilian" model semi-automatic AR-15 after producing the military M16.)[12] While the newscaster might be talking about a semiautomatic "assault rifle" they might be showing video of a full auto rifle being fired, thus distorting the public perception regarding semiautomatic weapons. A 1991 study concluded that nearly 80 percent of the news stories on "assault rifles" did not distinguish between fully automatic fire and semiautomatic fire, and that "assault rifles" cannot fire like a machine gun.[13]

Because the media has often been instrumental in dictating which events get coverage and which do not, sometimes the result of specifically biased political intent as referenced with KABC-TV, it would follow that researchers cannot exclusively use news stories as valid statistics for occurrences of specific types of crimes without also falling prey to distorted statistical data. In cases such as Everytown for Gun Safety and Mass Shooting Tracker it appears to be intentionally distorted.

It seems evident that the media manipulates people's perceptions in regards to Second Amendment issues, but I wanted to see if I could find any evidence suggesting it has actually had any effect in creating what appear to be illogical or emotionally constructed laws. I really didn't have to look too hard.

Bruce Lee

Does everyone remember seeing Bruce Lee kick the crap out of numerous people with nunchucks in movies such as Enter the Dragon and Fists of Fury in the early 1970's? For those of you living in a cave, nunchaku (nunchucks) are basically two rods or sticks about a foot long and roughly a one inch diameter with a cord or chain attached to one end of each stick.

Although there is some evidence of somewhat similar weapons evolving in ancient China, most modern research regarding the nunchaku suggests that they were primarily a farming tool for threshing rice and soy, which had made its way from China to Okinawa Japan during the 17th century.[14,15] Others have suggested the original tool was an Okinawan horse bit (muge.)[16] Weapons had been outlawed in Okinawa, so the farming tool was implemented into martial arts at the time as a means of defense, as the nunchaku would not be confiscated. It is a good example of how authorities can try to ban weapons all they want, but people will still find ways to use ordinary items to defend themselves. If you ban firearms will people use that butcher knife in the kitchen instead? Nunchaku being used in martial arts also made its way to the Philippines and was incorporated into Filipino Martial Arts systems. Dan Inosanto, a Filipino-American and a student of Bruce Lee's, had been trained in Filipino Martial Arts and introduced Bruce Lee to the nunchaku. It was subsequently adopted by Bruce Lee and used in numerous movies. Due to pop movie culture, the nunchaku has become one of the most recognized martial arts weapons.

First, I should note something about the legality of nunchaku overall. In the United States, there is no federal ban on nunchaku, but possession has been made illegal in many states such as New York, Arizona, California and Massachusetts.[17-20] In *Maloney v Rice* there was a constitutional challenge to New York's statutes that criminalize in-home possession of nunchaku. It was originally dismissed due to previous court precedent citing the Second Amendment only applied to Federal action, however after the *McDonald v. Chicago* case we previously covered, the U.S. Supreme Court granted a writ of certiorari on *Maloney v. Rice*, vacating the decision and sending it back to the court for "further consideration." According to a note on an NYU website set up for the topic which appears to be from Jim Maloney directly, "There has been no activity in the case since 2011 because the Magistrate Judge has ruled that I may not proceed with the deposition of the sole Defendant (Rice), and the Office of the County Attorney has not responded to my repeated requests that they identify another witness with knowledge of the matters on which I seek testimony." The case appears to be stalled at the moment as the District Court will not allow Maloney to depose the defendant (being a high level government official, the District Attorney of Nassau County), but the writ of certiorari by the Supreme Court after the *McDonald* precedent speaks volumes concerning a state ban on nunchaku; the right to own may very well be protected by both the Second and Fourteenth Amendments.

With Second and Fourteenth Amendment issues presently undecided regarding nunchaku at a state level leaving existing state laws intact, we'll look at California as an example of how some legal situations appear illogical. Possession of nunchaku in California is punishable by up to one year in county jail or prison. However, California has allowed a nunchuka exception for professional and licensed martial arts schools when sold to the school and used on the premises.[21] So in California you can teach people how to use nunchaku as a weapon, but you cannot possess them personally. In the article, "Nunchucks Are Banned in California...Except in Martial Arts Schools, Where They're All the Rage" , L.J. Williamson writes:

> The nunchucks ban was added to the California penal code in 1974, at a moment when the United States was in the kung-fu grip of a martial arts craze. Sparked by the 1973 release of Bruce Lee's Enter The Dragon and spurred by such pop phenomena as the TV series Kung Fu and the song "Kung Fu Fighting," martial arts fever was spiking, along with a faddish interest in martial arts weapons.[22]

So in California you can receive up to one year in jail for a pair of sticks on a string designed for threshing rice. But the real point being; how did we effectively arrive here? Do you remember the wave of nunchaku murders and violence that swept through the United States afterwards? No, me neither. It was nothing more than Bruce Lee kicking the crap out of a bunch of people in a few Hollywood movies and the fallacious belief that anyone can pick up a set of nunchaku and somehow immediately be some sort of "killing machine" leading to California's preemptive ban of nunchaku without a single shred of evidence that a nunchaku violent crime or homicide problem did, would or even could ever exist.

Is it possible the existing California law violates your Second and Fourteenth Amendment rights but somehow made it into California law anyway? Is the law an example of what Blackstone would call a wanton and causeless restraint of the will of the subject? With no evidence to support the need of a nunchaku law, it would be hard to answer with anything other than yes. The real irony being they weren't originally weapons, they had been historically integrated for self-defense *only because* weapons had been outlawed. It just goes to show how ridiculous public perception and legislative illogic can get. Two pieces of stick on a string, designed for threshing rice, used in relatively unrealistic fight scenes in a couple of fictional Hollywood movies...mere possession in California is a year in jail.

Molotov Cocktail

I started to question what the real probability of unknowingly possessing items which might break an existing law might actually be. It was pretty easy to find a scenario that could fit the bill. The NFA (Title II) restricts destructive devices. Title 26, U.S.C. Section 5845(f)(3), makes it unlawful for a person to possess "any combination of parts either designed or intended for use in converting any device into a destructive device as defined in subparagraphs (1) and (2) and from which a destructive device may be readily assembled." There is some ambiguity in the subsequent exceptions for already assembled devices not intended to be weapons (such as legal pyrotechnics), but no real exceptions for the individual parts if not already assembled into those otherwise legal devices. There may also be some ambiguity in the "designed or intended for use in" phrase. That would either include almost all or exclude almost all individual items necessary for making a destructive device, the latter making the subsection kind of moot. Many destructive devices are made with items designed for other purposes, such as ammonium nitrate fertilizer. "Intended for use in" becomes extremely subjective.

The ATF website (www.atf.org) specifically designates a Molotov cocktail as being a destructive device. As Wikipedia describes, "A Molotov cocktail is a breakable glass bottle containing a flammable substance such as gasoline/petrol or a napalm-like mixture, with some motor oil added, and usually a source of ignition such as a burning cloth wick held in place by the bottle's stopper." Let's go with the stricter napalm description here for an extra level of complexity. In the article *How to Make Napalm B: Chemical Synthesis of a Gelled Sol*, Anne Marie Helmenstine, Ph.D. describes how to make Napalm B with polystyrene foam and gasoline.[23]

Here's the thing: Say you possess a gas can with gasoline for your car or maybe your lawnmower; and you have polystyrene foam packing peanuts (not the biodegradable starch ones) maybe from something you ordered on Ebay; and you have any glass bottle such as that Kiwi-Strawberry Snapple you just drank or the Corona you just pounded; and you have a piece of flammable cloth such as a cotton T-shirt or pair of Levis; then technically you have all the makings of a Molotov cocktail and arguably are committing a felony. Under 26 USC § 5871 it states "Any person who violates or fails to comply with any provisions of this chapter shall, upon conviction, be fined not more than $10,000, or be imprisoned not more than ten years, or both."[24]

Would the ATF ever seriously try to convict you due to the scenario above? Most likely not as it would seem horribly absurd. Should the law more logically require the actual assembly of the items, or require "proof" of actual intent to make a destructive device (innocent until proven guilty, right) before becoming a crime? The number of U.S. citizens that possess all these items at any one time is probably astounding. Could they use this scenario as evidence to detain you when they can find no other valid reason to do so, in order to give them the time and reasonable cause to search for some other violations of law? Yes. Could they use it to increase the penalty on a lesser crime you committed? Yes. Could they use this as sufficient evidence to gain a warrant to search or raid your premises just as they did in what led to the Waco siege? Apparently so. Will that old military manual you legally own with the one chapter on incendiaries be used to confirm your guilt? Most likely. Will the fact that you also legally own firearms suggest that you might be intent on some type of government insurrection or be a "domestic terrorist?" Possibly.

How many news stories have you heard where the media goes on about a search of a "suspect's" home which finds a number of legal things that are suddenly used to imply the suspect's guilt? Something along the lines of "suspects apartment contained firearms, books on explosives, survival gear, and a copy of Sun Tzu's *Art of War.*" Assuming the weapons are registered if necessary, of course, these are all legal possessions being used to reinforce the guilt of someone at this point who is still just a suspect or has been charged with a crime, not yet convicted of a crime. Having a Playboy, some duct tape and a box of condoms at home does not provide any evidence that you are a rapist if accused of committing such a crime. Neither does possessing all the items to make a Molotov cocktail...but somehow there's an existing law which does appear to prohibit possession of merely the materials to construct one.

I'm sincerely not trying to suggest a "conspiracy theory" here in any way, but remember that Charles II in England didn't enforce the Militia or Game Acts strictly in the beginning either, years later however, James II did. A similar example of "finding" other laws to target a specific individual is Al Capone who was convicted for tax evasion when they could find no other evidence of his Prohibition based crimes. In fact, charges of violations of the Volstead Act from any crimes he may have committed during Prohibition were dropped at trial.[25]

My point being, the law already exists which could ultimately be abused, regardless if it is being abused today, and many of you have technically been in violation of that law and just didn't know it. Should we have a law that incriminates the possession of commonly owned and used items, merely because some people have a fear of potential bombs? You have to decide for yourself, but to me it appears to be a law that could easily be used against a non criminal which doesn't make logical sense and stems from an irrational fear that anyone possessing these items absolutely intends to build a Molotov cocktail.

Hunting and Sporting Purposes

What about the "hunting and sporting purposes " arguments being thrown around? It is true that past surveys have concluded that roughly 75 percent of the population says that hunting is one of the uses for their firearms, but we've seen that was not the intent of the Second Amendment.[26] The "hunting and sporting purposes" argument is a means of redirecting to another and only vaguely correlated argument that is easier to win. It is hard to argue that an AR-15, for instance, isn't protected by the Second Amendment. However, one might present an argument that an AR-15 isn't appropriate for hunting. A pro-gun enthusiast might immediately enjoin that argument and suggest it is. The argument then goes back and forth and people get caught up in wanting to be right in that argument. The problem is, it may be a very easy argument to show that an AR-15 isn't appropriate for hunting, and you've lost an irrelevant battle.

Let me give an example of this type of redirect. Say I'm the Pope, and being extremely Catholic I want to ban any type of contraceptives since I believe they are against 'God's" will (thank 'God' I'm not the Pope). I then state that condoms should be banned because they don't prevent STIs (sexually transmitted infections.) You immediately engage me in the argument and suggest that they do, which further validates the argument that condoms are for the prevention of STIs. I then point out that STIs are transmitted from genital to oral, oral to genital and oral to oral, none of which are prevented by a condom. Even more so, I suggest that when using a condom for traditional intercourse one might use saliva as lubrication.

I have just shown how STIs might be transmitted from one person to another even with the use of a condom. It doesn't even matter if STIs are easy to transmit in these manners or not, just showing the fluid exchange is another redirect. I have an army of straw men. I suggest a ban. You then argue that condoms are sometimes used by a single person and STIs can't be spread that way. I then graciously make a concession and say that any ban on condoms will have exemptions for self masturbation. You just lost the argument and I look like I compassionately compromised due to your last point. Condoms are now banned, except during self masturbation.

The thing is, condoms are contraceptives and only have moderate use preventing STIs as a byproduct of its primary use. The fact that they can't prevent the spread of STIs was irrelevant to their contraceptive purposes, yet you engaged me in a redirected argument and lost the entire battle. I got what I wanted in the first place, to ban condoms as a contraceptive. It is not much different in letting someone argue that rifles are only intended for hunting purposes and then suggest an AR-15 is not appropriate for hunting and should be banned. If you take the bait, you've already lost the war. Many people are fighting the wrong battle...the battle their opponent has already predetermined they can win, which is only moderately relevant to the overall war.

We've already seen that the Second Amendment was not intended to be merely a hunting and sporting right. Yet somehow the argument persists. After the passage of the Brady Act in 1993, retired chief justice Warren Burger wrote:

> Americans also have a right to defend their homes, and we need not challenge that. Nor does anyone seriously question that the Constitution protects the right of hunters to own and keep sporting guns for hunting game any more than anyone would challenge the right to own and keep fishing rods and other equipment for fishing – or to own automobiles. To 'keep and bear arms' for hunting today is essentially a recreational activity and not an imperative of survival, as it was 200 years ago. 'Saturday night specials' and machine guns are not recreational weapons and surely are as much in need of regulation as motor vehicles.[27]

At least he mentions defending your home. To be honest, I think I find the term "recreational weapons" to be more disturbing than the attempt to make people believe the Second Amendment is for "sporting purposes." Is that an unintended oxymoron, or just a phrase that accurately suggests a gun is merely a tool...like a fishing rod or an automobile?

Saturday Night Special

You don't hear about "Saturday Night Specials" much anymore unless you're a die-hard Skynyrd fan.[28] There's no legal definition for what constitutes a Saturday Night Special but the NRA defines it as "a slang term generally used to refer disparagingly to relatively compact, less expensive, small-caliber handguns."[29] A slightly different definition at the time was "junk guns" which were usually low caliber guns made with poor quality materials, typically made of Zamak zinc alloy, and low-cost manufacturing techniques.[30]

The GCA of 1968 banned importation of a lot of inexpensive handguns. American manufacturers started making them locally to fill the demand. These companies were labeled the "ring of fire" companies; Arcadia Machine & Tool, Davis Industries, Jennings Firearms (aka Bryco), Lorcin Engineering Company, Phoenix Arms, Raven Arms and Sundance Industries. All but one of the original "ring of fire" companies were defunct by 2003 (Phoenix Arms), though Raven Arms actually became Phoenix Arms after it was destroyed by fire and Jennings/Bryco was bought by Paul Jimenez, Bryco's former factory foreman, after Bryco filed for bankruptcy and became Jimenez Arms.[31] Phoenix Arms and Jimenez Arms are still making cheap guns out of Zamak at this time. In reality, it was really that one family, the Jennings, who started manufacturing them to fill demand. All the "ring of fire" companies were, or originated from prior affiliations with, the Jennings family.[32]

There were arguments for and against the cheaper handguns. Some argued that they were used more by blacks or the poor, with the obvious assumption that blacks or the poor committed more crimes.[33] In fact, the original Saturday Night Special moniker contained four words, formerly leading off with a racial slur which I decline to repeat here. The counter argument was that banning them prohibited poor blacks from being able to financially acquire guns for self-defense and was therefore racist.[34] Some argued the junk guns, due to their lack of quality, were not suitable for sporting purposes or self-defense. Robert Sherrill researched that claim and concluded that no junk gun had killed or seriously injured a user due to mechanical or design failures, though that research was published in 1973.[35]

It's sincerely mostly a moot point these days. In 2013 one state Representative, Luis Gutierrez (D-Ill.) did try to introduce a ban on "Saturday Night Specials" with bill H.R. 965. It was not his first attempt to do so. This attempt appeared to be mostly in response to Illinois having to permit concealed carry in the state. Mother Jones tried to cover the story, and I was actually kind of embarrassed for Gutierrez.[36] The most recent reference to "cheap" handguns Mother Jones gave in the article was a 2003 lawsuit filed by the NAACP against 45 gun manufacturers claiming they market cheap guns to impoverished communities. For the record, a Federal judge dismissed that lawsuit.[37] There was a reference to a study in Maryland conducted between 1990 and 1998 by the American Journal of Epidemiology that banning "junk guns" reduces death. Though the reference cited for that points to the Law Center to Prevent Gun Violence (we'll get back to them when we talk about Self-Defense) and not the research. If you look at the actual research, and not at the Law Center to Prevent Gun Violence's interpretation of it, that isn't what the research concludes. Depending upon time delay estimates of when the law is assumed to produce an effect, and depending upon the inclusion of certain outliers or covariates, the results ranged from a reduction of 11.5 percent in homicides to an increase of 15 percent in homicides in response to the Saturday Night Special ban.[38]

In the Mother Jones article, there was also a reference to the claim "Of the top ten most-traced crime guns by the ATF from 2000, half were junk guns" which also points to an article from December 1, 2013 by the Law Center to Prevent Gun Violence and not to the actual research to cite the claim.[39] So what does the actual ATF research suggest? If you look at the DOJ report from 1995 as an example, you'll see that 7 of the 10 most traced guns in 1994 were in fact "ring of fire" manufacturers. However, looking at the same report you'll see that only 6 percent of 1994 traces were from homicides. In fact, 72 percent of traces are listed as "weapons offenses" that were specifically not: Drug offenses (12%); Homicides (6%); Assaults (5%); Burglary (2%); or Robbery (2%). Only 29 percent of the traces appear to be on guns actually used in crimes, 72 percent appear to be the breaking of gun laws themselves, such as concealed carry without a permit or while being a prohibited person. The conclusions on homicides or violent crimes made from trace data are thus seriously flawed. The very same research by the Department of Justice suggests criminals prefer high-quality guns, in the largest caliber they can easily conceal.[40]

Glock changed everything with polymer frame technology and simplicity of design.[41] With relatively low cost, high quality, user friendly guns from manufacturers implementing Glock technology, there really just isn't all that much demand for cheap quality handguns anymore. When you can buy a new high quality Taurus, Ruger or Kel-Tec polymer frame .380 as low as $200, there's just no reason to buy a cheap quality Zamak gun of the same size and lower caliber at half the price anymore. The modern firearms can be small and inexpensive, but they certainly aren't "junk guns."

The research and statistics provided on "Saturday Night Specials" are mostly antiquated and irrelevant, especially after the *Heller* decision, but groups like the Law Center to Prevent Gun Violence continue to reference the information as though it is of relevance today. The one remaining consistency over time appears to be that criminals choose high quality, larger caliber handguns.

So, "Gimme Back My Bullets."[42]

Knife to a Gun Fight

Since we're talking about small concealable weapons (the Saturday Night Specials...not what you put in those condoms), I guess I should bring something up I have seen implied in a number of places. There is a common misconception that a firearm is always the dominant weapon in any scenario, and I wanted to make a point concerning that. There is what has become a common colloquialism that is often joked about, which I'm sure you've all heard, concerning "bringing a knife to a gun fight." The truth is, if you are less than roughly 15 feet away and have a holstered or concealed weapon, and your adversary has a knife already in their hand, then the joke may actually be on you because you may have just brought a gun to what will effectively be a knife fight.

At 15-21 feet away, if you've been well trained you may have a chance to get the weapon out and at least rocked into a weapons retention position where you can get off a shot, maybe even one extended on target, but at that closer range you are at a severe disadvantage. Granted you may not be able to draw your knife any quicker in situations where you're already behind the curve and the aggressor has their weapon out at that distance...but you tell me, as a general citizen would you be more likely during a suspicious but ambiguous moment of concern to be willing to have a less conspicuous foldable knife in your hand, or actually risk bringing out a loaded firearm to even low ready with no confirmation of a real threat? That may ultimately be a personal choice with no correct answer, but at less than 10 feet if the aggressor has not already drawn their weapon I might take the knife in my hand to stop their draw as opposed to a firearm still at my beltline.

At extremely close ranges, a quickly deployable dagger may be king. Under some specific circumstances, guns may not be the most effective weapon protected by the Second Amendment. It appears that a concealed handgun is typically a misdemeanor under most laws while a concealed dagger is typically a felony. Do you think there may be some justification for this, or possibly another example of illogically constructed laws? Either way, I just wanted to make a point that the Second Amendment doesn't only protect firearms.

Gun Culture

Even the term "gun culture" is somewhat of a media tactic. It originally came from an obviously biased article by historian Richard Hofstadter titled *America as a Gun Culture* in describing the United States as "the only modern industrial urban nation that persists in maintaining a gun culture."[43] I don't intend to take a stroll down the path of McCarthyism here, but after reading Hofstadter's article I can kind of understand why John Wayne had a fear of American Communists. Hofstadter is certainly entitled to his opinion, but it does appear to be pretty extreme. The article makes some questionable claims and seems to seriously distort some basic historical facts. Hofstadter refers to the Second Amendment as only a "collective right" and fallaciously cites the *Miller* case for support. He refers to the GCA of 1968 as a "feeble measure" and goes on to say "It seems clear now that the strategic moment for gun controls has passed and that the United States will continue to endure an armed populace, at least until there is a major political disaster involving the use of guns."

From the article, the historically most repeated section appears to be Hofstadter's claim that the 740,000 deaths from firearms in the 20th century up to 1964 were "considerably higher" than all battle deaths suffered by American forces in all the wars in American history. He excludes military deaths due to disease (and though unstated, it appears to exclude starvation or any other possible cause of death of troops) as though they weren't the result of being at war. Even excluding those 400,000-500,000 Civil War deaths possibly by disease, or those in any other war, the estimated American combat fatalities from the American Revolutionary War through to the Bay of Pigs invasion in 1961 comes to about 660,000. Those numbers are all estimates, as nobody really knows those numbers for certain.

If you include all military deaths as a result of war, including those possibly by starvation and disease as a result, it comes to about 1.4 million deaths over the same period. If we're going to compare loss of life due to gun rights to loss of life due to war, maybe we should include all the costs of war in the analysis?[44] It may sound like a significant fact at first, but the comparison really doesn't mean anything in regards to gun control. It is merely comparing two unrelated issues in order to aggrandize one of them. From the same numbers,

I could make a pointless counter claim that disease and starvation killed more American soldiers in all U.S. Wars than guns did over that same time period, and thus argue that guns aren't even that bad in war (that's even before excluding bombs, bayonets, chemicals etc. from the battle death numbers to truly reflect only gun deaths.)

He goes on to say "Many otherwise intelligent Americans cling with pathetic stubbornness to the notion that the people's right to bear arms is the greatest protection of their individual rights and a firm safeguard of democracy—without being in the slightest perturbed by the fact that no other democracy in the world observes any such "right" and that in some democracies in which citizens' rights are rather better protected than in ours, such as England and the Scandinavian countries, our arms control policies would be considered laughable." He is somewhat ambiguous about blaming the American frontier's lack of hunting restrictions allowing people to hunt anywhere to acquire a meal, but seems to quite clearly blame Indian (Native American) massacres, specifically, for the frontiersman's necessity to own a firearm which has led to this "gun culture" we have today. More than anything, though, it seems he blames the "antimilitaristic traditions of radical English Whiggery" of our Founding Fathers and their false belief that the "answer to civic and military decadence" was the militia and an armed populace. And yet here we are; a sovereign nation.

He is quite clearly indicating that there is no right to bear arms at an individual level, that the collective right basically stems from delusion and as such gun ownership is merely a circumstance of American history passed down through culture. The history we've covered shows that the right to bear arms may in fact have been cultural for nearly a thousand years, and the Framer's secured that as a

Constitutional right with the addition of the Second Amendment. Using the term "gun culture" today is clearly an attempt to circumvent the Second Amendment right entirely, just as Hofstadter meant to do in 1970.

Gun Show Loophole

Those suggesting there is a "Gun Show Loophole" argue that it provides convicted felons and other prohibited purchasers with opportunities to evade background checks, as they can easily buy firearms from private sellers with no accountability or oversight. The ability to buy firearms without a background check legally does exist. The implication, though, is that they can circumvent the law through some 'loophole", which just isn't the case. In reality, their argument suggests that the choice not to adopt a law on private party sales makes it easier to break a background check law, when in fact it just isn't the law. It is really just another "semantics" trick, as there is no evidence of any "loophole." The ease with which a buyer can see multiple private sellers at one location due to a gun show does not make an otherwise legal transaction illegal. Private party sales are still legal without a background check (though they cannot sell to someone they know would not pass one) and dealers with a Federal Firearms License (FFL) by law still have to do background checks at gun shows on all sales.[45]

Just a reminder: U.S. federal law requires those who are engaged in the business of dealing in firearms to have an FFL. Under the terms of the Firearm Owners Protection Act of 1986 (FOPA) individuals not engaged in the business of dealing firearms, or who only make occasional sales within their state of residence, are under no requirement to conduct background checks on purchasers or maintain records of sale...by specific design. The Gun Control Act of 1968 (GCA) originally restricted FFLs to conducting business only at the address listed on their license and were prohibited from doing business at gun shows. The FOPA subsequently allowed FFLs to transfer firearms at gun shows provided they follow the provisions of the GCA and other pertinent federal regulations. As of 1998, that includes doing the NICS background check on all FFL sales at gun shows.

In the ATF's *Following the Gun: Enforcing Federal Laws Against Firearms Traffickers*, the ATF's review of trafficking investigations showed that 14 percent of their investigations involved gun shows and flea markets (which included both licensed FFL dealers and unlicensed private sellers), involving approximately 26,000 illegally diverted firearms, while trafficking by "unlicensed sellers (not associated with gun shows and not straw purchasers) were the focus of about 20 percent of the investigations, involving over 22,000 trafficked firearms."[46] These statistics reference actual investigations where specific laws have been broken, not loopholes, and suggest that combined violations at gun shows are fairly equivalent to violations by private sellers not at gun shows, thus defeating the argument that gun shows provide a more prevalent means of breaking the law than any other private party transaction.

If someone wants to argue that private party sales should require a background check, that is an entirely different argument to make and possibly sound, but really has no relevance to any existence of a "gun show loophole" which makes breaking the law any easier. Of course, should private parties be required to do background checks on potential buyers, then they would need to be given the same access to the NICS database as an FFL, or they would effectively be restricted from selling their own firearms. This also might increase the level of violent crimes and possibly homicides where a felon decides to target a private seller of a firearm not to purchase it, but to forcibly show up and take it.

Is it "easier" for someone to get a DUI if they've been at a bar that sells alcohol? Probably so, but that does not make it illegal to sell alcohol, to consume alcohol, or to drive a car...you still have to intentionally break the law by driving under the influence and the "ease" of acquiring the alcohol does not create a "loophole." A bartender still has the responsibility to cut someone off if they know they are intoxicated, just like an FFL should not sell to a failed background check or admitted straw man or a private party sell to a potential buyer who has just admitted they are a prohibited person.

Though those arguing the loophole ideology would suggest "gun shows'" make it easier to break the law due to a localized market environment, would it not also make it easier to enforce those same laws as opposed to going location to location to enforce virtually the same number of violations evidenced by other private party transactions? If the intent is really to enforce the law on the illegal sales, and not just prohibit gun sales overall, wouldn't a forum marketplace like a gun show be easier to monitor than, say, all the homes of individual private sellers or home based FFLs?

The ATF defines a straw purchase as "the acquisition of a firearm(s) from an FFL by an individual (the "straw") done for the purpose of concealing the identity of the true intended receiver of the firearms."[47] Straw purchases can be illegal when made at a federally licensed firearm dealer. If the straw purchaser of the firearm lies about the identity of the ultimate possessor of the gun, he can be charged with making false statements on a federal Firearms Transaction Record. Straw purchases of used guns are not illegal, unless the gun is used in a crime with the prior knowledge of the straw purchaser.[48] The latter variant would have to be because background checks aren't required on private party sales anyway.

"Cop Killer" Bullets

For roughly 30 years I've been hearing about the infamous "cop killer" bullets. Sounds scary, huh? Before I looked it up, I remembered hearing that it was all about the Teflon coating that made them go through bullet proof Kevlar vests. I even remember a scene in the movie *Ronin*, where Robert De Niro gets shot through his body armor and then when the doctor pulls the bullet out of him he says they "sprayed the bullet with Teflon" thus explaining why it went through the vest. We have to ban "cop killer" bullets, right? Apparently we did...well, kind of.   The question is, do the "cop killer" bullets really exist or are they a mystical unicorn?

In the 1960's a company called KTW, founded by Paul Kopsch (an Ohio coroner), Daniel Turcos (a police sergeant), and Donald Ward (Kopsch's special investigator), started developing a special purpose handgun round for law enforcement capable of improved penetration against hard targets, such as windshield glass and automobile doors. In other words, they were designing an armor piercing handgun round for law enforcement. Traditional handgun ammo is lead based, as it carries a lot of mass and yet is soft and expands when it hits a target. Expansion is good in slowing threats from soft tissue targets because it "mushrooms" in the tissue and the kinetic energy stays in the body to do damage to organs and muscle. Without the expansion a harder bullet can go directly through the body and have little effect regarding stopping power, unless it actually hits a vital organ or damages bone structure. The soft lead is poor in penetrating hard targets though. For hard target and armor piercing penetration they needed a harder core, and initially settled on a steel core surrounded mostly of hard brass. The problem they had was that the hard brass excessively wore out handgun barrels because it did not conform to the rifling in the handgun barrel like lead or a softer copper jacket did. To extend the life of the gun barrels shooting the steel / hard brass round they decided to cover the bullet with Teflon. The softer Teflon did increase barrel life and it has been suggested that the Teflon diminished the deflection of the bullet off of hard targets as well, a secondary benefit. The Teflon, however, was not what made the round an armor piercing round.

And as usual in the gun debate, here is where ignorance once again steps in to create history. In 1982 NBC ran an episode on the bullets where it suggested the bullets were a threat to police, as it was assumed they would pierce through the ballistic vests which the police wore at the time. Ignorantly assuming the Teflon was the source of the bullets armor piercing properties, gun control organizations immediately started labeling Teflon coated bullets as "cop killers" and the media followed suit. As it turns out, a few of KTW's bullets could penetrate soft body armor under certain conditions, however testing concluded that the Teflon actually decreased the bullets penetration through Kevlar body armor.[49] According to research done by Kleck at the time of his publication, there is no evidence that a "cop killer" bullet has ever killed a single cop.[50] Keep in mind that these are only regarding handgun rounds, a significant portion of available rifle ammunition will already penetrate Kevlar soft body armor with no modifications.

So are "cop killer" bullets a unicorn? The moniker is horribly fallacious and deceiving, but their existence isn't entirely fictitious. They're more like a horse wearing a party hat, posing as a unicorn. "Cop killer" bullets don't really exist...but armor piercing handgun rounds do. The Federal Law didn't ban "cop killer" bullets or Teflon coated bullets, but banned all armor piercing rounds sans a few later exemptions such as the "green tip" 5.56 mm steel-core bullets in SS109 and M855 cartridges, which can be fired from AR-15 semi-automatic rifles, and .30-06 M2AP cartridges, which fit a range of rifles. But on a state level: North Carolina, Oregon, South Carolina and Virginia all fell for the Teflon "cop killer" fallacy and as of this writing still have bans on bullets based on no other distinction than a Teflon or similar coating.[51-54] (There are a couple more, but those states have other restrictions along with the Teflon.) Nearly 30 years later, as recently as March 12, 2015 the Los Angeles Times ran an editorial entitled "Ban these 'cop killer' bullets" after the ATF decided not to pull the two exemptions previously noted (handguns had subsequently been designed which fire those two rounds prompting them to reconsider the exemption.)[55] The bullets in question are armor piercing handgun bullets and yet nearly 30 years later the media continues referring to them by a fallacious moniker. Even after Kleck's research, I cannot find a single cop in the United States having being killed specifically from a Teflon coated armor piercing handgun bullet, but maybe you'll have better luck than I did.

Killer Cop Bullets

At which point we stumble across a conundrum regarding training. We want cops to be evaluated during training on the least common denominator for equal opportunity employment requirements, such that they are effectively tested and trained to the minimum necessary standards, so that an acceptable amount of people will pass the police tests.[56] Yet we want civilians to be held to the highest denominator, suggesting that certain weapons are problematic and that a portion of civilians can't possibly have the training to implement them safely, so they should be banned for everyone. We end up with police officers who are insufficiently qualified and arguments that citizens shouldn't be allowed to compensate for that fact by owning certain firearms to defend themselves.

On February 7, 2013, at least seven LAPD officers shot and wounded a 71 year old mother and wounded (by debris) her 47 year old daughter as they were delivering newspapers. LAPD had thought that the truck belonged to fugitive Christopher Dorner, who had recently killed the daughter and fiancé of an LAPD captain and shot and killed a police officer in Riverside, and opened fire on the vehicle without ever verifying their target.[57] LAPD Chief Charlie Beck said it was "a tragic misinterpretation" by officers working under "incredible tension." This is directly from the article:

> As the vehicle approached the house, officers opened fire, unloading a barrage of bullets into the back of the truck. When the shooting stopped, they quickly realized their mistake. The truck was not a Nissan Titan, but a Toyota Tacoma. The color wasn't gray, but aqua blue. And it wasn't Dorner inside the truck,

but Carranza and her mother delivering copies of the Los Angeles Times.[58]

In reality, what probably happened was that one officer that made an avoidable error; the remaining officers most likely responded as a result of fully believing they were being fired upon. Was this from insufficient firearm training requirements for the average police person or was it just a typical human over-reaction and one we are trying to restrict the average citizen from making through gun control laws? Furthermore, would these civilians have had either the legal or natural right to return fire upon the police in this scenario, if they had been legally armed?

Statistics suggest that police officers have somewhere around an 18 percent average hit rate on target when firing their weapons in actual gunfights. The average hit rate where fire is not returned is 30 percent.[59] If you include suicide and shooting animals, the NYPD hit rate went up to 34 percent in 2005.[60]

Though the suspect did shoot his intended target inside, every single injury outside the Empire State building on August 24, 2012 was due to NYPD police fire and not from the armed suspect. Sixteen rounds were fired, three passerby were hit with direct fire, 6 more from fragments. Witnesses suggest the police hit the suspect 3 times. In this case, at least they verified the suspect first and reports suggest that the suspect did fire upon them, but apparently NYPD just weren't very accurate.[61] If the police do more damage to bystanders than the suspect would have done, has society really gained anything by giving police firearms while trying to deny them to the average citizen? A common argument is that armed citizenry would be more detrimental than beneficial in scenarios such as mass shootings, but if the police are no more accurate than this, is it really a valid argument?

I want to be very specific here and reaffirm this to be a training issue argument, this is not an affirmation that the shooter should be blamed as Mass Shooting Tracker claims. Remember, Mass Shooting Tracker would have labeled this as a "mass shooting" even though the suspect only shot one person, his intended target. The shooter and the victim had both filed harassment complaints against each other previously.[62] Mass Shooting Tracker also assumes that police inaccuracy in shooting bystanders is the fault of the suspect, not the fault of the police.

These scenarios aren't to bash on the police force by any means, they put their lives on the line and have a tough job to do, but merely brought up to propose the hypothesis that we may have a double standard here. If the average citizen is giving up a portion of their Second Amendment rights on the argument that the police are well trained and there to protect them, should we not either provide our police officers with higher levels of firearms training than currently required and/or possibly concede that some members of society would voluntarily choose to be better trained with firearms than currently required of the average police officer and some existing firearm laws prohibit them from filling that beneficial role to society? (I've taken some classes from former and current LAPD SWAT members at International Tactical Training Seminars. They are not your "average" police officers, and I wouldn't want to be on the wrong end of Uncle Scotty's 1911 with even 200 yards between us.)

A corollary to this argument is that police officers do in fact have some firearm training and still have a relatively low hit rate on target. If a trained police officer can have such a low hit rate on target for whatever justifiable reasons (stress, fear, surprise, return fire) is that not an extremely strong argument for why the average citizen should have as much ammunition available to defend their lives as it takes...possibly taking a lot while under stress of attack? Anyone who has ever argued that a person shouldn't need more than say, 6 rounds, because if you didn't hit anything with the first 6 rounds you never will, has probably never had to defend their life or their loved ones while under gunfire. I think it's actually another "hunting and sporting purposes" argument. It may come from someone who spends most of their time shooting animals at a distance, who don't shoot back. I have never been in a gunfight, and hopefully never will be, but it doesn't take a rocket scientist to imagine the stress it must place upon a human being to maintain your composure while bullets are whizzing past your head.

Self-Defense Use

You knew someone would just outright argue against the self-defense use of a gun, right? When looking at self-defense use of a gun, there is one online article making the argument against the use that I tend to see spread around consistently which comes from the Law Center to Prevent Gun Violence titled *Statistics on the Dangers of Gun Use for Self Defense*.[63] The article references a few of the primary sources who have tried making an argument against self-defense use of a firearm, so we'll use it as an example. I'll include all of their references for the article in my references for this chapter, so you can follow up on the research on your own.[64-73]

I don't want to go into a point-by-point analysis of each reference cited regarding the argument. Much of the research they referenced has already been discredited in regards to the conclusions they attempt to make, and it would probably take most of another book to repeat that. Most of the back and forth on these statistics has already been done, therefore what I really want to focus on here is one specific issue proposed in their article. I believe that issue is most relevant to the topic of self-defense. Their main argument is that in comparison to the risks of gun ownership, guns are rarely used successfully for self-defense.

The article leads with this statement, "Guns kept in the home are more likely to be involved in a fatal or nonfatal unintentional shooting, criminal assault or suicide attempt than to be used to injure or kill in self-defense." Their citation is from *Injuries and Deaths Due to Firearms in the Home* by Arthur L. Kellerman (Somes, Rivara Lee & Banton.)[74] That statement may in fact be true, but notice how it compares not only shooting events but also criminal assaults, which do not necessitate an actual firing of a gun, to self-defense "shootings only" and not all successful self-defense uses of a gun. Presentation of the gun for self-defense would be the same as presentation of the gun for criminal assault. The intent is to imply that your gun is more likely to be used for a homicide or suicide than for self-defense. The problem follows that the opening statement is irrelevant to successful use of a gun for self-defense, as a shooting is not necessary for success. Kellerman isn't even accurately comparing deaths to deaths here.

Either way, there are 2 general problems with much of the research being referenced in the Law Center to Prevent Gun Violence article. One, most of the research referenced for the "guns kept in the home" argument was done by looking back upon historical homicides and suicides for evaluation. This focuses on "gun in the household" percentages where a homicide or suicide already occurred. That is by default a biased data set which assumes the hypothesis itself to be true; that a homicide or suicide "will" happen. What it really argues is that, in events where a homicide or suicide occurred, the presence of a gun in the household resulted in a higher probability chance that the homicide or suicide will have been from the gun. That is an entirely different argument. It does not make a sound argument that households possessing guns for self-defense have a higher risk of homicide and suicide (i.e. the dangers of gun use for self-defense.)

It would be like looking at all pregnancies and then evaluating how many conceptions there were with condoms in the home; then after finding that, let's randomly say 54 percent, of conception events had condoms in the home prior, trying to conclude that possession of condoms leads to a higher probability of conception than contraception. Without including the events where a condom successfully prohibited conception in the data set, avoiding pregnancy entirely, you cannot draw an accurate conclusion regarding the cause and effect of condoms on conception. Yet that is how this research has been conducted. (Yes, I reference condoms occasionally for comic relief.)

In fact, one of the very articles they reference from Charles Branas et al titled *Investigating the Link Between Gun Possession and Gun Assault* in 2009 points out that a National Research Council committee already found the previously released reports "do little to reveal the impact of guns on homicide or the utility of guns for self-defense."[75] Though Branas points out that previous research relied on existing homicides as I suggest above, his research on assaults basically makes the same error in relying on actual shooting events to define an assault. He concluded that "individuals who were in possession of a gun were about 4.5

times more likely to be shot in an assault than those not in possession. This however also does not include a single assault where someone possessing a gun used the weapon for self-defense in a manner in which nobody was shot such that the successful use of the gun in self-defense did not need to be reported.

To make the household argument correctly, we must first distinguish which households do and do not have guns and then search for subsequent homicides and suicides by gun in each set. This leads to a second problem in the research, determining which households "honestly" have guns. Again, unless there is a gun homicide or suicide, there is no real way to prove a gun was in a household without a confirming event. With the assault scenario it is even worse, as there is no way to know which citizens carry a gun and also no way to know when an assault took place if there was no shooting and the assault was never reported. There is an argument to be made that there is a propensity for people, where no gun crime has already been committed to force the then unnecessary agreement that a gun was present, not to disclose that they have a gun. Surveys will therefore most likely not be accurate. You can use data sets from states where full gun registration is mandated, but that could lead to extreme biases in either direction. It would be virtually impossible to truly determine which households (or individuals) have guns and which do not, and then subsequently determine the percentage of households with guns who have not had homicides. (Honestly I think suicide data is irrelevant here either way. What we're really evaluating is possible use of your gun (which you keep for self-defense) against you in successful attacks versus use of your gun in successful defenses. Though suicide is a problem, killing yourself is entirely opposite from desiring self-defense from an attack. You cannot argue that someone can use a gun for suicide and at the same time desire self-defense from that gun. The desire for self-defense in those cases has ceased to exist.) People have often tried to accurately obtain household data, but the procedures for either collecting the data sets or extrapolating the data never seem to pass scrutiny. Therefore what I want to do is look more specifically at self-defense uses of the gun, and ultimately at a statistic which nobody appears to dispute.

Going back to the article, it accurately points out that the research previously done by Kleck, through a phone survey that extrapolated results to conclude there were 2.5 million self-defense uses of a gun per year, was discredited in an article by David Hemenway titled *The Myth of Millions of Annual Self-Defense Gun Uses: A Case Study of Survey Overestimates of Rare Events.*[76] Regardless of the fact that it has been discredited, the NRA continues to cite this statistic as being credible. However, what this article then references as a valid statistic is the FBI justifiable homicide numbers. Again, those only represent successful self-defense uses of a gun where someone was shot and killed.

One of their closing citations references Violence Policy Center's *Firearm Justifiable Homicides and Non-Fatal Self-Defense Gun Use: An Analysis of Federal Bureau of Investigation and National Crime Victimization Survey Data.* This report references Hemenway's discrediting of Kleck's research, but coincidentally goes further to point out, "Hemenway notes, and numerous others agree, that the most accurate survey of self-defense gun use is the National Crime Victimization Survey (NCVS) conducted by the Bureau of Justice Statistics." No one appears to discredit this statistic as being too high, I can only find arguments that suggest it is too low. If that is the research that the anti-gun for self-defense clan wants to claim as credible, then let's look at what that research actually suggests.

I'll use information exclusively from Violence Policy Center (VPC) reports. Since they are one of the organizations citing the dangers of gun possession listed as a reference for the Law Center to Prevent Gun Violence article, there seems little risk they will attempt to discredit the very data they themselves are providing to support their argument. The NCVS research quoted by the VPC in *Firearm Justifiable Homicides and Non-Fatal Self-Defense Gun Use* estimates there were 338,700 "self protective behaviors" involving a firearm in attempted or completed violent crimes or property crimes over the 5 year period from 2007 to 2011.[77] That would be an average of 67,740 attempted self-defense uses (self protective behaviors) of a gun per year. Self-defense justifiable shootings are in fact historically low annual numbers. In their June 2015 report by the same name, the VPC points out that from 2008 to 2012 there were 1,108 justifiable homicides involving a gun. That would give us an average of 222 self-defense justifiable homicides per year. They cite references that there were 42,219 criminal homicides over that matching 2008 to 2012 time period. That would be an average of 8,444 criminal homicides per year.[78]

They are quick to point out that the ratio of criminal homicide to justifiable homicide is 38 to 1. Honestly, I will be quick to point that out as well as it substantially reinforces the benefits of self-defense use of a gun. Look at the numbers here. They cite 67,740 attempted self-defense uses of a firearm on average per year. They cite 8,444 criminal homicides on average per year. They cite only 222 justifiable homicides on average per year. The attempted self-defense use of a firearm outpaces the number of criminal homicides 8 to 1, and yet only produces 1/38th the number of deaths per year on average. Even if we make the unlikely assumption that every single criminal homicide had been met with a "self protective behavior" involving a firearm which subsequently failed to save the victim's life, that would still suggest a minimum of 59,296 scenarios on average annually where using a gun for self-defense was successful. Subtracting the 222 average annual justifiable homicides from that, we still have a minimum average of 59,074 successful uses of a gun for self-defense not resulting in death per year. So on average; for every criminal homicide committed, at minimum 7 people successfully used a gun for self-defense where NOBODY HAD TO DIE.

Okay, there may be a select few who are saying none of this matters either way because a person should never kill in self-defense, not even in situations where you are about to be raped or murdered. You have a right to feel that way about your own life, but you're going to have a hell of a time trying to convince the rest of the people they don't have a natural right to self-defense. I would suggest that if you really feel that way, it would be a nice gesture for humanity if you would put a sign in your front yard saying so, such that those intent on committing violent crimes will have a preference to go to your house instead of one inhabited by someone who actually values their own life over that of someone's intending to take theirs away. I certainly don't want you to die, but if you're willing to give your life to a killer then why not in proxy for an otherwise innocent victim? Just sayin'...

Credible data on self-defense use of a gun is still inaccurate (most likely understated) because some successful self-defense uses of a gun do not end in a homicide or injury and thus do not need to be reported to anyone. It is probably less than 2.5 million and greater than 67,740 per year. Even by the anti-gun for self-defense clan's own conservative numbers; self-defense using a gun is successful, dwarfs the number of criminal homicides by 600 percent, and still results in very few deaths. By their numbers, on average only 0.3 percent of all successful self-defense uses of a gun end in a homicide. If the major argument against all guns is death itself, how can you try to argue against the self-defense use of a gun merely because it does not produce "enough" deaths?

The posting of fallacious or antiquated data may not seem like a big problem at first, but the Law Center to Prevent Gun Violence submits Amici Curiae with these claims to the Courts which may affect the decisions of the judges in those cases if they believe the source to be credible.[79] It may fall under freedom of speech, but it isn't helping society resolve the problem. Continuing to spread this article from the Law Center to Prevent Gun Violence which references antiquated research containing discredited conclusions is like continuing to argue that the Earth is flat. It's time to get a new paradigm Lactantius.

Concealed Carry

There are some states that have "shall issue" concealed carry permits. There are also states, such as California, that have "may issue" concealed carry permits. As mentioned earlier, "'may" then becomes subjective and often results in a denial. In California I was once told it is "may issue" and May lives in Texas. This appears to have a distinct effect on crime. Many gun crimes are just the illegal carry or possession itself, and not otherwise committing another crime with a gun.[80] Remember the gun crime trace data? It is another one of those circular arguments that suggests more laws are necessary because people are breaking the gun restriction laws, not necessarily committing crimes with guns.

At least one study has confirmed that carrying concealed weapons actually has a beneficial effect overall. In *Crime, Deterrence, and Right to Carry Concealed*, John Lott and David B. M. Mustard conclude that, "Using cross-sectional time-series data for U.S. counties from 1977 to 1992, we find that allowing citizens to carry concealed weapons deters violent crimes and it appears to produce no increase in accidental deaths."[81] It is not uncommon to hear someone argue this has been discredited by *The Impact of Right-to-Carry Laws and the NRC Report: Lessons for the Empirical Evaluation of Law and Policy* by authors Aneja, Donohue and Zhang in 2011. They concluded that right to carry laws had no effect on crime except for a positive effect on assault.[82] In 2013, that research was repeated by Carlisle E. Moody, Thomas B. Marvell, Paul R. Zimmerman, and Fasil Alemante in *The Impact of Right-to-Carry Laws on Crime: An Exercise in Replication* which claims to correct a "serious omitted variable problem." Their conclusion was that right to carry laws "significantly reduce murder" but had no significant effect on other violent crimes.[83]

Having had some level of handgun training at this point, I do tend to favor the idea of mandatory training for gun owners who intend to carry, so they don't do more damage with their weapon than the event they are trying to defend themselves against. From some of the references we've already seen, evidence seems to suggest that proper training was the intent of the Framers as well. A number of states who allow concealed carry in some capacity do require a training course to get the permit. Some states do implement moderate competency tests merely to purchase a firearm. Requiring training does not appear to circumvent the intent of the Second Amendment right. I have been unable to find any statistics which would clearly define whether a higher trained society itself might reduce gun violence (as delineated from the number of people carrying concealed possibly reducing the number of crimes), might reduce gun homicides from gun related accidents, or actually increase the effectiveness of criminals overall when using guns in crimes. It might be argued that mandatory gun training be required of all citizens carrying weapons in public to see if it has any statistical impact going forward, but I have yet to see that be seriously proposed in the gun debate.

Removing Rights of Innocent People by Proxy

Current laws can effectively remove the rights of innocent people by proxy as well. Let's use another California example and suppose that your spouse gets 5150'd after becoming extremely intoxicated at home, neighbors call the police and they feel your spouse may be a threat to themselves or others. I should also point out that a 5150 is not being placed under arrest. No charges are filed, yet California law deems such an event as having been committed to a mental health facility and therefore the person is mentally deficient and prohibited from being in possession of firearms for five years. Not from the experience or evaluation from a psychiatrist or psychologist, merely the general impression of the arriving officers. That person can subsequently appeal in court to have their firearm rights reinstated. This appears a very loose interpretation of someone who is mentally deficient. According to section 8102 of California's Welfare and Institutions Code all firearms in the house will legally be confiscated no matter who owns the firearms.[84] Though the actual owner of the firearm has done nothing wrong, they must then go through a lengthy application process to the California Department of

Justice to reacquire their possessions. The Department of
Justice will do another background check on you and verify
that the firearms stated are currently registered in your
name. They then provide you a 'gold seal' letter to take to
pick up your firearms at whichever police station they are
being held. From the feedback I have received, it has been
suggested that they may also fire your weapons to maintain
a ballistic record. I have not been able to confirm or deny it.

While waiting for the entire process to run its course, which
can take months, the firearm owner has been deprived of
their Second Amendment rights and an ability to use their
firearms for self-defense without due process of law. This
may be one of those situations where the public good
outweighs the costs, but how do you subsequently reconcile
rights being taken away from an innocent person without
due process? Should the innocent person not be afforded the
right to remove their firearms from the household without
confiscation, possibly even ceasing to reside at the location?
But then again, isn't it quite possible the person who was
5150'd in this scenario to begin with was merely drunk and
disorderly...and not truly mentally deficient? They aren't
entirely without blame here, but were their Second
Amendment rights violated without due process as well?

I can't find a single instance where any U.S. states take away
drivers licenses because someone has a single previous drunk
and disorderly or public intoxication violation (if older than
21) suggesting that they are suddenly a DUI threat. That
isn't much different than taking away gun rights because
someone has a restraining order (if not from an actual act of
violence) or marijuana use (prescription or not), suggesting a
previous unrelated issue creates a predisposition to violate
an entirely different law in the future. Also, a single

accident or moving violation typically does not remove your driving rights.

Can you imagine if your spouse lost their driving privileges, or worse maybe your unemployed 16 year old daughter accidentally ran someone over and lost her driving privileges and was not subsequently incarcerated and remained at home possibly under house arrest, and every car in your household was taken away from you because there is a risk the suspended family member could have access to it and could possibly use it for further negligence? I've seen it happen with weapons in California. Though self-defense using a weapon is not uncommon, as evidenced by the NCVS statistics, the average person will obviously need to drive their cars more than defending their lives with their guns. Since there is at least some type of prior issue to segregate the person losing their rights from the rest of society, it is possible to argue these scenarios provide a greater benefit to society than the burden on individuals overall. The comparisons don't directly correlate, but it is food for thought while constructing any further gun-control legislation. We need to be certain we are really balancing the risks with reward, and not passing legislation purely due to emotional reaction, in some cases effecting innocent people.

We've also seen where events like natural disasters have led to people having their Second Amendment rights restricted and their firearms confiscated. We previously referenced Hurricane Katrina, where an armed state National Guard and local police went door to door and effectively confiscated registered owner's firearms. They claimed the action was to prohibit possible racial violence, but here again we have innocent people having their Second Amendment rights and ability to defend themselves restricted without due process of law specifically due to the "predicted" actions of others.[85]

Large-Capacity Magazines

We've already covered a number of issues regarding "large-capacity" magazines, and I'll try to not to repeat that at length as much as possible. As noted previously, the debate over magazine capacity probably has a wider effect on both gun rights and violent gun crimes than an "assault weapon" itself. In some states, "large-capacity" magazines are still restricted due to a perceived advantage in committing crimes, but does that inhibit your self-defense rights while defending yourself against another armed aggressor who doesn't follow the laws and fights with a higher magazine capacity? Remember the appellate court's decision regarding the NY SAFE Act? The Court felt that the fulfillment of the state's interest regarding public safety was arguably even stronger for the magazines than the "assault weapons" themselves but also felt the 7 round capacity limit could lead to those intent on doing harm loading their weapon with more than the permitted seven rounds while attacking a law abiding citizen who could not.

Evidence submitted to the Court reflected that "large-capacity" magazines were used in half the "mass shootings" since 1982 and that more people die when a "large-capacity" magazine is used. This first stems from research conducted by Mother Jones.[86] The research looks at the 62 "mass shootings" between 1982 and 2012 (that's right, only 62 "mass shootings" in 30 years) and includes all rifle and handgun magazines in excess of 10 rounds that would be deemed "large-capacity" and banned under the specific guidelines of a bill Diane Feinstein was proposing at the time. In 31 of the events, there were 42 guns that had magazines with capacities over 10 rounds. As Mother Jones admits, "The data includes all guns recovered at the scene in each case, though not all of them were used in the crimes." So really it is that "large-capacity" magazines were "present" at half of the "mass shootings" and not necessarily "used in" half of the "mass shootings." Semantics are important.

The second research comes from self professed god himself Mr. Bloomberg at Mayors Against Illegal Guns before they became Everytown for Gun Safety.[87] That ought to be enough right there to keep anyone from getting up and citing this research, but not wanting to be like Tim Sullivan and wanting to stick to sound logic, let's look at it anyway. The first thing I notice is that they claim 93 "mass shootings" between 2009 and 2013. Compared to the Mother Jones statistic, that would suggest they claim "at least" an additional 31 "mass shootings" happened in 2013 alone. That would be if all the 62 "mass shootings" Mother Jones claimed happened between 1982 and 2012 actually happened between 2009 and 2012. Are you seeing a problem here yet? Somebody isn't on the same page as the other.

The research shows that either "assault weapons" OR "high-capacity" magazines were used in at least 14 (15%) of the incidents. That's right, only 15 percent of mass shootings they cite involved either "assault weapons" or "large-capacity" magazines. Here's the biggest problem though: The research claims that there were 63 percent more deaths, 7.8 versus 4.8 per incident, than in other incidents when either an "assault weapon" or a "high-capacity" magazine were used. That supports absolutely nothing in regards to deaths from a "high-capacity" magazine on its own. Reading through the list they claim as "mass shootings", only 7 events reference "large-capacity" magazines:

> 6/7/13: Had (40) 30 round .223 round magazines. 5 killed, 4 injured. Had a gun converted to fire .45

caliber, three zip guns and an AR-15. Doesn't say which of the weapons were used for the murders.

12/14/12: Lanza at Newtown. (We looked at this one already) 30 round magazines. 27 killed.

8/5/12: The Sikh temple shooting. Shooter "reportedly bought three 19 round magazines when he purchased the gun." I'm not sure that "reportedly" should even count here. 6 killed.

7/20/12: Holmes at Aurora. Had 100 round drum (we'll talk about that in a minute.) 12 killed.

1/8/11: Loughner in Gabrielle Giffords shooting. Glock with 33 round magazine. (we'll talk about that in a minute too). 6 killed.

4/3/09: "At least one magazine with a 30-round capacity was recovered at the scene." 14 killed.

3/21/09: East Oakland. "Police said the assault weapon had a high-capacity magazine." 4 police officers killed.

Only 3 of the events referencing "large-capacity" magazines had an appreciably higher death count than the average. (The San Bernardino shooting on December 2, 2015 was not yet in their list, but that event would make it 4 and I'm willing to accurately include that in their favor. 14 were killed.) Only in a different news report about Lanza did we see that he made tactical reloads firing as little as 15 rounds from the magazines, and yet his death count doubles that of any other "large-capacity" magazine reference in the list. As mentioned previously, a 30 round magazine with under 10 rounds fired out of it in an event gives no valid logical argument that the "large-capacity" magazine in question had any relation to the outcome due merely to its capacity, if the larger capacity never came into play. Even using Mother Jones' and Everytown's statistics, it appears "large-capacity" magazines rarely create high death tolls.

On occasion, the Violence Policy Center is also credited as being a source for these claims.[88] Their report cites 50 "mass shooting" events using "high-capacity" magazines over the 35 year period from 1980 to present. They give no indication as to the number of "mass shooting" events that did not involve "high-capacity" magazines over the same time period and thus make no comparisons between those two sets of data, merely citing 50 events where "high-capacity" magazines were used. It certainly gives no indication as to how they came to the conclusion's title; *High-Capacity Ammunition Magazines are the Common Thread Running Through Most Mass Shootings in the United States*. The total dead (including the shooters) was 436 and the average death per event was 8.72. If you remove the 4 extreme events it brings the total down to 329, averaging 7.15 deaths per event; Sandy Hook (28), Virginia Tech (33), Luby's Cafeteria in Killeen, TX (24) and McDonalds in San Ysidro (22). But again, this is in comparison to what? Also, as is typically the case, nothing here addresses whether the "large-capacity" magazines were implemented and had an outcome in the shootings. I could go on with overall statistics, and other statistics do show that most instances of gun violence rarely involve a large number of shots being fired, but at this point it kind of seems like beating a dead horse.[89]

I will repeat one thing I said earlier though: At least a "large-capacity" ban is an across the board approach which does not merely rely on making the weapon less accurate or precise, exacerbating the lack of training many people have with the weapon. The magazine capacity restrictions on all rifles may in fact slow the shooting from an untrained shooter, from a more accurate longer range firearm, under a greater set of circumstances. It will do little to slow the shooting of a trained shooter. The overall outcome here may still be more of a benefit to society than a burden to Second Amendment rights. The burden, in this case, can mostly be overcome by training.

We have briefly mentioned assassinations of public figures and luckily this next one was unsuccessful. Gabrielle Giffords was a member of the U.S. House of Representatives from Arizona. On January 8, 2011 Giffords was critically wounded by a gunshot injury to the head in an attempted assassination by Jared Lee Loughner while at a public meeting talking to constituents.[90] Giffords' husband Mark Kelly, is a former U.S. Navy Captain and veteran of Desert Storm. As a result of the attack, Giffords and Captain Kelly have created Americans for Responsible Solutions, which operates both as a 501(c)(4) advocacy organization and political action committee.[91] I respect that their family has gone through tragedy and that they are taking a somewhat more realistic approach to solving the problem than many others after tragedy, and I do not intend to downplay her attack in any way.

On the two year anniversary of the shooting, in an interview with Diane Sawyer, Giffords and Captain Kelly announced their Super PAC and spoke of gun violence. In the interview, Captain Kelly says that he and Gabby are both gun owners and "strong supporters of the Second Amendment". In regards to the debate over "large-capacity" magazines, he said he doesn't believe they are necessary for the sport. I don't even have to say it, do I? Maybe Captain Kelly believes

Second Amendment rights are only for hunting purposes, as we are now led to believe, but at least *you* don't believe that at this point. Captain Kelly also claims, "An extended magazine is used to kill people…lots of people."[92] He talks about "common-sense" solutions and then seems to forget to use any. Captain Kelly's statements make a lot of misguided conclusions and contain a lot of flaws.

Unless you're beating someone in the head with it, I don't think the magazine is going to kill anybody at all. We've talked about this briefly already. I can only conclude that Captain Kelly must mean the cartridges those magazines contain are meant to kill people, the "large-capacity" magazine holding more of them thus increasing the likelihood of doing so. But are all firearm cartridges specifically designed to kill? That may seem like a silly question, but maybe it is not. Kleck referenced this issue specifically in Point Blank:

> Dr. Martin L. Fackler (1989), Director of the Wound Ballistics Laboratory at the Letterman Army Institute of Research, has noted that typical "assault rifles" fire smaller-than-average ammunition, and has shown through ballistics experiments that this ammunition has milder wounding effects than civilian hunting ammunition or regular infantry rifle cartridges. This is partly because the military cartridges commonly used in "assault rifles" have smaller, pointed bullets, which tend to produce smaller wounds, which are correspondingly less lethal. The more lethal hollow point or "dumdum" bullet often used in hunting ammunition was forbidden for military use by the 1899 Hague Peace Conference. In addition to serving life-saving humanitarian purposes, the smaller, pointed full-metal-jacketed bullet has military

advantages. By wounding rather than killing enemy soldiers, it not only removes the soldier from combat, but also requires the enemy to devote resources to evacuating and treating him. Further, the light weight of the bullets allows soldiers to carry more rounds. In short, rather than being designed to kill human beings, the military ammunition commonly used in assault rifles was designed in such a way as to reduce the likelihood it would kill.[93]

Though Kleck's analysis appears to address "assault rifle" rounds in general, I just want to note that the research by Fackler he cites is specifically on the 124 grain FMJ 7.62 x 39mm cartridge fired by Patrick Purdy with an AK-47 at the Stockton school shooting. In that shooting, 35 children were shot by Purdy but only 5 were killed. Fackler's research is addressing that result and the misconceptions that overstate the damages of an "assault rifle" round.[94] The 5.56 round (nearly identical to .223) was adopted by NATO in 1980 and is widely used in the AR-15 platform, as well as numerous other rifles.[95] Though they are of similar profiles, the 5.56 x 45 NATO round is about 30 percent less in diameter and typically a little under half the weight. The biggest point here is that the hollow and soft point rounds expand upon impact to create a larger wound channel than the diameter of the bullet itself, while the non hollow point full metal jacket rounds tend to yaw or tumble in the wound at some depth to create a bigger wound channel. The smaller 5.56 x 45 round does appear to do a little more damage than the 7.62 x 39, as it starts to tumble at about 5 inches of depth, while the 7.62 x 39 doesn't start to tumble until about 12 inches of depth.[96] This is why the AK-47 round went cleanly through many of the children shot without creating fatal damage; the kids just weren't 12 inches thick, so the bullet didn't have the depth of space under resistance to start tumbling and went straight through.

What Kleck is really trying to point out here is that the "non expansion" ammunition specifically, and not a specific caliber round, was prohibited by The Hague Convention in order to kill less people, as the subsequent wound profiles are typically substantially smaller on an equal caliber comparison.[97] Though the military can't presently use them, you can buy both 5.56 NATO and 7.62 x 39 rounds with hollow points. The point here again is that though all bullets are designed to shoot something, there are some such as those mandated of the military by The Hague Convention that were adopted with the intention of killing less people, and not more. Hunting ammunition often has expansion capabilities; in some cases the use of the military non-expanding FMJ rounds is actually prohibited for hunting so that a shot animal isn't merely wounded and left to suffer. I find it interesting that people can see humanitarian benefits in the latter example, while denying it exists in the first scenario.

Having already addressed the ideology which Captain Kelly implies about Second Amendment rights being for sport, let's look further at his "extended magazine" comment. The intent of an extended magazine is to be able to fire more rounds before reloading, period. It does not provide any other new intent to the magazine itself, it does not provide a new intent to the weapon, and it does not dictate a new intent to the shooter. A larger Pez dispenser does not change the purpose of the Pez dispenser to deliver candy, one piece at a time in succession. It only changes the number of pieces of candy you can get before reloading and does not suddenly imply an extended candy capacity in a Pez would be purely intended to make people obese...lots of people.

Let's look at a few of the prevailing assumptions that more rounds in a magazine are only ever required with the intent to kill lots of people, significantly faster than using multiple lower capacity magazines, and are always more beneficial than a lower capacity magazine.

I have often heard it suggested that in actual gunfights the last round fired wins the fight, though I'm not sure if that research exists. One thing we do know is that criminals don't necessarily play by the rules, so you could very well be defending your life in your home with 10 rounds in a magazine when a criminal has 30 or more. Maybe the intent here is still to kill (only to save your own life), but certainly not to kill lots of people, just the one(s) trying to kill you who may have brought the ability to fire more shots than you. We've already looked at the low hit rate of shots fired by trained police officers under fire. This would tend to suggest the old adage "If you can't do it with six, you can't do it at all" may not be sound. The restrictions on capacity don't account for training issues regarding your aim but also don't consider the level of stress one endures being fired at. It seems to kind of suggest that if your aim or concentration under fire isn't sufficient, you shouldn't have the right to have enough ammo to stay in the fight until the person trying to kill you fails to do so. He who has the most ammo, clearly has an advantage. Should that advantage be with the aggressor or the defender?

There is very little difference in speed between two 10 round magazines and one 20 round magazine.[98] Granted it takes a well trained person to be proficient at reloads, however, one cannot argue that the untrained can manipulate a firearm to achieve results of range and accuracy to its fullest extent with no training, and then argue that they could not be just as effective on reloads. Which leads us to how do you slow down a reload?

A bullet button alters your magazine release such that it requires something small, like the tip of one of those small pointed bullets described above, to activate the magazine release. It will slow down a reload a little as compared to a regular magazine release button but only by a matter of a couple of seconds, not minutes. It might be enough to create that reloading gap theorized to give bystanders a moment to attack a shooter. The bullet button restriction almost pre-supposes a restriction on magazine capacity as well. If you have a 30 round pre ban magazine (in states such as CA that prohibit them otherwise) have you really changed anything with any significant results? Worse, what if you are defending your life in the dark and can't reload your firearm quickly enough to save yourself from an attacker? If it inhibits an offensive attack, it most likely inhibits a defensive action as well.

There is also a point at which a "large capacity" magazine may become a tactical disadvantage instead of an advantage. In the July 20, 2012 Aurora Colorado shooting, James Holmes fired multiple weapons including a semi-automatic Smith and Wesson M&P 15 (an AR-15 clone) with a 100 round drum which malfunctioned after firing what sources say was 65 rounds. Reports suggested the drum jamming actually slowed down his assault before he switched to a handgun.[99] A number of more reliable 30 round magazines may have been more effective, less likely even a pocket full of 10 round magazines, and yet the general public calls for an immediate ban on 100 round drums suggesting larger magazine capacities are always more effective. According to Republican state Senator Bernie Herpin, if the 100 round drum had not jammed the death toll may have been much higher.[100]   Though Sen. Herpin appeared to have subsequently been crucified in the media for his statement, and I'll concede it probably does "sound" insincere on the surface to the uninformed, I would have to agree with his assessment. In fact, one of the survivors did claim he was only alive because the drum jammed.

Holmes got off 65 shots with the drum, so it isn't like it jammed after 3 or 4 rounds, but it brings up an interesting question.   If the public focuses on the capacity of the magazine, and totally neglects the fact that the magazine design failed and could not produce that functional capacity, is the outcry to immediately ban 100 round drums all that sound? Would a 500 round magazine on an AR-15 be even more deadly? If a 30 round magazine fails, you drop it and load a new magazine and only lose a few rounds of your ammunition. When his 100 round drum failed, he lost the use of ALL the remaining rounds for that weapon as well as the use of that weapon going forward. If he had chosen to take five or six 30 round magazines, he may have been able to fire substantially more shots from that more accurate longer range weapon, before having to switch to the Glock .40 handgun. The general public seemed to look at merely one factor; capacity.

As a final point regarding the "extended magazines" comment, many pistol and rifle magazines classified in legislation as "large-capacity" are actually the factory standard magazines originally designed for use with their respective weapons platforms and though they might be "large-capacity" magazines under an arbitrary definition now generally accepted, they are not necessarily "extended" beyond the manufacturer's original design intentions for the weapon. In many cases, "reduced-capacity" magazines were later created in response to enactment of the "large-capacity" magazine bans.[101]   In comparison, the 396 in the 1965 Corvette wasn't an "extended" engine as compared to the 327, it was just one of the stock options that year. Using the semantics "extended magazine" gives an impression the magazine has been modified beyond the intent of the manufacturer and is quite deceiving in the scope of any argument being made as to the magazine's legality or usefulness. A "large-capacity" magazine and an "extended" magazine are two different things. "Extended magazines" do exist and may be "large-capacity", but not all "large capacity" magazines are "extended" magazines. I doubt that Captain Kelly even realizes he's been acclimated to, and is himself now using, a semantics trick. I do, however, wish them both the best.

Assault Weapons

We've covered a few issues with "assault weapons" already, I guess we should begin here with some definitions.   An "assault rifle" is a select fire rifle which can switch between either semi-automatic or burst fire and fully automatic fire.[102] Burst fire typically ranges somewhere between 2 and 5 rounds fired for each pull of the trigger. The Germans did research which showed that most firefights happened within 400 meters and designed the Sturmgewehr 44 to be effective in those scenarios.   It was first adopted in 1944.[103] Sturmgewehr translates into English as "assault rifle" thus creating the name for the class of rifles.[104] A fully "automatic weapon" is a firearm that reloads itself and keeps firing until the trigger is released.[105] A "machine gun" is a firearm capable of shooting a continuous stream of bullets.[106] Though similar to a fully automatic weapon, a broader "machine gun" class might require a mechanical means to be continuously fired, such as turning a crank. A "sub-machine gun" is a lightweight automatic gun that shoots pistol ammunition, is usually fired from the shoulder or hip, and often has the capacity for shooting single rounds.[107] A "machine pistol" is a lightweight automatic submachine gun designed to be fired when held by one or two hands.[108] A "semi-automatic firearm" is a weapon that performs all steps necessary to prepare the weapon to fire again after firing but does not automatically fire an additional round until the trigger is released and re-pressed.[109]

First use of the term "assault weapon" in regards to a gun appears to have come from Assemblyman Art Agnos in 1985 while presenting a bill to ban semi-automatic firearms to the Assembly Public Safety Committee, saying "The only use for assault weapons is to shoot people." This followed the McDonald's shooting a year earlier in San Ysidro referenced previously. More than anything, it appears to have specifically been to target the sale of Uzis that could be converted to full auto fire. The reference to "assault weapons" almost seems circumstantial here, as the bulk of the references actually refer to the weapons as "assault type" guns.[110]

So exactly how do we define what is an "assault weapon" then? Merriam Webster defines it as "any of various automatic or semiautomatic firearms; especially: assault rifle."[111] Of course they also define "assault"; *a*: a violent physical or verbal attack *b*: a military attack usually involving direct combat with enemy forces.[112] We've seen the definition of "assault weapon" from the Federal Assault Weapons Ban. As an example, a .223 rifle with a solid wood stock and 10 round removable magazine would not be an "assault weapon" but a .223 rifle with an adjustable stock, pistol grip and 10 round removable magazine would be. We've seen the NY SAFE Act restrict that definition in the state of New York even more severely than the Federal Assault Weapons Ban originally did. In NY, the rifle with the pistol grip and removable magazine is an "assault weapon" having one military style feature.

Unfortunately, in the past people like Dr. Gary Kleck have used the abbreviation "AR" in their writings to designate an "assault rifle."[113] This appears to have led to the false assumption by many that the "AR" in AR-15 also means "assault rifle", and possibly provided more support for banning the AR-15. AR was actually a common prefix Armalite used on all their weapons.[114] For instance, the AR-17 is a semi auto 12 gauge shotgun and the AR-7 a .22 caliber survival rifle that breaks down and stores in the stock of the weapon. Though not as Kleck intended in using the abbreviation, it is another one of those semantics tricks used to manipulate public opinion.

It's actually interesting to watch how the semantics slowly evolved over time. It started out as "assault-type" weapons. At some point after Agnos' comment, it morphed into "assault weapons" and no longer "assault type" weapons, with the media often deceivingly presenting them as fully automatic rifles. "Assault weapon" was used as a semantics trick to make you believe the semi-automatic rifle was a military full-auto "assault rifle" because it was styled like an assault rifle and therefore also intended for military style "assaults." Thus an assault style rifle became known as an "assault weapon" and the inaccurate semantics accepting the use of the word "assault" for the civilian class of weapons stuck over the years.

It has now appeared to come full circle. The media can't say the weapons used in the San Bernardino shooting on December 2, 2015 were bought as "assault weapons" because they were legally not "assault weapons" by CA definition when purchased, but later modified. "Officials said they believe one of the San Bernardino gunmen, Syed Rizwan Farook, asked Marquez to buy the two "assault-style" rifles back in late 2011 or early 2012 so that Farook's name would not be on file in connection with the high-powered rifles."[115] So what they are calling them at the time of purchase is "assault-style" rifles. Technically, the fact that they are merely "assault-style" weapons has been correct the whole time, but now the correct moniker actually appears to have an entirely different meaning. After 30 years of "assault weapons" semantics, what the people now seem to hear is "assault (weapons) style" firearm. These weapons were "styled" just like "assault weapons." In essence, they're now using a semantics trick to reference the previous semantics trick to, once again, make legal guns sound like they should be illegal. When in reality, assault "style" firearms were all they ever were to begin with.

Towards the end of the Korean War in 1952 the Hitchman report suggested a "pattern-dispersion" principle would help increase hits at ranges up to 300 yards.[116] This was understood to suggest that a full auto infantry rifle would be beneficial. Read: the speed of untargeted random fire would be of benefit in close quarter combat situations. After the Vietnam war, it was concluded that full auto fire was ineffective and wasted ammunition. The military subsequently switched to rifles that were selectable between semi-auto fire and 3 round bursts. Today, the military is adopting the M4A1(semi and full auto) in place of the M16A4, one reason being the burst feature isn't required anymore, as modern training focuses predominantly on semi-automatic fire anyway.[117] The real irony here is that while segments of the population are worried that civilian rifles are too much like full auto and 3 round burst military assault rifles, the military has progressively headed towards dropping the implementation of those features and focuses predominantly on the semi-auto firing of the civilian models.

It seems like the public fear of machine guns is really in "hearing" them fire so quickly and a couple of aggrandized media reports. As the Brady Campaign pointed out (we'll talk about them in a moment), the speed of fire between the two is extremely negligible. The gain of control in specifically targeting each shot with semi-automatic fire is beneficial. Unless you're just laying down cover fire, which is not going to be the case with most civilian uses, every shot should really count. I've seen arguments be made for full auto for law enforcement use, but knowing that they are accountable for every single round that leaves their weapon, I doubt random cover fire is all that acceptable and I'm not sure why they'd want to risk the inaccuracies of 3 round burst or full auto.

Before we talk about scenarios where the argument may be dependent on various levels of training, I should point out another phenomenon that seems to creep into the gun debate. There is an element of "armchair quarterback" mentality that takes place regarding firearms. People inherently assume that anyone who picks up a weapon can immediately have the accuracy of a sharp shooter and the situational focus of a Navy SEAL. It's just not the case. It's like Dr. Garen Wintemute, Professor of Emergency Medicine at UC Davis School of Medicine, who stated that with a .50 caliber rifle, "I could be, if there weren't some stuff in the way, I could be at the base of the Washington Monument and pick off a target on the west side of the Capitol, no problem."[118] The shot he is referencing is about 1.4 miles in distance. There have only ever been 4 recorded kills reported by the military with a .50 caliber rifle, by trained snipers, at that range; Corporal Rob Furlong (2,657 yd March 2002), Corporal Arron Perry (2,526 yd March 2002), Sgt. Bryan Kremer (2,515 yd. March 2004), Gunnery Sergeant Carlos Hathcock (2,500 yd February 1967.)[119-122] Though Wintemute actually said the weapon had a one and a half mile killing range, only Furlong's shot was a full 1.5 miles. I'm guessing Wintemute also thinks he can duplicate the achievements of Michael Jordan, John Von Neumann and Ron Hyatt...no problem. The ignorance is seriously mind-boggling.

We've already discussed how the military style "assault weapons" features aren't cosmetic, and that the advantage of those with some features over those without is moderate. They predominantly affect accuracy and precision, and again an accurate and precise gun is a safer gun overall. The bullets for semi-auto and "assault weapons" versions are often the same and thus have the same ballistics, there is maybe a slight difference in multi round accuracy firing repeatedly with a more accurate and precise weapon due to better control. The AR-15 specifically is a modular weapons platform in regards to features tests, those features can quickly and easily change.

I bring up accuracy and precision again because the Court appears to switch logic at times. The assumption by the Court when talking about features like adjustable stocks, forward grips and muzzle brakes or flash suppressors is that a "mass shooter" can repeatedly shoot at targets quicker due to the benefit from those features, thus appearing to argue that being able to better take intentional aim is beneficial to a shooter. However, they then basically do an immediate flip and switch their argument to be that pistol grips and thumbhole stocks are more deadly because it is mechanically easier for a shooter to "spray fire" from the hip. So which is it? Are the features that allow quicker target acquisition more lethal, or are features that allow non targeted "spray firing" more lethal?

Now each individual feature might have a different benefit for a different shooting scenario, and that doesn't discredit the argument against each feature individually, but there actually is an underlying consistency in the Legislature's and Court's logic from both shooting style alternatives: The Legislature and Court seem to be continuously hung up on the repetition of shots and seem entirely ignorant as to accuracy or precision of shots having any relation to lethality in a shooting. They appear to merely judge "how fast" one can shoot into a space. When the Courts view "assault weapons" features, they clearly don't see those features as accuracy enhancing features; they merely see them as speed of repeat fire features.

Why is it that people always seem to believe the movies and that spray firing, or merely rapid firing, is somehow the most efficient means of hitting a target? If you really want to believe the movies, go back and watch how much ammunition Rambo actually wastes. Spray firing is random, and the number of hits is entirely dependent upon the density of the crowd of people that are being shot at. If I'm ever in an "active shooter" scenario, I hope like hell the shooter is shooting randomly. If he's taking intentional aim at specific targets, and putting multiple rounds in each, I'm going to be a lot more worried about my outcome.

Seriously, go to the fair and find one of those balloon dart games. Close your eyes and throw 20 darts at the board quickly and see how many you hit. The balloons aren't even trying to get away by moving around. Now open your eyes and for 20 throws take intentional aim at individual balloons but still at as quick a pace as you controllably can. Which method do you think the results will favor? I point this out not because I think it has any bearing on the conclusions of the court cases specifically, because as the Court points out the law must only fulfill the governmental objective substantially and not perfectly. I bring this up because I have come to realize it is a fallacious perspective that has somehow become the norm in what does or does not make a weapon more "dangerous" or "lethal" than other weapons. It's the same assumption the Hitchman report made, later to be found inaccurate in actual application.

Everything came to a head with the Federal Assault Weapons Ban we've talked about already. Instead of talking about statistics independently, let's look at the report required of the ban and see what the conclusions were. It contains references to percentages pertinent to the debate. We'll just cite those.

Updated Assessment of the Federal Assault Weapons Ban: Impacts on Gun Markets and Gun Violence, 1994-2003. [123]

The first thing the report concedes is that "The ban is directed at semiautomatic firearms having features that appear useful in military and criminal applications but unnecessary in shooting sports or self-defense (examples include flash hiders, folding rifle stocks, and threaded barrels for attaching silencers)." That hunting and sporting purposes argument just will not go away, will it? At least it includes self-defense purposes, but makes a serious leap in assuming that these features are not beneficial for self-defense. I think we've already concluded that many of them are. The report does not address whether that is a sound argument in regards to self-defense; the report only addresses the potential for societal good without regards for any burden placed upon society as a result. That is still a valid reason for debate. Just note that this is an evaluation on half of the full argument, though in that regard it does appear that Koper and his group did a relatively sound job.

Ultimately, their conclusions were mostly inconclusive. More specifically, they concluded that making any conclusions would be premature. Even then they note that any anticipated favorable outcomes would have been relatively small, possibly even undetectable, given that assault weapons are rarely used in crimes to begin with. "Assault weapons" were used in roughly 2 percent to 8 percent of gun crimes prior. "Large-capacity" magazines were used in roughly 14 percent to 26 percent of gun crimes prior. This pretty much parallels the same percentages of their total share in overall gun ownership statistics. Here is the entire Chapter 9 summary:

> Although the ban has been successful in reducing crimes with AWs, any benefits from this reduction are likely to have been outweighed by steady or rising use of non-banned semiautomatics with LCMs, which are used in crime much more frequently than AWs. Therefore, we cannot clearly credit the ban with any of the nation's recent drop in gun violence. And, indeed, there has been no discernible reduction in the lethality and injuriousness of gun violence, based on indicators like the percentage of gun crimes resulting in death or the share of gunfire incidents resulting in injury, as we might have expected had the ban reduced crimes with both AWs and LCMs.
>
> However, the grandfathering provision of the AW-LCM ban guaranteed that the effects of this law would occur only gradually over time. Those effects

are still unfolding and may not be fully felt for several years into the future, particularly if foreign, pre-ban LCMs continue to be imported into the U.S. in large numbers. It is thus premature to make definitive assessments of the ban's impact on gun violence.

Having said this, the ban's impact on gun violence is likely to be small at best, and perhaps too small for reliable measurement. AWs were used in no more than 8% of gun crimes even before the ban. Guns with LCMs are used in up to a quarter of gun crimes, but it is not clear how often the outcomes of gun attacks depend on the ability to fire more than 10 shots (the current limit on magazine capacity) without reloading.

Nonetheless, reducing crimes with AWs and especially LCMs could have nontrivial effects on gunshot victimizations. As a general matter, hit rates tend to be low in gunfire incidents, so having more shots to fire rapidly can increase the likelihood that offenders hit their targets, and perhaps bystanders as well. While not entirely consistent, the few available studies contrasting attacks with different types of guns and magazines generally suggest that attacks with semiautomatics – including AWs and other semiautomatics with LCMs – result in more shots fired, persons wounded, and wounds per victim than do other gun attacks. Further, a study of handgun attacks in one city found that about 3% of gunfire incidents involved more than 10 shots fired, and those cases accounted for nearly 5% of gunshot victims. However, the evidence on these matters is too limited (both in volume and quality) to make firm projections of the ban's impact, should it be reauthorized.[124]

Here are some of the individual conclusions I think are most important in the analysis along with some additional supporting quotes:

Assault weapons are only used in a small percentage of crimes to begin with "though AWs still seem to account for a somewhat disproportionate share of guns used in murders and other serious crimes."[125] When they are used in crimes it is mostly assault pistols and not assault rifles, the same followed for their statistics regarding reductions in use from the ban. There was some evidence that criminals prefer assault pistols. "Perhaps the best evidence of a criminal preference for AWs comes from a study of young adult handgun buyers in California that found buyers with minor criminal histories (i.e., arrests or misdemeanor convictions that did not disqualify them from purchasing firearms) were more than twice as likely to purchase APs than were buyers with no criminal history (4.6% to 2%, respectively) (Wintemute et al., 1998a). Those with more serious criminal histories were even more likely to purchase APs: 6.6% of those who had been charged with a gun offense bought APs, as did 10% of those who had been charged with two or more serious violent offenses. AP purchasers were also more likely to be arrested subsequent to their purchases than were other gun purchasers."[126] From a societal good perspective, the logic on banning assault pistols may appear to be sound, the banning of an assault rifle does not.

The real issue, though, as we've already discussed is with the "large-capacity" magazines and not the weapons platform itself. "Hence, use of guns with LCMs is probably more consequential than use of guns with other military style features, such as flash hiders, folding rifle stocks, threaded barrels for attaching a silencers, and so on."[127] On that issue, there is still no tangible evidence that "large-capacity" magazines truly have a direct impact on injuries or deaths because data does not segregate the number of shots actually fired from each magazine, in many cases the size of the magazine used is not even recorded by police. Koper and his group argue that should change; I would have to agree.

Overall, gun crimes resulting in deaths didn't change during the ban; either there was no true correlation or people just used other weapons to create the same crimes. "But a more casual assessment shows that gun crimes since the ban have been no less likely to cause death or injury than those before the ban, contrary to what we might expect if crimes with AWs and LCMs had both declined. For instance, the percentage of violent gun crimes resulting in death has been very stable since 1990 according to national statistics on crimes reported to police. In fact, the percentage of gun crimes resulting in death during 2001 and 2002 (2.94%) was slightly higher than that during 1992 and 1993 (2.9%)."[128] In regards to using other weapons, they said "Although criminal use of AWs has declined since the ban, this reduction was offset through at least the late 1990s by steady or rising use of other guns equipped with LCMs."[129] Again, this seems to reference "large-capacity" magazines as the major factor in deaths.

There's really no difference between a semi-automatic rifle and a semi-automatic rifle with military features. "In other respects (e.g., type of firing mechanism, ammunition fired, and the ability to accept a detachable magazine), AWs do not differ from other legal semiautomatic weapons."[130] Honestly, I think in reality we've seen that pretty much goes for fully automatic rifles as well. I think this really confirms we're talking about accuracy and precision enhancing features, and not merely features that increase the speed of fire appreciably. In regards to speed of fire itself being an asset, "As a general point, the faster firing rate and larger ammunition capacities of semiautomatics, especially those equipped with LCMs, have the potential to affect the outcomes of many gun attacks because gun offenders are not particularly good shooters."[131] On this one, I'm not sure that is an entirely sound argument. That's the exact same interpretation the Hitchman report made in 1952, later concluded to be false by the military after Vietnam. The speed with which one can merely fire into space has been shown not to have a direct correlation to lethality. "Spray and pray" does not increase your probability of striking a target, it only slightly reduces the time in which probability can work in your favor. Even then, there is no "law of averages" suggesting that the next shot is more likely to hit a target than the previous one...that is a density of crowd variable. It is only the capacity to continue firing that has a direct correlation. Regardless, it does seem to confirm that capacity regulations in society may still be sound, as they can affect the untrained shooter disproportionately.

A New York Times / CBS News Poll on Terrorism and the 2016 Presidential Race from December 4-8 in 2015 found that, for the first time in 20 years, a majority of Americans do not support an "assault weapons" ban. In the four years from 2011 to 2015, the support in favor of a ban dropped from 63 percent (34% specifically in opposition to a ban) to 44 percent (50% specifically in opposition to a ban.) As an aside, the same poll shows that 50 percent believe that stricter gun laws would help prevent gun violence either "some" or "a lot" while 48 percent believe it would help either "not much" or not at all." In contrast, 75 percent believed better mental health screening and treatment would help.[132]

The Administration of President Barack Hussein Obama II

There is a common argument that the current political administration wants to ban all firearms. The rebuttal is made that suggesting some gun control does not imply that a complete ban is desired, and that it is an irrational fear. Are some people correct in thinking that a full ban is what is ultimately intended, or is it an unsupported argument? Let's take a look at Barack Obama's comments over time to see what you think.

President Obama, Sept. 9, 2008: "I just want to be absolutely clear, alright. So I don't want any misunderstanding. When ya'll go home and you're talking to your buddies, and they say, "Ah, he wants to take my gun away," you've heard it here — I'm on television so everybody knows it — I believe in the Second Amendment. I believe in people's lawful right to bear arms. I will not take your shotgun away. I will not take your rifle away. I won't take your handgun away. ... So, there are some common-sense gun safety laws that I believe in. But I am not going to take your guns away. So if you want to find an excuse not to vote for me, don't use that one. Cause that just ain't true."[133] Keep in mind this was 5 years after the Federal Assault Weapons Ban came to an end, but only 3 months after *Heller* and before the scope of that decision was really understood by the general public.

During the second Presidential debate in 2012, President Obama had this to say, "What I'm trying to do is to get a broader conversation about how do we reduce the violence, generally. Part of it is seeing if we can get an assault weapons ban re-introduced, but part of it is also looking at other sources of the violence, because frankly, in my hometown of Chicago there's an awful lot of violence, and they're not using AK-47s. They're using cheap handguns."[134]

Is an "assault weapons" ban taking away some shotguns and rifles from society? It appears to. Or does this imply a grandfather clause for pre-owned weapons? Maybe this is only taking some of them away from future buyers and not taking them away from present owners? Here again, keep in mind this was not only after it became widespread knowledge that the 2008 *Heller* decision specifically protected handguns, but was also after the 2010 *McDonald* decision held that protection applied to the states as well. More importantly, this quote was made after the appellate court had heard the *Moore v. Madigan* appeal and was currently in deliberation, which would decide if Obama's home state of Illinois would be required to allow concealed carry. To be absolutely fair here, I'll even reference the FactCheck.org article that tries to argue that Obama didn't "Flip-Flop" on gun control so you can check that out yourself, though it was written in February 2013 before the most recent Obama quote from 2015 that we'll see below.[135] At this point, maybe there is not a clear flip-flop; maybe the statement is merely a political plug for the Assault Weapons Ban of 2013 Feinstein was about to introduce in Congress, and a last ditch effort to get the appellate court to side with Illinois in the *Moore v. Madigan* appeal.

In response to the Umpqua Community College shooting on October 1, 2015, Obama had this to say about gun control laws. "We know that other countries, in response to one mass shooting, have been able to craft laws that almost eliminate mass shootings. Friends of ours, allies of ours -- Great Britain, Australia, countries like ours. So we know there are ways to prevent it."[136]

Does that constitute a "flip-flop" or even a tangible change in ideology from Obama since 2008? This statement was clearly after handgun ownership was confirmed to be a national constitutional right both inside and outside the home, after *Moore v. Madigan* forced Illinois to allow concealed carry confirming it as a constitutional right and after Diane Feinstein's Assault Weapons Ban of 2013 bill was defeated in Congress. Let's look at the requirements for Great Britain's "Shotgun Certificate" as an example of exactly what kind of restrictions they put in place:

> Applications for a shotgun certificate must include a completed application form as provided for by the Firearms Rules;

> four passport-sized photographs, one signed by a referee (reference) that it is a true likeness of the applicant; and

> a signed statement by a referee that the information contained in the application is correct and that they know of no reason that the person should not be allowed to possess a shotgun.

> The person providing the signed statement must "(a) be resident in Great Britain, (b) have known the applicant personally for at least two years, and (c) be a member of Parliament, justice of the peace, minister of religion, doctor, lawyer, established civil servant, bank officer or person of similar standing."

> Shotgun certificates may be granted by the chief officer of police if he is satisfied that the applicant's possession of a shotgun will not pose a danger to public safety or the peace. Certificates will not be granted if the chief officer of police

(a) has reason to believe that the applicant is prohibited by this Act from possessing a shot gun; or

(b) is satisfied that the applicant does not have a good reason for possessing, purchasing or acquiring one.

The term "good reason" for possession of shotguns includes reasons connected with the certificate holder's profession, sport or recreation, or shooting vermin. The requirement for "good reason" to possess a shotgun was introduced after the Hungerford massacre and concerns that weapons were being purchased for self-defense.[137-143]

I really like the part about the type of individual and their societal standing that has to give you a reference, having known you for two years and verifying the picture you submit is of you. I had to look three or four times to make sure you don't have to be Protestant. If similar laws were adopted here, and say you moved from Texas to California; would you have to reside in California for two years in order to have a high ranking societal member living in California provide the reference for you, thus limiting your ability to have a firearm in California for at least the first two years? Most importantly, did you catch the footnote here: "The requirement for 'good reason' to possess a shotgun was introduced after the Hungerford massacre and concerns that weapons were being purchased for self-defense." The requirement was added to reduce concerns that weapons were being purchased for self-defense?

Do I even have to point out the fact that Great Britain and Australia actually aren't exactly "countries like ours?" Their governments are both constitutional monarchies, the United States is a constitutional republic. In fact, both countries have the same (Protestant) monarch; Queen Elizabeth II. Though sovereign, Australia (officially the Commonwealth of Australia) is a Commonwealth Realm of Great Britain. There is a reason the United States is not currently a Commonwealth of Great Britain.

This is one example of the types of gun control laws President Obama is now suggesting we follow. Reading this, do you think a concern about the potential for what might effectively be a full weapons ban being proposed is unwarranted? After having read the history of the Second Amendment, do you think the requirements above would violate your Second Amendment rights if implemented in the United States? How do you feel about banning guns for self-defense purposes?

Do you remember that No-fly list argument from Everytown for Gun Safety? President Obama recently made this exact same argument in a statement to the people, "Right now, people on the No-Fly list can walk into a store and buy a gun. That is insane. If you're too dangerous to board a plane, you're too dangerous, by definition, to buy a gun." Our President actually suggested we deny people who are only "potential terrorists or criminals" their Fifth Amendment rights of Due Process in spite of the fact the No-fly list had already been ruled unconstitutional.[144,145]

I hate to resort to a possible expression of Godwin's Law, but haven't we seen another nation do that before? Do we really want to set precedent that constitutional rights can be removed from people by a "secret" government agency without Due Process of the Fifth Amendment? If we allow the Fifth Amendment to be circumvented, then there is no longer a legal avenue with which the accused can fairly and publicly fight oppressions by the government. It could easily be argued this last section could have gone in the chapter on Insurrection.

Brady Campaign to Prevent Gun Violence

You may argue the President is being taken out of context in suggesting we follow the paths of Britain and Australia. Well, is there evidence that any current groups have campaigned with the ultimate intent of banning all firearms? The Brady Campaign to Prevent Gun Violence is a 501(c)(3) non-profit. It was originally founded by Dr. Mark Borinsky, a victim of gun violence, in 1974 as the National Council to Control Handguns. Nelson "Pete" Shields soon joined the group in 1976 after his eldest son, Nick, was shot in what has become known as the Zebra murders. Shields became Chairman in 1978. The name was changed to Handgun Control, Inc. in 1980. We've already addressed Jim Brady's shooting during the unsuccessful assassination attempt of Ronald Reagan; Jim and Sarah Brady joined the organization in the mid 1980's.[146] The Brady Campaign to Prevent Gun Violence adopted their current name in 2001.

There is no doubt that people who have become understandably biased after being a victim of gun violence, or suffering the loss of a loved one to a gun death, tend to fight for the greatest restrictions. What ultimately became The Brady Campaign to Prevent Gun Violence is no different. In 1976, while still the National Council to Control Handguns, Nelson "Pete" Shields stated the following:

> "We're going to have to take one step at a time, and the first step is necessarily -- given the political

realities -- going to be very modest... [W]e'll have to start working again to strengthen that law, and then again to strengthen the next law, and maybe again and again. Right now, though, we'd be satisfied not with half a loaf but with a slice. Our ultimate goal -- total control of handguns in the United States -- is going to take time. . . . The first problem is to slow down the number of handguns being produced and sold in this country. The second problem is to get handguns registered. The final problem is to make possession of all handguns and all handgun ammunition-except for the military, police, licensed security guards, licensed sporting clubs, and licensed gun collectors-totally illegal."[147]

It appears the organization started off pretty extreme. It may no longer be relevant in The Brady Campaign as it stands today, but it does show the group once existed with the intent of banning gun possession to a large portion of society. It is hard to argue that nobody desires to achieve such goals.

Under its different monikers, the group has had some notoriety over the years. The National Council to Control Handguns is actually credited with outlawing "cop killer" bullets and the import of parts for Saturday Night Specials (of course the latter seems to have created the ring of fire companies as a byproduct.)[148] Now I'm glad we covered those issues first. So the organization banned one thing that doesn't actually exist.

They have also been credited as successfully pushing for the legislation of plastic guns under H.R. 4445, the Undetectable Firearms Act of 1988.[149] The Act banned guns with less than 3.7 oz of metal content. Though it was originally targeting the polymer framed Glocks, no such guns designated under the bill appear to have existed at the time. But hey, it's "common sense" to make gun laws to keep guns that don't exist from being able to go through metal detectors undetected, right? So now we have two things that they've gotten banned that don't actually exist. They're on a roll.

Of course that didn't stop the movies from perpetuating the myth: "That punk pulled a Glock 7 on me. You know what that is? It's a porcelain gun made in Germany. It doesn't show up on your airport X-ray machines here and it costs more than what you make in a month" – John McClane in Die Hard 2 (1990).150 The Glock 7 doesn't exist, but with new 3D printing technology it may actually become a real issue today. Roughly 27 years later, I can just hear someone at The Brady Campaign finally running around the office yelling, "Well,Yippee ki-yay, motherf...er!"

We've already referenced the Brady Bill being passed in 1993. Immediately after their success with passing the Brady Bill, HCI attempted to pass further legislation which would create a database of every registered gun owner subsequently deemed Brady II. In claimed support of that bill, there is reported to have been a leaked memo from HCI from December 30, 1993. I cannot find any evidence discrediting the memo as being authentic, or any claims by HCI that it is not real. Though I have found numerous references to the article, or uses of HCI quotes from the article in the media...we've seen how trustworthy the media is. Caveat emptor on this one regarding legitimacy.

Pete Shields had passed away earlier in 1993, but because this memo virtually parallels his previous quote and is argued to be real from citable sources, I decided to go ahead and include it. It's not really about the authenticity here, it is about the perceptions it created supposedly being a "leaked" authentic memo. One section defines roughly a ten year plan for handgun restrictions through licensing fees, "Handgun License Fees Year 1 to 2: Program can begin at a relatively low cost to discourage non-compliance: Suggested Fee Schedule: $50 - $75 annual fee Year 3 to 4: Fees would be raised to reflect the cost of enforcement and discourage new ownership: Suggested Fee Schedule: $150 - $250 annual fee Year 5 to 8: If private ownership has not been prohibited by this time then fees can be gradually increased to discourage private ownership: Suggested Fee Schedule $550- $625 annual fee."[151]

In another section of the memo they suggest, "Military Assault Weapons: The confusion by the general public between semi-automatic weapons can work in our favor. Constantly dropping the words - submachine gun, fully automatic, machine gun, military weapon, high tech killing machine are good debater's tricks to instill a sense of dread over these weapons. Ultimately people will learn to dread these weapons just like chemical warfare weapons and toxic waste dumps." It actually encourages using the very semantics tricks we've seen the media subsequently use. That is another reason I decided to reference it, there is evidence it was actually implemented. Here is their stated goal with requiring licensing, "Our eventual goal is to reduce the number of licensees to zero. The revenue itself can be utilized to achieve this goal."

Again, it's hard to say if this was a real memo or not. It does parallel the initial ideology of Pete Shields. It does reference actual semantics tricks known to still be in use today. Either way, it's no wonder gun owners fear people want to disarm the American public if being presented with this memo, seeing other verifiable signs that appear to also support this memo's authenticity.

In the past, the Brady Campaign has argued against semi-automatic weapons, including the Federal Assault Weapons ban in 1994, under their previous moniker. They state that there is really no difference between fully automatic and semi-automatic weapons. "The only difference between an ˋautomatic and a semi-automatic assault weapon is about 3.5 seconds."[152] I would have to agree. By the very same logic though, it kind of negates the "large capacity" magazine ban ideology. Much like with a trained person changing magazines in an AR-15, the time difference is minimal. Do 3 seconds make a tangible difference in a multiple shooting, or do they not? Although, as I've suggested already, mere speed of firing doesn't equate to much in regards to acquiring repeat targets except in the minds of the uninformed people. Evidence doesn't suggest that machine guns, though used in isolated locations and periods of time in the past century, equate to higher death rates when used.

Let's look at the Brady Campaign's website and see what they have to say today. From their website, here is their objective:

> Brady has announced the bold goal to cut the number of U.S. gun deaths in half by 2025, based on an innovative and exciting strategy that centers on the idea of keeping guns out of the wrong hands through three impact-driven, broadly engaging campaigns: (1) a policy focus to "Finish the Job" so that life-saving Brady background checks are applied to all gun sales; (2) to "Stop 'Bad Apple' Gun Dealers" – the 5 percent of gun dealers that supply 90 percent of all crime guns; and (3) to lead a new national conversation and

change social norms around the real dangers of guns in the home, to prevent the homicides, suicides, and unintentional shootings that happen every day as a result.[153]

I'm going to look at them in reverse order. Objective number 3 is "to lead a new national conversation and change social norms around the real dangers of guns in the home, to prevent the homicides, suicides, and unintentional shootings that happen every day as a result." As such, I guess it is not surprising they go on to distort research we have already covered. "A gun in the home is 22 times more likely to be used to kill or injure in a domestic homicide, suicide, or unintentional shooting than to be used in self-defense." They cite Kellerman's research, which we've already addressed as being seriously flawed.[154] At least the Law Center to Prevent Gun Violence compared the homicides, suicides and unintentional shootings to justifiable homicides as Kellerman's research actually did, and only presented the false conclusion in a way to make it sound deceiving. Not only is the Brady campaign citing discredited research here, they aren't even accurately citing what the discredited research claimed to conclude. Guns in the home, where no previous event has already happened, is a virtual impossible data set to define and you cannot use a biased data set that presupposes the event will happen by evaluating only historic events where it did. We've also seen that self-defense uses of a gun are highly successful, with only a negligible percent of those uses having to end in death.

Objective 2 is "to "Stop 'Bad Apple' Gun Dealers" – the 5 percent of gun dealers that supply 90 percent of all crime guns." They claim that "research shows that 90% of guns used in crimes were supplied by just 5% of dealers."[155] The problem is that it isn't the "same" set of dealers comprising that percentage year after year. This comes from a 2000 report from the ATF titled *Commerce in Firearms*.[156] It covers the distribution of crime gun traces among current dealers in 1998. When considering all retail dealers (retail gun dealers and pawnbrokers), 7.2 percent of dealers accounted for 89.5 percent of the traces, which meant they had as little as 2 traces lead back to them. This comprised of 6,056 dealers. If you really cut off the fat though: 1,020 dealers (1.2%) had 10 or more traces comprising 57.4 percent of all traces; 332 dealers (0.4%) had 25 or more traces comprising 39.6 percent of all traces; and only 132 dealers (0.2%) had 50 or more traces, which comprised 27.2 percent of all traces. If you exclude the pawnbrokers, like the Brady Campaign did, it results in only 99 retail gun dealers (0.1%) accounting for 30.4 percent of all crime gun traces.

I'm not suggesting there isn't a problem "in 1998", but it does not imply that 5 percent of dealers are "bad apples." The statistics suggest there are clearly "bad apple" dealers out there, but it is not as widespread among dealers as the Brady Campaign is trying to suggest in their campaign. I think it might be hard to suggest that because a dealer at some point in their history sold 2 guns that were later used in crimes in 1998 that they are somehow law breaking gun dealers. The following year, it is likely to be an almost entirely different set of dealers who had 2 traces back to them, and not the same set of dealers at all. The longer you are in business, the higher probability that a gun you sold will be used in a crime, it doesn't mean the dealer broke the law. To be very clear, every year the list of dealers with 2 traces will change and not be the same set of dealers that the Brady Campaign claims are a specific set of "bad apple" repeat offenders. You have to look at which dealers are repeatedly on the list, and the number of trace guns per year, to evaluate who is a "bad apple" and The Brady Campaign does not address that.

Even then, having 10 crime gun traces could be merely circumstantial to location, such as being Chuck's Gun Store in Chicago where crime rates are really high. In fact, the Brady Campaign brings that up in another version of the claim on one of their website pages titled *Why Do Nearly One in Five Crime Guns in Chicago Originate at Just Four Gun Dealers?*[157] In reality, half of one percent are probably "bad apple" dealers, but it isn't actually an epidemic like the Brady Campaign makes it out to be. It's just not the same "5 percent" of gun dealers on the list year after year. All that report suggests is that, in any given year, roughly 7.2 percent of all gun dealers will have, at some point in their history, sold 2 guns that were used in crimes that year. Only 14.3 percent of all dealers had ever sold a gun that was used in crime in 1998. In other words, only 14 percent of dealers accounted for 100 percent of gun traces in 1998.

Why did I highlight "1998" above? The research they cite comes from a report dated February 2000. Due to the Tiahrt Amendment blocking the ATF from sharing source data on crime guns with anyone outside of law enforcement, there is no publicly available data to trace crime guns back to dealers since 2003. The amendment was intended to cut down on politically motivated lawsuits against firearms dealers.[158] The Brady Campaign is not only misinterpreting the data, they are also merely "assuming" the data would be consistent more than a decade later. The whole argument is pure fallacious propaganda either way. Speaking of politically motivated lawsuits, let's look at a lawsuit specifically dismissed as being such.

In 2014, as a result of the Aurora Colorado shooting by James Holmes, on behalf of the parent and step-parent of one of the shooting victims, Brady Center lawyers filed suit against the companies Lucky Gunner LLC, The Sportsman's

Guide and BTP Arms owner Brian Platt. These were the sources from whom Holmes purchased the ammunition, magazines, and body armor he used in the shooting. In 2015, the judge in the case dismissed the suit on the grounds that such a lawsuit is in violation of both Colorado law and the federal Protection of Lawful Commerce in Arms Act, because the guns and ammunition obtained from the online companies worked as claimed. He also ordered the plaintiffs to pay the legal costs of the defendants, which came to $203,000. Judge Matsch commented, "It is apparent that this case was filed to pursue the political purposes of the Brady Center," further adding that it "appears to be more of an opportunity to propagandize the public and stigmatize the defendants than to obtain a court order."[159]

So what about Objective number 1, "a policy focus to 'Finish the Job' so that life-saving Brady background checks are applied to all gun sales." Well, results do tend to suggest that the background checks required of the 1993 Brady Handgun Violence Prevention Act have had a positive effect overall.

By 2000 the background checks on FFLs, which were required under the Brady Act, had prohibited more than 500,000 attempts by prohibited individuals from buying firearms from FFLs.[160] The Federal Bureau of Investigations claims that there have been 1,258,427 denials through the NICS from November 30, 1998 to November 30, 2015.[161] The Brady Campaign cites statistics from the Bureau of Justice Statistics, which includes both NICS denials by the FBI as well as state and local agencies from the pre-ban period of 1994 through December 31, 2012, to be 2.4 million.[162] I'm going to go with the FBI data here, because I do not know the specific state or local statutes that prohibited a person beyond their restriction on the NICS list. They may be oppressive restrictions not supported by the federal government overall.

Regardless, we can still conclude that roughly 1.3 million prohibited people were denied sales through the NICS because of the Brady Bill. Let me clarify that because some, such as the NRA, argue that this does not represent evidence of success. One of their arguments is that criminals will not obey the laws and thus this regulation does not affect them. However, the law is designed to stop prohibited individuals from legally buying firearms through FFLs. At least 1.3 million prohibited individuals still attempted to legally buy firearms and were prohibited from doing so as of the end of 2015. Their other argument is that some criminals will get guns anyway. Yes, a portion of those denied may have still been able to acquire those weapons through private party transactions or other means, but that adds no valid argument that the law did not successfully prohibit over 1.3 million prohibited people from legally buying firearms through dealers as intended.

The Bill appears to have been successful, but as we've already seen, there is a lot of room for interpretation in exactly "who" is a prohibited person. If background requirements were to be conducted in a biased manner regarding groups who are prohibited (such as non-Protestants), the benefits would cease to exist. It makes me wonder why an additional 1 million people were denied at state and local levels beyond the NICS checks on a federal level.

It needs to be pointed out that this does not mean registration, permits, or tracking procedures for firearms are being logically condoned or supported along with the Brady Bill's background check success. These different gun control measures need to be evaluated independently on their own merits. It is not uncommon for a group to argue against background checks and then cite the adverse affects of registration to support their argument. Those are two different arguments.

I can find no valid argument or statistics which support that serial numbers on firearms have a correlation to gun crimes, nor any correlation to prohibiting the Second Amendment rights of the people. They do appear to have some benefit in solving gun crimes after the fact, thus I would have to conclude that, overall, serial numbers on firearms fulfill the better good of society while not prohibiting the rights of the people. I can find no statistical evidence to support the argument that registration or permits provide any benefit to keeping firearms out of the hands of prohibited people or reduces gun crime, especially with background checks already done. Though registrations and permits might also help with the solving of pre-existing gun crimes, there does appear a valid argument that registration and permits give a lot of power to discriminate and disarm specific groups or all of society, much like what happened in England. This may excessively prohibit the rights of the people beyond any gain for the public good. We've already looked at actual standing laws that fit this description. I do believe there is a way to provide tracking after a crime while avoiding registrations...but you'll have to wait until Chapter 8 to hear it.

Looking at the Brady Campaign during the length of time I spent writing this book, my perceptions of them have changed slightly. Don't get me wrong, it still turns my stomach to read some of the claims they try to make. The recent lawsuit seems to reflect upon their intentions derogatorily. Going through their entire website, though, they do seem to provide some credible statistics geared at areas that mostly do not appear to be intended to be a gun grab. Some of the issues are real issues that should be addressed. Suicide is a problem we should seek to avoid, regardless of the tool used. Negligent shootings are a problem we should seek to avoid. Cutting the number of gun deaths in half by 2025 is an admirable goal, so long as it doesn't increase non-justifiable homicides by other tools at the same time as a result.

Though they are distorting some data to support their objectives, I am no longer convinced they are doing it maliciously like Everytown for Gun Safety and Mass Shooting Tracker. I think they might actually believe that all the data they are referencing is valid and their conclusions sound. It very well may be that those running The Brady Campaign to Prevent Gun Violence have an abundance of cardiac muscle and a deficiency in grey and white matter. They definitely appear to have toned down the full gun ban rhetoric over the years. They've done and said some stupid things, but they do also provide some good to society overall. The Brady Bill resulting in the NICS background checks has proven to fulfill its intended purpose. Their argument to extend those checks to private party transactions appears sound.

National Rifle Association

Though I have brought up the Brady Campaign for both good and bad issues, it would still be unbalanced if I didn't also bring up the National Rifle Association. The National Rifle Association was originally created in 1871 to "promote and encourage rifle shooting on a scientific basis." In 1934 the NRA formed the Legislative Affairs Division due to repeated attacks on Second Amendment rights.[163] They have tremendous lobbying power which is praised by many pro-gun advocates and detested by many anti-gun supporters. In some circles, they do have a reputation for creating fear in their members in order to bring in donations.[164] They also have a reputation for denouncing any and all gun control measures. I do have to admit that reading Wayne LaPierre's comments in an editorial to USA today, quoted on the NRA website, he does seem to use a lot of very poor logic in denouncing a universal background check, which we've already confirmed has been used successfully regarding FFLs.[165] There are so many issues with his statement, I'm going to have to include the whole thing:

> It seems so reasonable. In the minds of many, "universal background checks" for firearms transactions sounds like a good idea.
>
> But is it really? No.
>
> No idea is good if it doesn't work. No legislation is reasonable if it fails to accomplish its purported goal — to prevent violent criminals and the mentally ill from acquiring firearms.
>
> Criminals won't participate in a "universal" system. They'll always steal or get their guns, and everything else they want, on the black market. Reasonable people know that criminals will never be part of the "universe."
>
> Even when felons do try to buy a gun and are flagged by the system, they're almost never stopped. In 2010, out of 76,000 denied purchasers, only 44 were prosecuted nationwide for illegally attempting to

purchase a gun. That universal failure endangers us all.

The mentally ill won't be included in the system. For the past 20 years, government has failed to include records even for those who have been judged mentally ill by a court.

It's unreasonable to assume that the federal government will require medical professionals — who treat those suffering from autism, schizophrenia, anger management issues and more — to add records of their patients to a massive federal database.

Imagine the outcry over privacy rights! Those records will never be part of the "universe."

The only "universe" will be law-abiding, sane, decent, non-threatening Americans who have already participated in the check system for two decades now. It will be the names of good people — and only their names — that will go into a database, subjected to potential federal registration and abuse of privacy.

No, there is nothing at all "universal" about the proposed background check — and nothing reasonable about legislation that doesn't include criminals and the mentally disturbed in its "universe."

The nearly 5 million members of the NRA support what would make us all safer: the immediate protection of all of our schoolchildren, fixing our broken mental health system, and certain prosecution of every criminal with a gun.

> Those are good ideas that thoughtful Americans, responsible members of Congress and law-abiding gun owners can support.

This seems a very weak argument at best, and extremely manipulative at worst. After reading this book, I hope "reasonable people" will know to search for evidence themselves as opposed to making assumptions. It is true that criminals will acquire guns through illegal means, and we've already seen how presently having no law requiring background checks on private party transactions is not a loophole, but a different law is still being broken by the prohibited person (assuming they already know they are prohibited) and not by the seller who is unaware of the buyer's history. Thus, this is currently one of the very methods LaPierre is referencing when he says criminals will always get their guns. If criminals were forced into the black market to acquire their guns, that actually means the universal background check would have prohibited criminals from buying them in private party transactions. In fact, we noted above how the background checks required by FFLs have prohibited at least 1.3 million attempts by prohibited individuals from buying firearms from 1993 to present. LaPierre himself just admitted the system prohibited 76,000 transactions in 2010. This goes to show that prohibited individuals did still attempt to buy guns legally and were denied. Did some of those go on to acquire guns through more difficult means? Possibly yes, but that has no bearing on the legislation's merit itself as it did prevent these prohibited individuals from acquiring a firearm, at least from one specific source. Is that not what most people admit the intent of legislation is, stopping prohibited people from purchasing firearms while not restricting law abiding citizens?

If it prohibits criminals from obtaining firearms as easily, while not restricting any private citizen, then the benefits to society may outweigh the costs. The fact that criminals are not arrested after being caught by the present background check system, though a valid and important argument to make on its own, also has no bearing on the fact that those transactions were in fact caught and stopped a sale to a prohibited individual. Any lack of enforcement of the law is a different argument. It may be true that those mentally deficient are not always reported and thus detected under a background check due to restrictions on release of medical records, but the results of the legislation do not require that it has a 100 percent success rate at flagging all prohibited persons in order to have an impact. If it prohibits only restricted felons from purchasing a firearm, the legislation could be deemed successful.

The other error LaPierre makes is that a universal background check system is not the same as a registration or licensing system where purchaser's names are recorded in a database. Those are two independently different types of gun control measures, as we've previously addressed, and LaPierre is trying to redirect you with a straw man to an entirely different argument; which is that registration and licensing punish regular citizens and inhibit their privacy while doing nothing to criminals. Statistically, LaPierre may be correct in his "redirected" argument here as well. However, the original Brady Handgun Violence Prevention Act did not require either registration or licensing, which is why the Brady Campaign immediately proposed a subsequent bill in 1994 that was dubbed Brady 2, which would have required these things if it had passed.[166] It did not pass.

It is entirely possible to extend a universal background check to private party transactions with the required database containing no more than prohibited individuals without any other citizen required to have their purchase documented. For LaPierre to suggest that background checks for prohibited persons don't include criminals, when evidence including his own stated statistic clearly shows they already have, is nothing short of ludicrous. I would also like to point out that "certain prosecution of every criminal with a gun" would include any person, including an NRA member, who is breaking any type of firearm regulation in any way. This would include anyone who breaks laws directed at guns themselves, such as carrying without a required permit, having inadvertently converted your AR15 into an "assault weapon" due to too many excluded features in the state of California, New York, Connecticut or maybe owning a handgun without a permit in New York, and not merely acts of crimes involving firearms such as rape, robbery and murder. Though the comments above do appear to be extremist (or at least the extreme use of straw man arguments to take an extreme position), at least they offset the extremism by groups such as Everytown for Gun Safety and Mass Shooting Tracker. Still, though the debate may be both polarized and yet balanced by the offsetting extremes, this feeds and perpetuates the problem and does not resolve it.

I really don't think it is necessary to continue pointing out the extremism of the NRA, you could write an entire NRA "Encyclopædia Britannica" set on regulations they have opposed. I don't like their extremism; I don't like their fear mongering to raise money. However, they also do a lot of good for society in regards to firearm training and education…and it is not a trivial amount. The United States could definitely use more firearms education. If the supposed "war on guns" were to end, and both sides came to an accord, I do believe the NRA could go back to providing beneficial services to society. I do believe it would be possible to see a day where the NRA actually gets grant money from the federal government for firearm education, as opposed to the NRA using fear mongering tactics to raise enough money to fight the federal government.

(I have kept the section on the NRA short, not because of favorable sentiment for them or fear of recourse from them, but because going into great detail regarding that which most people are already aware kind of feels like pissing up a rope.)

After everything I've seen researching this book, none of these groups will get my membership or my donations unless they were to drastically change their ideologies over time. All seem to perpetuate excessive fear while denying statistical evidence regarding firearms. How is that truly helping anyone?

𝕮𝖍𝖆𝖕𝖙𝖊𝖗 VIII

Conclusion

"They who can give up essential liberty to obtain a little temporary safety, deserve neither liberty nor safety." – Benjamin Franklin [1]

We have looked at the true genesis of the Second Amendment right, and have found that it was intended as both an individual right and a collective right. We have seen the Courts, and thus the people's, impression of that wax and wane over time; at first supporting only the collective right and only recently confirming the individual right, with an almost strange newly adopted perception that a collective right does not exist now that we've acknowledged the individual right. We have seen how the concept of the militia was originally created and has been repeatedly restructured over time. The most recent major change to the militia created the National Guard of the states, but still left in existence a "reserve" militia composed of the people. There is still a collective right of the people to keep and bear arms as members of that militia. We have seen clear evidence of how the individual right is necessary for the collective right to exist in this case, and that a collective right was absolutely intended to provide the citizens of this country the security of having the tools necessary when and if the government our founding fathers set up ceased to function as an effective Democratic Republic and veered off into tyranny and oppression by taking measures not supported by the majority of the people.

We have watched legislation go from requiring the right to keep and bear arms being mandatory for all who would comprise the militia of the people; to having the U.S. government argue in court that the Second Amendment secured the right to military weapons only; to doing an entire flip and creating legislation banning weapons that are even "styled" like military weapons; to an overall stance that there is no collective right at all, at times actually ridiculing those citizens who believe the collective right exists or believe it could ever be effective against our government with its current military. We have witnessed our government presenting legislation regarding the Second Amendment as though the right was designed merely for "hunting and sporting" purposes, and have seen evidence to show that ideology was declined for inclusion in constructing the amendment. We have seen clear shifts of power from the Legislative to the Executive branch. The President can create and indefinitely maintain participation in international military campaigns without a Congressional Declaration of War. There have been mild shifts of power by Congress from the U.S. Government to international organizations like the United Nations and NATO.

There are other events and actions that suggest some moderate tyranny either is or has been placed on the people and that government power has been abused. The equivalent of military force was used to raid a compound of people who were never afforded the luxury of Fifth

Amendment rights before such a great measure of force was imposed upon them. The United States now has the standing army a majority of our founding fathers feared. To maintain this requires the constant creation of an enemy who is perceived to constantly and imminently threaten our national sovereignty; it has most likely truly created that enemy as a self-fulfilling prophecy. The fear of exactly such an enemy has led to substantially larger "secret" agencies in our government such as the National Security Agency (NSA) and subsequently "secret" lists such as the Terrorist Watch List. Evidence shows that these government secrecies have already been implemented in a way that violates citizen's Constitutional Rights. We've seen President Obama use these as a call for gun control measures to restrict Second Amendment rights in spite of Fifth Amendment protections of Due Process. We've seen President Obama reference gun laws of other nations he suggests we should adopt which would ultimately segregate Second Amendment rights by class, needing a high ranking member of society to vouch for you; laws which also prohibit the use of firearms for self-defense purposes. We have had federal restrictions on classes of firearms that had virtually no correlation to any statistical evidence that they were used on a tangible scale to commit violent gun crimes. Though the government mandated report on the first "Assault Weapons" ban suggested it had no impact towards its intended goal of reducing violent crimes over the 10 year period and might only ever have undetectable effects if continued, we constantly see segments of our government re-propose the exact same legislation.

Though there is definitely a sound argument to be made for an increasing fear of government tyranny and oppression, evidence does not suggest the government is acting wholly outside the desire of the majority of its citizens. What we do see is evidence that the politically aligned media have great power in distorting the perceptions of the people, and therefore the demand of their elected representatives to take specific actions. We've seen how organizations like the National Rifle Association, Everytown for Gun Safety, the Law Center to Prevent Gun Violence, the Brady Campaign to Prevent Gun Violence, Americans for Responsible Solutions, and Mass Shooting Tracker all feed the media with adequate misrepresentations of statistical data, semantic manipulation and a mass of fallacious propaganda to drive the people's perceptions to the extreme poles of debate on an issue through emotionally charged misinformation. This leads to extremist laws bouncing back and forth depending on which political party has the greatest pull at the moment. If the people do not have accurate information, they cannot make an accurate vote. The more fear the people feel, the more rights they tend to give up to vanquish the perceived threat. This is exactly how tyranny begins. The more rights people willingly give up in the shifts back and forth, the more likely one of the political parties will ultimately step up to abuse that lack of rights in such a way as the majority of the people justifiably feel the government action was against their collective will. That then gets reinforced against the masses through military force.

This impact has created two groups of people which hinder the Second Amendment debate. There are those who want their guns at any cost. They argue for absolutely no gun laws out of fear of government tyranny, in spite of existing facts that they can be moderately burdened through regulation without removing the right. Then there are those that want all guns out of society at any cost. They appear to have no regard for future consequences and how they affect the rights of the people regarding self-defense both individually and collectively, driven from a fear of tyranny from other citizens, in spite of existing facts that firearms are not the real problem and may only need to be moderately, but appropriately, regulated. Each side tries to present their arguments as though they are presenting unbiased evidence in an honest debate, but they mostly just distort data to try to support their true underlying belief and disguise it as though they do not have an extremist agenda. It is always the extremist views that get the most media attention. Everyone not on the polar extremes of that debate suffers the consequences.

At the present moment, however, there is no real evidence to suggest that the government is defying the will of the majority. It is still more of a media propaganda problem, misinforming the people in regards to pertinent facts. Considering a justifiable Insurrection against the government of the United States, at the present time, would be nothing other than an act of mere rebellion. Unfortunately though, the overall trend does appear to be headed in the direction of government tyranny. Though the trend in the Judicial has recently been favorable for the Second Amendment, the Legislative appears mostly divided between the extreme ideologies and the trend from the Executive appears to be headed in the direction of increased restrictions. Since the Judicial power tends to trail the Legislative and Executive by a large time gap, the current dynamic is probably a bad combination for the people overall.

We need to accept that a gun is a tool, nothing more. A dangerous tool if abused, but still just a tool. Many people do not want to accept this, and there is a reason why. The moment we accept this as truth, we have to address our societal delusions. We have to address what makes an otherwise normal and well balanced human being suddenly decide to murder people. We have to address what it is in our society that leads to such behavior. We seriously have to consider whether we too could one day succumb to a feeling that we need to kill other people for some reason, though we truly believe that we are personally sane and a good human being. We need to address the real delusions behind our belief systems. We need to seriously ask ourselves why Christian hates Muslim and Muslim hates Christian because they each believe in some "deity" or ancient set of writings. We need to seriously ask ourselves why there is a segment of society where white hates black and black hates white. We need to seriously ask ourselves whether perpetuating childish fantasies like Santa Claus, the Easter Bunny and Tooth Fairies are really fun and harmless builders of imagination, or perpetuating an acceptance of delusion in adults as they grow older if we do not clearly make distinctions between fun fables and facts. We need to ask ourselves Economic questions such as why we adhere to specific forms of government; such as the pursuit of material goods inherent in Capitalism or the somewhat necessary disregard for unequal initiative or talent inherent in the pursuit of mass equality in Socialism. Are either perspectives actually good or evil, or merely differences of opinion? The way I chose to describe them is even merely one opinion of their characteristics. We need to ask ourselves why, in such a modern society, some groups of people feel they need to commit crimes in order to merely survive.

We need to ask ourselves why, as human beings, we fear that which we do not understand instead of desiring to gain knowledge regarding that which we do not know. These are the solutions not only to understanding gun violence, but violence overall. Once we truly understand it, then we can talk about solutions. Until we honestly admit to ourselves what the real problem is, we're really just arguing about what color to paint the guillotine. If all guns disappeared today, violence and crime would continue. The underlying problem we refuse to address is that a tangible percentage of our society suffers with psychosis...and the remaining percentage suffers with the consequences.

Having looked at the overall evidence for and against the issues in regards to a debate on the Second Amendment versus how much of that Right to set aside for the benefit of society overall in implementing firearm legislation, what follows is my proposal for reconstructing the gun laws in this country.

Extend background checks to private party transactions

Create an addition to the NICS database where potential buyer and seller go online, enter identifying information, and get an immediate verification from the database with a unique verification number good for 30 days. There can be no charge for these as they may need to be repeated frequently before an individual buyer and individual seller come to terms and it cannot unduly burden the buyer or seller financially. Buyer must go through a background check; seller is merely getting a valid verification number linked to their identity. The buyer's and seller's information and the verification numbers are printable by home computer, or a company that can do so if the buyer or seller does not possess a computer, internet and printer. These must be printed out along with copy of photo ID and provided to the other party in advance or at time of private party sale. Seller then checks database to make sure name and verification number of buyer match before completing the sale. This should be even quicker than the initial request, as the match between ID and verification number should already be linked in the system during those 30 days. Seller must document the serial number or international ID of the firearm on their copy of the buyer's information. Buyer and seller must keep the printout and copy of photo ID for X number of years (maybe the same as tax records.) You close out your verification number for the sale by entering the other party's verification number in the NICS system. Though it will link a buyer and seller, the firearm itself is not reported. These verification numbers could be required to be present in private party online classified ads to buy and sell, same with an FFL license number for online sales by FFLs. All this can be accomplished in advance no matter where the private party transaction ultimately takes place, with only a very minor inconvenience to proceed with the sale. It is substantially less inconvenient than having to go through an FFL for all private party transactions and the repercussions that has on limiting an efficient, fair and yet safe market. Will two people who are willing to break the law occasionally come together to conduct an illegal sale? Of course, but this still reduces the number of sales where a seller would not agree to sell to a prohibited person, but ultimately did so not knowing the buyer was prohibited. And that is the intent, a reduction of sales to those who are prohibited people.

Let people provide this service at gun shows: search database, check ID, and make the printout. Set a reasonable fee that can be charged by private vendors for this service at a kiosk. The weapon itself is never part of the verification process other than in the first sale by an FFL. The record keeping requirement in this manner does not serve as a registration or tracking measure directly on private citizens and only as an ability to trace the path of the sales after the fact if a specific firearm was used in a crime at a later date. This would appear to fulfill the United Nations desire that countries establish tracking mechanisms, without actually violating the rights of citizens prior to a crime being committed. It also puts an end to the ludicrous comparison to the No-Fly List and the problems that restricting "suspected" criminals without Due Process, thus vacating Fifth Amendment rights, would set in legal precedent. Citizens should be notified the moment they are first placed in the NICS database as restricted to allow them to seek redress prior to attempting to buy a weapon and being denied.

Again, this does not mean direct registrations or tracking. Historically, registrations for tracking purposes have been shown to often be abused in ways which become avenues to restrict or illegally revoke the Second Amendment rights of law abiding citizens. This would provide the necessary background checks, and ultimately reflect that Dick sold something to Jane, but wouldn't disclose exactly what was transferred. A trace on a specific weapon would thus have to begin at an FFL with their initial sale, followed by requests for the required supporting sales information from each private party in succession throughout the trace. It does not, however, allow the government to know that Jane now has three AR-15s and one 1911.

Get rid of virtually all current "assault weapons" restrictions (in states that still have them)

Most restrictions by the "features test" definition merely limit the accuracy and precision of the weapon. Doing so is ridiculously ignorant. What the legislation adopting features test definitions are actually arguing for is less accurate and precise weapons for everyone. Accuracy and precision do not directly correlate to lethality. Someone might intend to shoot someone threatening their life, the inaccuracies in the weapon thus leading them to miss and shoot an innocent bystander. A more accurate and precise gun is a "safer" gun.

We should stop using the phrases "assault rifle" and "assault weapon" entirely. A rifle is fully automatic, select fire, semi-automatic or manual single shot (bolt and lever action etc.)...period. "Assault" is defined by the intent of the person using the weapon, not by the weapon itself.

Folding stocks and barrel lengths under 16" should be allowed; these are actually concealment issues. Either make concealment illegal without a concealed permit, or extend concealed carry laws to include rifles and shotguns or create a second class of concealment. Strengthen laws for illegally concealing a rifle or shotgun. Shorter barrels might be suitable for home defense scenarios due to confined space, especially for a shotgun. Though a rifle arguably could be too much gun for home self-defense due to over-penetration, those wishing to own only one firearm to suit multiple purposes are inconvenienced by that prohibition while the gain to society by the prohibition is extremely limited. Other than initial concealment, it adds no more additional utility to a criminal than it does to a civilian responding in self-defense. It is easier to conceal a large handgun than a small rifle or shotgun. They are all more potentially fatal at close range, which is what illegal concealment is intended to get you; within close range to a target.

Telescoping Stocks, pistol grips, additional front grips, flash suppressors and muzzle brakes (and thus threaded barrels) all are accuracy and precision enhancing features. A more accurate and precise weapon is a "safer" weapon. They are as good for self-defense as for criminal acts and vice versa. The greatest benefit of Economic utility in those features still lies with the self-defense shooter attempting to save their own life.

A grenade launcher really isn't part of the weapon itself. It is another weapon attached to the weapon. However, this is really a destructive devices issue, not a firearm feature issue. A bayonet is pretty much the same scenario. A dagger on a rifle is really just a heavy spear.

It does appear the use of "machine pistols" in gun crimes was reduced by the Federal Assault Weapons Ban. Though it is still predominantly dependent upon magazine capacity, when "assault weapons" were used in crimes it was predominantly "machine pistols." It might be more of a benefit for society than a burden to have a ban on "machine pistols" exclusively, both fully automatic and semi-automatic. This is specifically in reference to "machine pistol" type firearms, not handguns with magazines in the grip.

Proper training can only go so far to alleviate the problems with an inaccurate or imprecise weapon. You can never be more accurate than your tool will allow. The ultimate argument around the use of these weapons by an active shooter is really about the capacity to fire multiple rounds from an accurate weapon, so:

Magazine Capacity

I have been unable to find a single piece of evidence that truly confirms that magazine capacity has anything to do with lethality, even if turns out to be a valid statistic that they were "used" in half of all "mass shootings" and not merely present. Even the statistic now often cited suggesting more people die in an event with a large-capacity magazine is ultimately flawed. It may be that shooters who practice shooting more frequently and are thus more accurate may be more likely to own traditional 30 round capacity magazines when choosing to commit a crime. In fact, as a corollary to the traditional argument; the larger the capacities of each magazine, the more ammunition the shooter may lose access to if the magazine fails. That is actually a benefit to the victims in an active shooter scenario, the loss of implementable ammunition by the shooter.

Though a trained shooter can fire three 10 round magazines or one 30 round magazine from an AR-15 style rifle with literally only fractions of a second difference, the untrained shooter cannot. Therefore 10 round magazine restrictions may in fact have a beneficial effect on society overall to slow the shooting from an untrained shooter in an active shooter scenario. In this particular case, the subsequent burden on a lawful user is overcome by proper training. If you are going to use your weapon for self-defense, there is no argument that you should not have proper training in its use. That is a responsibility or burden that falls on you personally.

Background checks on all sales of all rifle magazines above 10 rounds should be adopted in cases where the detachable magazine is not an integral part of the design of the rifle. In the case of many handguns, the design of the weapon itself is around a magazine capacity in the grip as an integral part of the weapon design. As such, any handgun magazine that has the ability to hold more rounds than the manufacturer designed should be subject to a background check at time of purchase. The burden may be placed on items such as single round extensions for existing magazines, but it does not unduly burden the initial design intent of the handgun. This could also be circumvented in ways such as buying a government model 1911 magazine for use in a commander model 1911, but this doesn't go beyond the magazine capacity of the original design of the 1911. A 20 round magazine for a 1911 would subsequently need a background check. What we can, however, achieve with a method such as this is restrict a prohibited person who may already have access to a rifle or handgun from subsequently being able to purchase a large number of higher capacity magazines just prior to committing an intended crime.

Banning 30 round magazines entirely appears to have very limited hopes for success in achieving a specific goal while not over burdening the individual's rights. A 30 round rifle magazine could be prohibited in regards to public carry as could the handgun magazines in excess of manufacturer design, and yet be unregulated for home property use. I want to be very distinct here in what I'm suggesting; detachable rifle magazines capable of holding more than 10 rounds which are loaded with ammunition, regardless if they are in the weapon or not, should be prohibited in public only. A self-defense shooter should have every available round conceivable at their disposal when trying to save their own life or the life of a loved one from a life threatening attack on personal property, after also acquiring proper training of course. They have the same right to self-defense in public as at home, but the benefit to society vs. the burden on individuals by restricting them in public is substantially greater than the same evaluation on private property. Again, that burden placed on public carry is mostly overcome by training. You could argue that if no "large-capacity" magazines existed at all then criminals couldn't find them illegally. That may be a valid argument, but if you really think you could round up all the existing "large-capacity" magazines in existence in the United States such that the premise would be true and thus the argument sound, I think you're highly delusional.

Training does not mostly overcome the time sensitive restriction a bullet button creates. It is designed expressly to complicate the functional use of the weapon. With the magazine capacity restrictions in place, they should not be legally required.

Machine Guns

In regards to full-auto assault rifles and (non-machine pistol) sub-machine guns specifically; historically they were rarely used in homicides even prior to the ban, and typically only saw appreciable use during Prohibition and mildly during the Miami "drug wars." Even then, it was really a magazine capacity issue and not the speed of fire. Speed of fire between full-auto and semi-auto is negligible. Worse, it really is quite easy to convert many semi-auto rifles to full-auto fire anyway; yet we rarely hear of it being done. Segregating between the two truly creates a false sense of perception thus resulting in a false sense of security by banning only one. The real fear of machine guns is that they "sound" more terrifying when fired. One might argue that full-auto is intended to get more rounds on target faster, and if you're SWAT maybe you have trained to really implement that fraction of a second gain. In reality, for the average person it just promotes a "spray and pray" shooting approach which has been shown to be less effective. If feels less predictable and thus scarier, but I'd rather take my chances with a shooter spray firing from a full auto sub-machine gun with a 30 round magazine, than a shooter with 30 rounds and a semi-auto taking time to precisely aim at specific targets. Unless you're getting a free endless supply of ammo, I don't know why anyone would prefer full-auto. If you truly believe you "need" a full-auto rifle then this is the one scenario where I think the penis envy argument might actually hold true; but who are we to judge.

I guess I should also note that those Prohibition era Tommy Guns, being sub-machine guns, fired .45 ACP rounds and not the smaller .223. Though they weren't any more likely to kill people overall merely due to fully automatic fire, they could arguably do a lot more property damage in a short period of time. That's also bad for society. That said, I think the magazine capacity suggestions above regarding public carry would remove the issue with assault rifles and sub-machine guns. I think the ban on assault rifles and (non machine pistol) sub-machine guns should be lifted as it has set a bad precedent for irrational gun control. I think they should require registrations, such as the NFA restrictions currently in place, but without a lengthy "tax stamp" request process. The registration is not because they are more lethal but merely because they truly do appear to have been mostly used for terrorizing the public through their irrational excess fears of full auto fire. They aren't successful at creating more homicides, but they are successful in creating more public panic when used. I can really see no sound argument to then legalize larger, non hand held, higher caliber machine guns for civilian use. In that particular case, the benefit to society by a ban appears to outweigh the Second Amendment burden placed on an individual. If you think you personally need to own a weapon to bring to a battle that can shoot down an aircraft in self-defense; that aircraft might not be your biggest problem.

Ammunition

Armor piercing rounds which can be fired from a handgun should require a background check. There should be extended penalties for use of armor piercing rounds in a violent gun crime.

Suppressors

There is no evidence to suggest that a suppressor, being a firearm accessory, is protected by the Second Amendment. However, rarely do they ever make a firearm silent. Even though they are extremely easy to make, they are still rarely used in crimes. Making them easier to own could be beneficial to society in allowing more people to become proficient and trained with their firearms by reducing the problem with noise ordinances making it hard to have firearm ranges in convenient locations. Suppressors should be removed from the NFA and require only background checks. There should be extended penalties for use of suppressors while committing crimes, and at present there are.

Body Armor

The rights for civilian use of body armor should be federally secured. Body armor (at least rarely) kills anyone on its own. It isn't a weapon, it is a defense to a weapon and as such should not require a background check. In fact, those prohibited from owning firearms should still be entitled to some forms of self-defense if being shot at when not committing a crime, especially since they really don't have the legal right to shoot back. Banning body armor would not resolve any real crime concerns or limit overall deaths, as criminals could still illegally acquire and use these items while the law abiding citizen could not. Should a young person with a felony, possibly going back to school to change their life at a community college or vocational school which might be in a bad neighborhood, be restricted from carrying books in a Kevlar lined backpack merely because they are a felon? Would that not be considered body armor? There should be extended penalties for use of body armor while committing certain crimes, and at present there are for violent crimes and drug trafficking.

Make Concealed and Open Carry federally secured

Require a proficiency course and mandatory "shall issue" licensing for both concealed and open carry in public. Firearms on public property would require no personal licensing, except in certain limited conditions such as when children are in the home (mentioned below.) Private businesses should be able to prohibit carry at their locations. For public locations we should then re-evaluate our restrictions on carry between open carry and concealed carry. As example, there appears to be a sound argument for allowing concealed carry on public school property. However, open carry on school property might create a constant sense of panic and fear among children (and Liberal extremists.) In this way, proficiency is established in ALL public carry of firearms, concealed and open carry.

This is not an argument that more guns are good. This is an argument that more people proficient with firearm use is good, and gun owners not proficient in firearm use is bad. It is an argument that a perceived armed and trained populace is better than a perceived unarmed populace in regards to dissuading criminals from proceeding with a violent crime. There should be extended penalties for licensees who subsequently commit violent gun crimes.

Offer free federally funded basic firearm training programs for anyone who wants to own a firearm

This allows the people to acquire the proper training, without stigma or fear of being ostracized, thus overall reducing the ignorance in firearm mechanics and use in firearm owners. It should not be an embarrassment to seek firearm training. It will also reduce the fear of firearms due to ignorance. Expecting the people who would make up, what is now part of the reserve militia, to know how to properly use a firearm does appear to be the understanding of the framers of the Second Amendment. This should be federally funded, as it is a societal good. I'm going to go out on a limb here and guess that making the changes I suggest would free up a lot of excess funds currently being spent which could be used to provide this free service.

Legal recourse for the negligent death of a child

Penalties for the negligent death of a child or possession of a firearm by a (possibly pre-teen) child should be severe. We need more firearm education for children, especially in a home with a weapon. We need research on more ways a household with a child can maintain security of the weapon without the need to fully restrict that weapons immediate use for self-defense. If we make the changes I suggest, we could focus more efforts towards research on these issues.

Most of my suggestions are designed towards pre-crime education and self-defense preparation, and post-crime restrictions of rights (background checks, punishments etc.). Even a "perceived" armed and trained populace can have beneficial effects on reducing crime, even if the majority of lawful citizens do not choose to do so. Peer pressure has an amazing effect on controlling societies. I do not believe these suggested laws would turn the United States into the Wild West.

There is no arguable gun law which could truly stop a person from legally buying a firearm and then later becoming suicidal using that firearm, except a complete ban of firearms. That is not acceptable under the Second Amendment, nor does it do justice to those suffering with depression.

There is no arguable gun law which could truly stop a person from legally buying a firearm and then later becoming homicidal using that firearm, except a complete ban of firearms. That is not acceptable under the Second Amendment, nor does it do justice to those suffering from other emotional issues or ideologies; bigotry, anger, delusions, extremism, etc.

Many of our current gun laws have virtually no correlation to reducing violent gun crimes. They appear to be valid examples of a wanton and causeless restraint of the will of the subject. I'm not going to argue that these are "common sense" gun control laws that I propose here, as common sense is merely a semantics trick which intends to place a value judgment on one's own beliefs. What I offer here is a solution which I believe the facts appear to support without resorting to "wanton and causeless restraint."

Here are some of the problems I see with the no gun control clan holding an extreme "shall not be infringed" position

First off, historic precedent repeatedly shows that it can be infringed. You don't see prisoners open carrying Glocks in prison, do you? Individual Rights cannot be infringed without Due Process, but they can be infringed. Restrictions on machine guns have been ruled not to infringe the Second Amendment right to keep and bear arms because you still have the ability to bear other arms. There is also no question that we have set a precedent in this country that some rights can be burdened for the greater good of society overall.

Second, just like you may believe many of the statistics from the National Rifle Association to be credible, a majority of our nation also believes the fallacious statistics presented by Everytown for Gun Safety and Mass Shooting Tracker and do not question their validity; a majority of our nation believes that background checks should be extended to private party transactions; a majority of our nation now believes that "mass shootings" are an epidemic.

But most importantly, you think you are standing on a strong foundation after recent court precedents and continue to push for more stringent interpretations of the Second Amendment due to your perceived strength of position. What you are standing on is a sheet of thin ice on a pond. It is true that *Heller, McDonald* and *Moore v Madison* suggest you have an individual right, in and out of the home, and Fourteenth Amendment protections of that right on a state level. What they do not suggest is that the right cannot be infringed by restrictions upon that right which do not nullify the entire right overall.

At present, New York has arguably the strictest gun control regulations the nation has ever seen on a large scale, combining the long standing Sullivan Act with the new NY SAFE Act. The appellate Court has already ruled that the NY SAFE Act is Constitutional. It will go to the Supreme Court.

If 79 year old Justice Scalia dies with a Democrat in office before the Supreme Court hears that case, you can probably kiss the majority of your gun rights bye-bye. Even if he doesn't, in the Heller decision Scalia already suggested that the restriction on types of weapons or weapons features would be held to be constitutional, meaning that pre-emptive restrictions on the Second Amendment right can be adopted which severely diminished the scope of the right. This might also suggest that registrations would be deemed legal as they do not actually restrict your Second Amendment rights, merely require you to report that you embrace them and disclose with which exact weapons you choose to do so. Either way, there is at least a high probability that the NY SAFE Act will be deemed Constitutional by the Supreme Court.

No matter what you think, the moment that happens you can be damn sure we will get those regulations Federally, maybe even more severe, unless there is an alternate solution before that time. And there is a point at which the pull on Congress by the constituents is stronger than the push given by the NRA, lobbyists and Political Action Committees. A majority of the people are demanding change. If the Supreme Court rules the NY SAFE Act Constitutional, and we haven't already addressed the problem in the minds of the majority of society, you may get a large and uncomfortable change.

Extremists need to come back from the fringes. If you continue to defend against all gun restrictions indeterminately, and continue to fail to provide alternate solutions which meet the current demands of the majority of society overall, then you're going to lose your rights, plain and simple. You can bitch and moan about it like babies when it happens; you can be one of the few that take to arms at that time and actually increase societies demand for more gun control; or you can actually take actions now that might avoid the outcome entirely. You need to help adopt alternate gun laws that appease the majority of the people before it's too late, thus diminishing the majority push on Congress to adopt more dramatic solutions.

The ice is about to break and if you don't change your position you're going to drown. I'm trying to throw you a life preserver here.

Here are some of the problems I see with the ban all guns crowd holding an extreme "all gun deaths are violent crimes" position

Let's finally just be honest about it. The real argument you're making here is to basically revoke the Second Amendment, or at least the individual right. The Second Amendment is in the original Bill of Rights. Could we really even revoke, or even severely amend, one of the first 10 amendments in the Bill of Rights? If we can, that sets a scary precedent. It would mean we can severely alter any of the rights that were required to ratify the Constitution itself, and not merely limit those rights for societal good in ways that do not overly burden the right. With the exception of the Sixteenth Amendment on Prohibition which was repealed, it seems we typically make amendments to secure rights to groups that were not previously secured and not to actually vacate existing rights of the people. I guess arguably the Eighteenth Amendment removed your right to keep all your money, but funding the government isn't exactly the same thing as creating an actual amendment to prohibit private or public consumption of alcohol by the people, now is it? What would get thrown out next, Due Process? Apparently the current administration is attempting to suggest that. Maybe Freedom of Religion? Well, one Presidential candidate just argued for "a total and complete shutdown of Muslims entering the U.S."[2]

If you truly fear Ted Nugent and those like him, you should really want to secure your Second Amendment rights to defend yourselves from the hyper-armed Republican Extremists, because nothing you ever do is really going to get rid of their guns. You seriously believe that non-slave owners were willing to go to war and die for slavery, but don't think actual gun owners will be willing to do the same if you try to take their guns? If gun rights were to escalate like slave rights did into a Civil War, you'd all be dead in an afternoon. Your last thought being; they can't shoot an unarmed person. Your perfect world concept is nice, but you cannot force unwilling people to live in your perfect world without...well, force. You seem to have no concept of what guerrilla warfare might be like in this country, especially if such things as a religious or racial war broke out, even without a "gun rights" war.

If you get your way, you will have little resources to defend or secure your rights from an armed aggressor. That aggressor may be another government, it may be your government, or it may just be a majority of the people on a witch hunt. Are you absolutely sure you are not a member of a group that could one day be ostracized, having a majority of the nation claim that your group is the problem that needs to be dealt with; black, white, ethnic, male, female, Christian, Muslim, Jew, blonde, brunette, tall, short, ugly, attractive, circumcised, capitalist, socialist, rich, poor, educated, ignorant, promiscuous, infected, smoker, addicted, handicapped, obese, anorexic, delusional, rational, sterile, geriatric, Belieber? I could go on, but I think you get the point. If you seek to abandon your unalienable rights, your rights may one day abandon you.

Having come to the end of this book, I know that I do not care specifically about guns one way or another. A gun is merely a tool and it may or may not be the best available tool to use in a scenario at any given moment. If I should end up in a scenario being placed under threat, I'm going to use the tool I have available to me at all times; my brain. I will use that to implement any other available resource at that moment to take whatever measures I can to overcome that scenario in the best manner that can be expected under those particular circumstances. I will be the best I can hope to be with what I have available; with or without a gun.

What bothers me are not just the restrictions placed upon people limiting their ability to defend themselves from domestic and foreign threats; but the societal delusions we refuse to address, the false fears that lead people into taking irrational actions, the extremist ideologies that often lead to horrific outcomes, the oppression of civil rights and unwarranted restraints on liberty which gain no overall benefit to society, the use of propaganda to misinform the public, the rewriting of history such that future generations do not have the proper knowledge to choose not to make the same mistakes of historic societies and the misuse of strength upon the weak. What I care about are the innocent people these issues threaten, and I want them to have the best tools available to avoid such threats placed upon them both individually and collectively.

What I have come to understand in writing this book, is that most people falsely perceive the Second Amendment to merely be about militias or the keeping and bearing of certain types of arms. Those people are horribly missing the point.   The Second Amendment is about preserving the ability to defend your unalienable human rights by force, when all peaceful means of defense have failed.

References

Introduction

[1] Ideas and Opinions by Albert Einstein (1954), where they appear in the section "Aphorisms for Leo Baeck."

[2] A deity is a being, natural, supernatural or preternatural, with superhuman powers or qualities, and who may be thought of as holy, divine, or sacred. The preternatural or praeternatural is that which appears outside or beside (Latin præter) the natural. In contrast to the supernatural, preternatural phenomena are presumed to have rational explanations that are unknown.[Atheism is, in a broad sense, the rejection of belief in the existence of deities. Agnosticism is the view that the truth values of certain claims—especially claims about the existence or non-existence of any deity, as well as other religious and metaphysical claims—are unknown and (so far as can be judged) unknowable.- all Wikipedia]

[3] Barry Bruce-Briggs. The Great American Gun War. 1976. The Public Interest 45:59

[4] Morris, Edmund. Dutch: A Memoir of Ronald Reagan. 1999. Random House p.394

[5] Verordnung des Rates der Volksbeauftragen über Waffenbesitz, Reichsgesetzblatt 1919, Volume I, § 1, page 31–32.

[6] Harcourt, Bernard E (2004) "On the NRA, Adolph Hitler, Gun Registration, and the Nazi Gun Laws: Exploding the Culture Wars (A Call to Historians)" p 20-21.

[7] Alex Seitz-Wald (January 11, 2013). "The Hitler gun control lie." Salon.com. http://www.salon.com/2013/01/11/stop_talking_about_hitler/, Retrieved November 24, 2015.

8 Halbrook, Stephen P. (2000) "Nazi Firearms Law and the Disarming of the German Jews." Arizona Journal of International and Comparative Law, Vol 17. No. 3. p.528

𝔓art I: Historical Progression of the Second Amendment Ideology

𝖈𝖍𝖆𝖕𝖙𝖊𝖗 I

1 Santayana, George; Life of Reason, Reason in Common Sense, Scribner's, 1905, p.284

2 Michael Rhys Powicke, Military Obligation in Medieval England: A Study in Liberty and Duty. Greenwood Pub Group (1962) pp.563-565

3 Joseph E. Olson and David B. Kopel. All The Way Down the Slippery Slope: Gun Prohibition in England and Some Lessons For Civil Liberties in America. 22 Hamline L. Rev. 399-465 (1999) William S. Hein and Company

4 See Game Act of 1671, 22 & 23 Car. 2, ch. 25 (Eng.)

5 Harris, Tim, Revolution: The Great Crisis of the British Monarchy, 1685–1720, Penguin Books, Ltd., 2006. P. 271–272. ISBN 0-7139-9759-1][Ashley, Maurice, The Glorious Revolution of 1688, Charles Scribner's Sons, New York, 1966.p. 110–111. ISBN 0-340-00896-2

6 The Bill of Rights, 1 W. & M., Sess. 2, ch. 2 (1689)

7 An Act for the further Limitation of the Crown and better securing the Rights and Liberties of the Subject (The Act of Settlement). 12 and 13 Will 3 c. 2

8 Anonymous Account of the Convention Proceeding, 1688, Rawlinson MS D1079, at fol. 8, Bodleian Library, Oxford.] [Anonymous Account of the Convention Proceeding, 1688, Rawlinson MS D1079, fol. 10, Bodleian Library, Oxford

9 4 & 5 W. & M., ch. 23 (1692)

10 5 Ann, ch. 14 (1706)

11 Declaration of Independence.   Continental Congress, ratified July 4, 1776

12 Merrriam-Webster. Inalienable: "incapable of being alienated, surrendered, or transferred." http://www.merriam-webster.com/dictionary/inalienable. Retrieved January 2, 2016

13 Dictionary.com. Natural Right: "any right that exists by virtue of natural law." http://dictionary.reference.com/browse/natural--rights. Retrieved January 2, 2016

14 Merrriam-Webster. Legal Right: "a claim recognized and delimited by law for the purpose of securing it" http://www.merriam-webster.com/dictionary/legal%20right. Retrieved January 2, 2016

15 Blackstone, William, Sir, Commentaries on the Laws of England 4 v. First Edition. Oxford : Printed at the Clarendon Press, 1765-1769

16 Donald S. Lutz and Charles S. Hyneman, "The Relative Influence of European Writers on Late Eighteenth-Century American Political Thought," American political Science Review 189 (1984): 189-197

17 Commentaries, 1:139

[18] Commentaries, Vol. I, p. 140

[19] Commentaries, Vol. I, p. 121-122

[20] Commentaries Vol. II, p. 412

[21] George St. Tucker, Blackstone's Commentaries: With Notes of Reference, to the Constitution and Laws, of the Federal Government of the United States; and of the Commonwealth of Virginia. In Five Volumes. With an Appendix to Each Volume, Containing Short Tracts Upon Such Subjects as Appeared Necessary to Form a Connected View of the Laws of Virginia, as a Member of the Federal Union. W.Y. Birch, and A. Small, R. Carr. 1803

[22] David B. Kopel. The Second Amendment in the Nineteenth Century. BYY Law Review (1998) p. 1370

[23] The reference to "Art. 4" reflects the fact that the Second Amendment was originally the Fourth Amendment before the original first two amendments were dropped

[24] Annotating the Commentaries in footnotes 40 and 41.

[25] William Rawle, A View of the Constitution of the United States 125--26 1829 (2d ed.)

[26] W. Blizzard, Desultory Reflections on Police: With an Essay on the Means of Preventing Crimes and Amending Criminals 59-60 (London 1785)

Chapter II

[1] Richard Henry Lee. Walter Bennett, ed., Letters from the Federal Farmer to the Republican, at 21,22,124 (Univ. of Alabama Press,1975)

2   Schoolhouse Rock! Preamble. 1976.
http://www.schoolhouserock.tv/Preamble.html

3   The Writings of Thomas Jefferson: Being His Autobiography, Correspondence, Reports, Messages, Addresses, and Other Writings, Official and Private, H.A. Washington, ed., 1853-1854, 9 vols.

4   United States Constitution. Ratified June 21,1788

5   James Madison in convention, August 23, 1787, the Avalon Project, Yale Law School

6   Thomas Jefferson [letter to James Madison, 12/20/1787, [The Writings of Thomas Jefferson: Being His Autobiography, Correspondence, Reports, Messages, Addresses, and Other Writings, Official and Private, H.A. Washington, ed., 1853-1854, 9 vols.

7   (Federalist Papers #46) The Influence of the State and Federal Governments Compared, From the New York Packet, Tuesday, January 29, 1788. James Madison

8   (Federalist Papers #29) Concerning the Militia, From the Daily Advertiser, Thursday, January 10 1788, Alexander Hamilton

9   Joshua Kendall. The Forgotten Founding Father: Noah Webster's Obsession and the Creation of an American Culture. Berkley Trade; Reprint edition (2012). ISBN: 0425245454

10   Noah Webster in "An Examination into the Leading Principles of the Federal Constitution", 1787, a pamphlet aimed at swaying Pennsylvania toward ratification, in Paul Ford, ed., Pamphlets on the Constitution of the United States, at 56 (New York, 1888)

11   Elliot, Jonathan. The Debates in the Several State Conventions on the Adoption of the Federal Constitution. Vol. 3, June 16,

1788. pg 425

[12] (Federalist Papers #29)

[13] Thomas Jefferson, Proposal Virginia Constitution, 1 T. Jefferson Papers, 334,C.J.Boyd, Ed., 1950

[14] Walter Bennett, ed., Letters from the Federal Farmer to the Republican, at 21,22,124 (Univ. of Alabama Press,1975

[15] Elliot, Jonathan. The Debates in the Several State Conventions on the Adoption of the Federal Constitution. Vol. 3, June 16, 1788. pg 169

[16] Charles Hale, Debates and Proceedings in the Convention of the Commonwealth of Massachusetts (1856), p. 86.

[17] Annals of Congress, House of Representatives, 1st Congress, 1st Session: p.451

[18] Bernhard, Winfred E.A. Fisher Ames: Federalist and Statesman, 1758-1808. Chapel Hill: University of North Carolina Press, 1965

[19] Letter from Fisher Ames to F. R. Minot (June 12, 1789), in id. at 53-54.

[20] Garry Wills, A Necessary Evil: A History of American Distrust of Government, Simon and Schuster, 1999, pages 253–254.

[21] Annals of Congress, House of Representatives, 1st Congress, 1st Session; p.669

[22] Journal of the Senate of the United States of America, Vol 1: p.71

[23] Journal of the Senate of the United States of America, Vol 1: p.77

[24] Journal of the House of Representatives of the United States of America, Vol 1: p. 305

[25] Militia Act of 1792, Second Congress, Session I. Chapter XXVIII Passed May 2, 1792, providing for the authority of the President to call out the Militia

[26] Schecter, Barnet (2010). George Washington's America. A Biography Through His Maps. New York: Walker & Company. p. 238. ISBN 978-0-8027-1748-1.

[27] Boyd, Steven R. " Popular Rights, The Whiskey Rebellion and the Meaning of the First Amendment." 1982 p.78

[28] Letter to Jefferson, c. 1798. The Writings of James Madison. Edited by Gaillard Hunt. 9 vols. New York: G. P. Putnam's Sons, 1900--1910.] and [The Founders' Constitution. Volume 3, Article 1, Section 8, Clause 11, Document 8. http://press-pubs.uchicago.edu/founders/documents/a1_8_11s8.html, The University of Chicago Press

[29] By United States, Benjamin Brown French, John B. Colvin; Laws of the United States of America: From the 4th of March, 1789 to the 4th of March, 1815, Volume 4; published by John Bioren and 2. John Duane; R.C. Weightman; 1816; pg 115

[30] George M. Dennison, Martial Law: The Development of a Theory of EmergencyPowers, 1776-1861, 18 AM. J. LEGAL HIST. 52, 56-58 (1974).

[31] H.R. 4986: National Defense Authorization Act for Fiscal Year 2008". GovTrack.us. 2008. Retrieved January 24, 2008.

[32] Quimby, Robert S. (1997). The U.S. Army in the War of 1812: An Operational and Command Study. East Lansing: Michigan State University Press.,v

[33] Donald R. Hickey (2012). The War of 1812: A Forgotten Conflict. U. of Illinois Press, p. 80.

[34] Toll, Ian W. (2006). Six Frigates: The Epic History of the Founding of the U.S. Navy. New York: W.W. Norton. ISBN 978-0-393-05847-5. pp. 456,467.

[35] Suppression of the Rebellion Act of 1861, ch. 25, § 1, 12 Stat. 281, 281 (current version at 10 U.S.C. § 332 (2000))

[36] Merriam-Webster. Insurrection: "an act or instance of revolting against civil authority or an established government." http://www.merriam-webster.com/dictionary/insurrection. Retrieved January 2, 2016

[37] Merriam-Webster. Revolt: "to fight in a violent way against the rule of a leader or government" http://www.merriam-webster.com/dictionary/revolt. Retrieved January 2, 2016

[38] Merriam-Webster. Rebellion: "*1* : opposition to one in authority or dominance. *2 a* : open, armed, and usually unsuccessful defiance of or resistance to an established government; *b* : an instance of such defiance or resistance" http://www.merriam-webster.com/dictionary/rebellion. Retrieved January 2, 2016

[39] U.S. Constitution, Article I, Section 9

[40] The Militia Act of 1862, 12 Stat. 597, enacted July 17, 1862

[41] War Extracts p. 199-221, American Military History Url: http://www.history.army.mil/html/bookshelves/resmat/civil_war/extracts/the_civil_war_1861_(pg_199-221).pdf

[42] Bornstein, David (April 14, 2011). "Lincoln's Call to Arms". Opinionator.blogs.nytimes.com. Archived from the original on July 13, 2011.

[43] Chambers, ed. The Oxford Companion to American Military History, 181] [James W. Geary, We Need Men: The Union Draft in the Civil War (1991)

[44] Joseph G. Bilby, A Revolution in Arms: A History of the First Repeating Rifles, Westholme Publishing 2005 ISBN: 1594160171

[45] Greeley, Horace; Leon Case (1872). The Great Industries of the United States. J.B. Burr & Hyde. p. 944. ISBN 1-85506-627-0

[46] Revenue Act of 1861, sec. 49, 12 Stat. 292, at 309 (Aug. 5, 1861).

[47] Bill of Rights Transcript, Archives.gov, Url: http://www.archives.gov/exhibits/charters/bill_of_rights_transcript.html, Retrieved 2013-02-06

[48] The Enforcement Act of 1871 (17 Stat. 13)

[49] Scaturro, Frank (1999). President Grant Reconsidered. Lanham, Maryland: Madison Books. pp. 71–72. ISBN 1-56833-132-0

[50] National Archives. *The Charters of Freedom: "A New World is at Hand."* http://www.archives.gov/exhibits/charters/bill_of_rights_transcript.html. Retrieved January 2, 2016

[51] Text at Wikisouce. http://en.wikisource.org/wiki/Page:United_States_Statutes_at_Large_Volume_20.djvu/177. Retrieved January 31, 2013

[52] Jennifer Elsea, The Posse comitatus Act and Related Matters: A Sketch. The Navy Department Library. June 6, 2005.

http://www.history.navy.mil/library/online/posse%20comit.htm.
Retrieved: 2013-02-06

[53] The Militia Act of 1903 (32 Stat. 775)

[54] Dick, Charles William Frederick at the Biographical Directory of
the United States Congress.
http://bioguide.congress.gov/scripts/biodisplay.pl?index=D00030
2 Retrieved January 2, 2011

[55] Graham A. Cosmas, An Army for Empire: The United States
Army and the Spanish–American War (1971) ch. 3–4

Chapter III

[1] Wilson v. State, 33 Ark. 557, at 560, 34 Am. Rep. 52, at 54
(1878)

[2] New York Penal - Article 400 - § 400.00 Licenses to Carry,
Possess, Repair and Dispose of Firearms

[3] Revolver Killings Fast Increasing, New York Times, January 30,
1911

[4] Peter Duffy. 100 Years Ago, the Shot That Spurred New York's
Gun-Control Law. The New York Times. January 23, 2011,
Url: http://cityroom.blogs.nytimes.com/2011/01/23/100-years-
ago-the-shot-that-spurred-new-yorks-gun-control-law/.
Retrieved: 2013-02-06

[5] Richard F. Welch. 2009. "King of the Bowery: Big Tim Sullivan,
Tammany Hall, and New York City from the Gilded Age to the
Progressive Era."

[6] Bar Hidden Weapons on Sullivan's Plea, New York Times, May
11, 1911

[7] Peter Duffy. 100 Years Ago, the Shot That Spurred New York's Gun-Control Law. The New York Times. January 23, 2011, Url: http://cityroom.blogs.nytimes.com/2011/01/23/100-years-ago-the-shot-that-spurred-new-yorks-gun-control-law/. Retrieved: 2013-02-06

[8] Kleck, Gary & Kates, Don B. *Armed: New Perspectives on Gun Control.* Prometheus Books 1991. P. 130

[9] Anthony Smith, Machine Gun: The Story of the Men and the Weapon That Changed the Face of War, Macmillan. 2004

[10] Owen Rust, Size of U.S. Mitary Since WWI. Yahoo! Contributor Network. 2012-01-27. http://news.yahoo.com/size-u-military-since-wwi-185632617.html. Retrieved February 7, 2013

[11] Frank N. Shubert. Mobilization. U.S. Army Center of Military History. http://www.history.army.mil/documents/mobpam.htm. Retrieved February 7, 2013

[12] Howard Clark Kee, Christianity: A Social and Cultural History. 2nd ed. (Prentice Hall, 1998) p. 486

[13] The National Firearms Act ("NFA"), 72nd Congress, Sess. 2, ch. 757, 48 Stat. 1236, enacted on June 26, 1934; National Firearms Act of 1934, 48 Stat. 1236-1240 (1935), 26 U.S.C. § 1132 (1935), now codified beginning at 26 U.S.C. § 5801 (1998)

[14] Prohibition and the Rise of the American Gangster, The National Archives. Blogs.archives.gov/prologue/?p=8258, retrieved 1/16/2013

[15] In 1953, the name change to the "Internal Revenue Service" was formalized in Treasury Decision 6038. 1953-2 C.B. 657 (August 21, 1953), filed with Division of the Federal Register on August 26, 1967. Compare Treas. Department Order 150-29 (July 9, 1953)

[16] "History of ATF from Oxford University Press, Inc. · 1789—1998 U.S". Atf.gov. Retrieved 2013-02-07

[17] History of the National Firearms Act, Bureau of Alcohol, Tobacco & Firearms. Url: http://www.atf.gov/firearms/nfa/. Retrieved February 7, 2013

[18] Murder Statistics from Statistical Abstract of the United States, U.S. Department of Commerce

[19] Michael S. Brown (August 6, 2001). "The strange case of the United States v. Miller". Enter Stage Right – A Journal of Modern conservatism.

[20] Benedict Crowell, Assistant Secretary of War (1919). America's Munitions, 1917-1918. Government Printing Office, Washington D.C. pp. 185–186

[21] Anthony Smith, Machine Gun: The Story of the Men and the Weapon That Changed the Face of War, Macmillan. 2004

[22] Robert John McCarthy. History of Troop A Cavalry, Connecticut National Guard and its service in the Great War as Co. D, 102d Machine Gun Battalion. Tuttle, Morehouse. 1919; Christopher Lee, The Boals of Boalsburg: Two Hundred Years of a Pennsylvania Heritage, Published in 1989 by in Pennsylvania Heritage Magazine, a publication of the Pennsylvania Historical and Museum Commission.

[23] *United States v. Miller*, 307 U.S. 174 (1939), Brief filed by the United States, March 1939

[24] Ibid

[25] History of the National Firearms Act, Bureau of Alcohol, Tobacco & Firearms. Url: http://www.atf.gov/firearms/nfa/. Retrieved February 7, 2013

[26] Owen Rust, Size of U.S. Mitary Since WWI. Yahoo! Contributor Network. 2012-01-27. Url: http://news.yahoo.com/size-u-military-since-wwi-185632617.html. Retrieved February 7, 2013

[27] Bard, Mitchell G., U.S.-Israel Strategic Cooperation: The 1968 Sale of Phantom Jets to Israel. Jewish Virtual Library. https://www.jewishvirtuallibrary.org/jsource/US-Israel/phantom.html#N_20_. Retrieved Novermber 24, 2015

[28] Kelley, Michael; Here's How Much America REALLY spends on Israel's Defense; Business Insider; September 20, 2012; http://www.businessinsider.com/heres-how-much-america-really-spends-on-israels-defense-2012-9. Retrieved January 26, 2013

[29] Foreign Military Financing Account Summary. State Dept., http://www.state.gov/t/pm/ppa/sat/c14560.htm, Retrieved November 9, 2015

[30] The Six-Day War: 40 Years Later; Abraham H. Foxman; National Director of the Anti-Defamation League; This article originally appeared in New Jersey Jewish Standard on May 25, 2007

[31] Hijacked "Transcript". http://www.pbs.org/wgbh/amex/hijacked/filmmore/pt.html. Retrieved February 7, 2013

[32] Gun Control Act of 1968 (Title I) [The Gun Control Act of 1968 (GCA or GCA68), Pub.L. 90-618, 82 Stat. 1213, enacted October 22, 1968] and NFA of 1968 (Title II) (amended as 26 U.S.C. ch. 53)

[33] *Haynes v. United States*, 390 U.S. 85 (1968.)

[34] John F. Kennedy Assassination Homepage, Warren Commission Report, Page 645-646". Retrieved February 7, 2013

[35] Peter Kihss. The New York Times. Malcom X Shot to Death at Rally Here. February 22, 1965

[36] Gladwin Hill, Kennedy is Dead, Victim of Assassin; Suspect, Arab Immigrant, Arraigned; Johnson Appoints Panel on Violence, The New York Times, June 6, 1968

[37] Earl Caldwell. Martin Luther King Is Slain in Memphis; A White Is Suspected: Johnson Urges Calm. The New York Times. April 5, 1968

[38] *"Department of the Treasury Study on the Sporting Suitability of Modified Semiautomatic Assault Rifles"* https://www.atf.gov/file/57521/download April 1998. Retrieved November 24, 2015.

[39] Department of the Treasury Study on the Sporting Suitablilty of Modified Semiautomatic Assault Rifles. April, 1998

[40] Arthur Herbert. Open Letter To All Federal Firearms Licensees. U.S. Department of Justice. Bureau of Alcohol, Tobacco, firearms and Explosives. September 21, 2011

[41] Michael Mandelbaum. Vietnam: The Television War. MIT Press Vol. 111, No. 4, Fall 1982

[42] Jeff Mason and Laura Macinnis. Obama calls treatment of Vietnam War veterans "a disgrace". Reuters. May 28, 2012

[43] Firearms Owners' Protection Act of May 19, Pub.L. 99–308, 100 Stat. 449, enacted May 19, 1986, codified at 18 U.S.C. § 921 et seq

[44] Right to Keep and Bear Arms, U.S. Senate. 2001 Paladin Press. ISBN 1-58160-254-5

[45] Kleck, Gary; Targeting Guns: Firearms and Their Control, Aldine Transaction 1997

[46] James Kelly. South Florida: Trouble in Paradise. Time. November 23, 1981

[47] Pub.L. 103–159, 107 Stat. 1536

[48] Wayne King. Sarah and James Brady; Target: The Gun Lobby. The New York Times. December 9, 1990

[49] Neil Rawles (February 2, 2007). *Inside Waco* (Television documentary). Channel 4/HBO.

[50] Transcript of the affidavit of Davy Aguilera, Special Agent Bureau of ATF, used by the BATF in order to obtain a search warrant of the Branch Davidian center in Waco, TX. February 25, 1993. Before Dennis G. Green United States Magistrate Judge Western District of Texas

[51] Bovard, James "Not So Wacko." May 15, 1995. The New Republic: "Rolland Ballestros, one of the first ATF agents out of the cattle trucks, told Texas Rangers and Waco police shortly after the raid that he thought the first shots came from agents aiming at the Davidians' dogs."

[52] Robert Bryce. "Prying Open the Case of the Missing Door." August 18, 2000. The Austin Chronicle. http://www.austinchronicle.com/issues/dispatch/2000-08-18/pols_feature9.html.

[53] Daniel Klaidman & Michael Isikoff. A Fire That Won't Die: As the surprises keep coming, Reno names a special counsel to sift the ashes of the Waco fiasco and answer the big question: did

federal agents disobey orders against using deadly force, then lie about it? Newsweek. July 20, 1999

54 Frank Pellegrini. What Is the FBI Trying to Tell Us About Waco?. Time. August 26, 1999

55 US Treasury Department July 13, 1995 Memorandum to the Press "Weapons Possessed by the Branch Davidians

56 Hearing Before the Subcommittee on Administrative Oversight and the Courts Of the Committee on the Judiciary United States Senate. July 26, 2000. Serial No. J-106-99

57 McVeigh's Apr. 26 Letter to Fox News; 4/26/2001/ http://www.foxnews.com/story/0,2933,17500,00.html; Retrieved January 27, 2013

58 Adams, Jane Meredith. Sparked By School Massacre, Gun Debate Still Rages. Chicago Tribune, May 29, 1995

59 Reilly, Mollie. Gavin Newsom Wants California Voters To Take On The NRA. October 15, 2015. The Huffington Post. http://www.huffingtonpost.com/entry/gavin-newsom-guns_561ff791e4b028dd7ea72cb2. Retrieved December 28, 2015

60 Public Safety and Recreational Firearms Use Protection Act, H.R.3355, 103rd Congress (1993-1994), Government Printing Office. Retrieved February 7, 2013

61 Federal Assault Weapons Ban. Wikipedia. http://en.wikipedia.org/wiki/Federal_Assault_Weapons_Ban. Retrieved February 7, 2013

62 Militia "1580-90; < Latin mīlitia soldiery, equivalent to mīlit- (stem of mīles) soldier + -ia -ia." http://dictionary.reference.com/browse/militia. Retrieved December 28, 2015; Military "1575-85; < Latin mīlitāri (s),

equivalent to *mīlit-* (stem of *mīles*) soldier + *-āris* –ary."
http://dictionary.reference.com/browse/military?s=t.   Retrieved
December 28, 2015.

[63] Benedict Crowell, Assistant Secretary of War (1919). America's
Munitions, 1917-1918. Government Printing Office, Washington
D.C. pp. 185–186

[64] Jennifer Bendery. Diane Feinstein Introduces Assault Weapons
Ban, Urges Public To Help It Pass. Huffington Post. January
24, 2013.

[65] S.150 - Assault Weapons Ban of 2013

[66] Robert Evans, 6 things You Won't Believe Are More Legal Than
Marijuana, September 16, 2010, Url:
http://www.cracked.com/article_18732_6-things-you-wont-
believe-are-more-legal-than-marijuana.html,   Retrieved
February 6, 2013

[67] Greeley, Horace; Leon Case (1872). The Great Industries of the
United States. J.B. Burr & Hyde. p. 944. ISBN 1-85506-627-0

[68] Steven Wilson, The Galing Gun, Military.com, October 31, 2005,
http://www.military.com/forums/0,15240,79614,00.html,
Retrieved January 6, 2013

[69] Encyclopedia Britannica: Sir Hiram Stevens Maxim,
http://www.britannica.com/EBchecked/topic/370419/Sir-Hiram-
Maxim

[70] Pistol, Caliber .45, Automatic, M1911 Technical Manual TM 9-
1005-211-34 1964 edition. Pentagon Publishing. 1964.][Taylor,
Chuck (1981). Complete Book Of Combat Handgunning.
Boulder, CO: Paladin Press. p. 200] [Hogg, Ian V.; John Walter
(2004). Pistols of the World (4 ed.). David & Charles. p. 225

⁷¹ Joseph E. Olson and David B. Kopel. All The Way Down the Slippery Slope: Gun Prohibition in England and Some Lessons For Civil Liberties in America. 22 Hamline L. Rev. 399-465 (1999) William S. Hein and Company

⁷² *McDonald v. Chicago*, 561 U.S. ___ (2010)

⁷³ McCune, Greg (July 9, 2013). "Illinois Is Last State to Allow Concealed Carry of Guns", Reuters. Retrieved July 20, 2013.

⁷⁴ Jones, Ashby (July 9, 2013). "Illinois Abolishes Ban on Carrying Concealed Weapons", Wall Street Journal. Retrieved July 20, 2013.

⁷⁵ McDermott, Kevin, and Hampel, Paul (July 11, 2013). "Illinois Concealed Carry Now on the Books — But Not Yet in the Holster", St. Louis Post-Dispatch. Retrieved July 20, 2013.

⁷⁶ DeFiglio, Pam (July 9, 2013). "General Assembly Overrides Veto, Legalizing Concealed Carry in Illinois", Patch Media. Retrieved July 20, 2013.

⁷⁷ "Sandy Hook Shooter Adam Lanza Wore Earplugs", Dave Altimari and John Lender, The Hartford Courant, January 6, 2013, Retrieved October 29, 2015, http://www.courant.com/news/connecticut/newtown-sandy-hook-school-shooting/hc-sandyhook-lanza-earplugs-20130106-story.html

⁷⁸ "New York passes first U.S. gun control bill since Newtown massacre". CBS News. 15 January 2013. Retrieved October 29, 2015.

⁷⁹ The New York State Senate website, www.mysenate.gov, http://www.nysenate.gov/legislation/bills/2013/s2230, Retrieved October 29, 2015

[80] The New York State Senate website, www.mysenate.gov, http://www.nysenate.gov/legislation/bills/2013/s2230, Retrieved October 29,2015

[81] The United States Court of Appeals for the Second Circuit http://www.ca2.uscourts.gov/decisions/isysquery/f2d25915-8bec-4a52-8bfa-d84df8c4dfee/3/doc/14-36_14-319_opn.pdf#xml=http://www.ca2.uscourts.gov/decisions/isysquery/f2d25915-8bec-4a52-8bfa-d84df8c4dfee/3/hilite/

𝔓art II: But Things are Different This Time

𝔠hapter IV

[1] The Alchemist, HarperCollins paperback, 1998, p. 156

[2] Declaration of Independence.   Continental Congress, ratified July 4, 1776

[3] Middlekauff, Robert. The Glorious Cause: The American Revolution, 1763–1789. (2005) ISBN 13:978 0-19-516247-9 pg. 111–120.

[4] Miller, John C. Origins of the American Revolution. (1943) pg. 149–153

[5] Jared Ingersoll (1749-1822). University of Pennsylvania. http://www.archives.upenn.edu/people/1700s/ingersoll_jared.htm 1] and [Jared Ingersoll to Thomas Fitch, 11 Feb. 1765". Prof.Jeffery Pasley, University of Missouri-Columbia. http://pasleybrothers.com/mocourses/texts/Barre.htm.]   and ["Jared Ingersoll, Pennsylvania". The National Archives

[6] Col. Charles J. Dunlap, Jr. (1995). "Revolt of the Masses: Armed Civilians and the Insurrectionary Theory of the Second Amendment". 62 TENN. L. REV. 643. http://scholarship.law.duke.edu/cgi/viewcontent.cgi?article=5203

&context=faculty_scholarship&sei-redir=1. Retrieved January 26, 2013

7 CNN iReport; joshdb50/ 2012-12-27;
   url: http://ireport.cnn.com/docs/DOC-902515

8 Imam, Jareem and Saidi, Nicole; CNN; "Marine to senator: No ma'am, I won't register my guns", January 4, 2013; url: http://www.cnn.com/2013/01/04/us/marine-gun-letter-ireport/index.html

9 George Bush Presidential Library and Museum. Address Before a Joint Session of the Congress on the Persian Gulf Crisis and the Federal Budget Deficit. September 11, 1990. http://bushlibrary.tamu.edu/research/public_papers.php?id=2217&year=1990&month=9. Retrieved February 1, 2013

10 Ibid

11 UN at a Glance. http://www.un.org/en/aboutun/index.shtml. Retrieved February 1, 2013

12 Radia, Kirit. United Nations Authorizes Strikes in Libya; Gadhafi Vows Offensive. ABC News. March 17, 2012. Retrieved: February 1, 2013

13 North Atlantic Treaty Organization. http://www.nato.int/cps/en/SID-727086F9-8E641654/natolive/what_is_nato.htm

14 "Libyan Rebels Pledge Free and Fair Election". Reuters India. March 29, 2011.] ["A Vision of a Democratic Libya". The Guardian (London). March 29, 2011. Retrieved February 1, 2013

15 http://www.nato.int/cps/en/natolive/what_is_nato.htm. Retrieved; February 1, 2013

[16] United Nations.
http://www.un.org/press/en/2013/sc11131.doc.htm.
Retrieved December 12, 2015

[17] United Nations *Programme of Action Implemantation Support System*: PoA-ISS.
http://www.poa-iss.org/InternationalTracing/ITI_English.pdf.
Retrieved December 12, 2015

[18] Somin, Ilya. *Using Article 5 of the North Atlantic Treaty to legalize the war against ISIS*. Washington Post.   11-15-15.
https://www.washingtonpost.com/news/volokh-conspiracy/wp/2015/11/15/using-article-5-of-the-nato-treaty-to-legalize-the-war-against-isis/. Retrieved November 28, 2015

[19] Farmer, Ben. *Who were the terrorists? Everything we know about the Isil attackers so far*. The Telegrath. November 20, 2015
http://www.telegraph.co.uk/news/worldnews/europe/france/11996120/Paris-attack-what-we-know-about-the-suspects.html.
Retrieved November 20, 2015

[20] Public Law 107-56. From the U.S. Government Printing Office

[21] "The Homeland Security Act: The Decline of Privacy; the Rise of Government Secrecy". Bill of Rights Defense Committee. Retrieved January 2, 2013

[22] Keller, Susan Jo (September 27, 2007). "Judge Rules Provisions in Patriot Act to Be Illegal". New York Times.

[23] Greenwald, Glenn; MacAskill, Ewen (June 6, 2013). "NSA Prism program taps in to user data of Apple, Google and others". The Guardian (London).

[24] Barton Gellman and Ashkan Soltani (30 October 2013). "NSA infiltrates links to Yahoo, Google data centers worldwide,

Snowden documents say". The Washington Post. Retrieved November 29, 2015

[25] "U.S. NSA's phone spying program ruled illegal by appeals court". Reuters. May 7, 2015. Retrieved November 29, 2015

[26] Schuster, Steve. Authority of NSA to collect bulk phone data ends. ABC2 WBAY.com. November 29, 2015. http://wbay.com/2015/11/29/authority-of-nsa-to-collect-bulk-phone-data-ends/. Retrieved November 29, 2015

[27] Michael Moore, Fahrenheit 9/11 (documentary). Timestamp: 01:01:39–01:01:47

[28] Rachel Maddow. Drift: The Unmooring of American Military Power. Crown, 2012

[29] Stephen P. Halbrook. "Only law enforcement will be allowed to have guns: Hurricane Katrina and the New Orleans firearm confiscations" (DOC). George Mason University Civil Rights Law Journal

𝕮𝖍𝖆𝖕𝖙𝖊𝖗 V

[1] Bennet-Smith, Meredith. Huffington Post. "Bryan Fischer: God Did Not Protect Connecticut Shooting Victims Because Prayer Banned In Schools". 12/15/2012. video url: http://youtu.be/is2x7QTZ8AI. http://www.huffingtonpost.com/2012/12/15/bryan-fischer-god-did-not-protect-connecticut-shooting-victims-prayer-banned_n_2303903.html. Retrieved January 2, 2015

[2] Alexandersen, Christian. 'We need to turn our nation back to God': Pa. legislators ask people to pray for the United States. November 17, 2015. http://www.pennlive.com/politics/index.ssf/2015/11/we_need_to_turn_our_nation_bac.html. Retrieved December 21, 2015

[3] Constitution of the United States of America – Bill of Rights – First Amendment

[4] Constitution of the United States of America – Article VI

[5] http://www.masonicinfo.com/member.htm

[6] History of 'In God We Trust'. U.S. Department of the Treasury. https://www.treasury.gov/about/education/Pages/in-god-we-trust.aspx. Retrieved December 21, 2015

[7] Inquisition. New Advent. http://www.newadvent.org/cathen/08026a.htm. Retrieved December 21, 2015

[8] Destination America: The Earth is the Lord's (Episode Three). PBS. http://www.pbs.org/destinationamerica/usim_wy_01.html

[9] Greenwood, Tim. The Myth of the Separation of Church and State. https://www.tgm.org/mythofseparation.html. Retrieved December 21, 2015

[10] United States Bill of Rights. Drafted 8 June – 25 September 1789; Signed 28 September 1789; Articles three through twelve ratified 15 December 1791; Article two ratified 5 May 1992 as the Twenty-seventh Amendment to the United States Constitution. https://en.wikisource.org/wiki/United_States_Bill_of_Rights. Retrieved December 21,2015

[11] Santana, Rebecca. Scalia dismisses concept of religious neutrality in speech. AP December 2, 2016. http://news.yahoo.com/scalia-dismisses-concept-religious-neutrality-speech-202953789.html. Retrieved December 3, 2016

𝕮𝖍𝖆𝖕𝖙𝖊𝖗 VI

[1] Carlyle, Thomas. *Chartism.* J. Fraser, 1840. P.10

[2] Nolo. http://www.nolo.com/legal-encyclopedia/homicide-murder-manslaughter-32637.html

[3] Peters, Jeremy W. (2014-04-15). "Bloomberg Plans a $50 Million Challenge to the N.R.A.". *New York Times.* Retrieved November 27, 2015

[4] http://everytownresearch.org/school-shootings/

[5] Gun-Free School Zones Act (as amended) [104 Stat. 4789 aka 104 Stat. 4844] & Gun-Free Schools Act of 1994 as part of the Improving America's Schools Act of 1994 [20 U.S. Code § 7151 - Gun-free requirements]

[6] Gun in kindergartener's backpack goes off at Memphis elementary school. CBS News. August 20,2013. http://www.cbsnews.com/news/gun-in-kindergarteners-backpack-goes-off-at-memphis-elementary-school/. Retrieved November 27, 2015

[7] School shooting tragedy averted in Ga., CBS News. August 20,2013. http://www.cbsnews.com/news/school-shooting-tragedy-averted-in-ga/. Retrieved November 27, 2015

[8] Student shot at Widener University may have been targeted. CBS News. January 20,2014. http://www.cbsnews.com/news/student-shot-on-widener-university-campus/. November 27, 2015

[9] Man Shoots Estranged Wife in School Parking Lot. NBC Chicago. April 21, 2014. http://www.nbcchicago.com/news/local/Man-Shoots-Estranged-

Wife-in-School-Parking-Lot-256119341.html.
Retrieved November 27, 2015

[10] Delong, Katie & Sachs, Jenna. Milwaukee police: 10-year-old girl "caught in the crossfire" & shot on playground. April 21, 2014. http://fox6now.com/2014/05/21/milwaukee-police-source-11-year-old-girl-shot-in-the-head-on-the-playground/. Retrieved November 27, 2015

[11] http://everytownresearch.org/issue/online-gun-sales/ Retrieved November 29, 2015

[12] ATF. https://www.atf.gov/firearms/qa/may-nonlicensee-ship-firearm-through-us-postal-service. Retrieved December 12, 2015

[13] https://about.usps.com/postal-bulletin/2011/pb22321/html/updt_001.htm. Retrieved December 12, 2015

[14] http://www.dhl-usa.com/content/dam/downloads/us/express/shipping/terms_and_conditions/prohibited_restricted_commodities.pdf. Retrieved December 12, 2015

[15] https://www.ups.com/content/us/en/resources/ship/packaging/guidelines/firearms.html Retrieved December 12, 2015

[16] http://www.fedex.com/us/freight/rulestariff/prohibited_articles.html. Retrieved December 12, 2015

[17] ATF. https://www.atf.gov/firearms/qa/may-nonlicensee-ship-firearm-common-or-contract-carrier. Retrieved December 12, 2015

[18] http://everytownresearch.org/reports/felon-seeks-firearm-no-strings-attached/. Retrieved November 29, 2015

19 http://everytownresearch.org/. Retrieved November 29, 2015

20 http://everytownresearch.org/gun-violence-by-the-numbers/

21 https://www.fbi.gov/about-us/cjis/ucr/crime-in-the-u.s/2014/crime-in-the-u.s.-2014/tables/table-20.   Retrieved November 27, 2015

22 http://everytownresearch.org/issue/guns-in-public-places/. Retrieved November 29, 2015

23 Holan, Angie Drobnic. Crime rates in Florida have dropped since 'stand you ground,' says Dennis Baxley. Politifact Florida. 3/23/2012. http://www.politifact.com/florida/statements/2012/mar/23/dennis-baxley/crime-rates-florida-have-dropped-stand-your-ground/. Retrieved November 27, 2015

24 http://everytown.org. Retrieved November 29, 2015

25 Senate Bill 3930 Military Commissions Act of 2006 (as passed by Congress), S.3930, September 22, 2006

26 Biesecker, Michael & Fram, Alan. *Paul Ryan Balks Over Blocking Gun Sales To People On Terror Watch List.* Huffington Post. 11-20-2015. http://www.huffingtonpost.com/entry/guns-terror-watch-list_564fec70e4b0258edb31b652. Retrieved November 27, 2015

27 Clark, Dave. *How the US plans to welcome 10,000 Syrian refugees.* Business Insider. 9/12-2015. http://www.businessinsider.com/afp-how-the-us-plans-to-welcome-10000-syrian-refugees-2015-9. Retrieved November 27, 2015

28 Wing, Nick. *7 Ways That You (Yes, You) Could End Up On A Terrorist Watch List.* Huffington Post. 7/25/14.

http://www.huffingtonpost.com/2014/07/25/terrorist-watch-list_n_5617599.html. Retrieved November 27, 2015

[29] Jung, Helen. No-fly list appeals process unconstitutional, federal judge in Portland rules. 6/24/14. http://www.oregonlive.com/portland/index.ssf/2014/06/no-fly_list_appeals_process_un.html#incart_m-rpt-1.   Retrieved November 27, 2015

[30] *Mohamed v. Holder.* United States District Court Eastern District of Virginia Alexandria Division.   No. 1:11-CV-0050. Filed April 4, 2015

[31] Shamsi, Hina. Until the No Fly List Is Fixed, It Shouldn't Be Used to Restrict People's Freedoms. December 7, 2015. https://www.aclu.org/blog/speak-freely/until-no-fly-list-fixed-it-shouldnt-be-used-restrict-peoples-freedoms.   Retrieved December 12, 2015

[32] Mokdad v. Lynch. United States Court of Appeals for the Sixth Circuit. No. 14-1094. Filed 10/26/2015

[33] Loeb, Robert and Weybrecht, Matthew.   Government Bid to Shut Down Challenge To No Fly List Grounded. November 5, 2015. https://www.lawfareblog.com/government-bid-shut-down-challenge-no-fly-list-grounded. Retrieved December 12, 2015

[34] Peters, Jeremy W. (2014-04-15). "Bloomberg Plans a $50 Million Challenge to the N.R.A.". *New York Times.* Retrieved November 27, 2015

[35] Mayors Against Illegal Guns, *New Poll Shows NRA Members Strongly Support Common-Sense Gun Laws.* Mikebloomberg.com. July 24, 2012. http://www.mikebloomberg.com/news/new-poll-shows-nra-

members-strongly-support-common-sense-gun-laws/. Retrieved December 3, 2015

[36] Hunt, Earl (2011). Human Intelligence. Cambridge: Cambridge University Press ISBN 9780521707817

[37] Nation of Change. http://www.nationofchange.org/defining-mass-shooting-1345908412. Retrieved December 2, 2015

[38] Morris, Mike. *1 person dead, 3 others wounded in DeKalb shooting.* AJC.com. January 29, 2015. http://www.ajc.com/news/news/one-dead-three-wounded-in-dekalb-shooting/njy7R/. Retrieved December 2, 2015

[39] *Arrest made in South Bend shooting that injured 4.* WSBT.com/ May 3, 2015. http://www.wsbt.com/news/local/update-arrest-made-in-south-bend-shooting-that-injured-4/32785308. Retrieved December 2, 2015

[40] *4 injured in shooting in SE Bakersfield.* Bakersfieldnow.com. November 6, 2015. http://www.bakersfieldnow.com/news/local/Shooting-near--342248321.html. Retrieved December 2, 2015

[41] Sweat, Candace. *Two dead, five injured in shooting at Hope Mills party.* January 11, 2015. http://www.wral.com/two-dead-five-injured-in-shooting-at-hope-mills-party/14346149/. Retrieved December 2, 2015

[42] Lemon, Ken & Suskin, Greg. *Second person dies after 3 shot Sunday night in Pageland. WSOCTV.com.* October 26, 2015. http://www.wsoctv.com/news/news/local/two-people-shot-one-killed-chesterfield-county/nn9BT/. Retrieved December 2, 2015

[43] *Four people injured in shooting outside Deja Vu Showgirls nightclub.* ABC10. March 30, 2015. http://www.abc10.com/story/news/local/stockton/2015/03/29/four-

people-shooting-deja-vu-night-club/70644684/.   Retrieved
December 2, 2015.

[44] *1 dead, 3 others wounded in SW Houston shooting.* KHOU.com.
November 24, 2015.
http://www.khou.com/story/news/crime/2015/11/24/1-dead-3-
others-wounded-sw-houston-shooting/76299510/.   Retrieved
December 2, 2015

[45] Lipinski, Jed.   *17 people shot in Bunny Friend Park Sunday
night: NOPD.* NOLA.com. November 22, 2015.
http://www.nola.com/crime/index.ssf/2015/11/at_least_10_victim
s_of_bunny_f.html. Retrieved December 2, 2015

[46] Ramseur, Antoinette & Morlock, Jackie. Five people wounded
in early morning shooting at Portsmouth lounge. WTKR.com.
January 13, 2015. http://wtkr.com/2015/01/13/early-morning-
shooting-at-portsmouth-lounge-leaves-5-people-injured/.
Retrieved December 2, 2015

[47] Randall, Michael.   5 people shot at in Newburgh bar on
Broadway. November 23, 2015. Times Herald-Record.
http://www.recordonline.com/article/20151123/NEWS/151129781
. Retrieved December 2, 2015

[48] 2015 #49
http://www.ledger-enquirer.com/2015/03/10/3607030_five-
wounded-during-tuesday-morning.html

[49] 2015 #41
http://wncn.com/story/28228144/at-least-2-shot-at-tarboro-
barber-shop

Chapter VII

[1] Only general references to Robert Young's Sanka ad appear to exist and not retrievable historic video. In this particular case, I chose Robert Young's quote because 1) I've actually seen the commercial myself; and 2) I did not want to cite Peter Bergman's 1986 Vicks Formula 44 commercial in error as having originated the general "I'm not an X, but I play one on TV" disclaimer. If you have a problem with that, change the reference to Peter Bergman. The point remains the same. http://www.dailymotion.com/video/x36pho_vicks-44-with-peter-bergman_shortfilms. Retrieved December 14, 2015

[2] Kimmey, Samantha, The Raw Story, www.rawstory.com, January 18, 2013. Video url: http://youtu.be/zxGhG_F0kj8. Retrieved December 14, 2015

[3] Bogus, Carl T., The Hidden History of the Second Amendment (Winter 1998). U.C. Davis Law Review, Vol. 31, p. 309, 1998; Roger Williams Univ. Legal Studies Paper No. 80. Available at SSRN: http://ssrn.com/abstract=1465114

[4] Dred Scott v. Sandford, 60 U.S. 393 (1857)

[5] Duwe, Grant. A Circle of Distortion: The Social Construction of Mass murder in the United States, Western Criminology Review, 6(1) 59-78, (2005)

[6] Duwe, Grant. Mass Murder in the United States: A History. McFarland (2007) p.173. ISBN: 0786431504

[7] Duwe. Mass Murder in the United States: A History.

[8] Ibid p. 101, p.161-162

[9] Ibid p. 172

10 Ackerman, Robert .M. *Mass Murderers Prefer Semiautomatic Rifles*. The New York Times. March 2, 1989. http://www.nytimes.com/1989/03/02/opinion/l-mass-murderers-prefer-semiautomatic-rifles-365989.html. Retrieved December 17, 2015

11 Kleck, Armed p.184] [Bea, Keith. U.S. Congressional Research Service, assault weapons: Military-Style Semi Automatic Firearms Facts and Issues, Report 92-434 GOV (1992)pp. 38-39

12 *"A Historical Review of Armalite"* (PDF). ArmaLite, Inc. 1999-04-23. Retrieved 2008-07-16.

13 Tamryn Etten, "Gun Control and the Press: A Content Analysis of Newspaper Bias," (paper presented at the annual meeting of the American Society of Criminology, San Francisco, November 20-23, 1991

14 Donn F. Draeger & Rober W. Smith (1969). *Comprehensive Asian Fighting Arts*. ISBN 978-0-87011-436-6.

15 Mendel, Bob. The Nunchaku: Lethal Weapon or Flashy Toy? Even the Experts Disagree. August 1984. P.19

16 Levitas, Alex. *The real history of the nunchaku.* http://nunchaku.tripod.com/about_e.htm. Retrieved December 27, 2015

17 2006 New York Code - Criminal Possession Of A Weapon In The Fourth Degree

18 Arizona Revised Statutes Title 13 Section 3101

19 California Penal Code Section 12020

20 Massachusetts General Laws Part IV Title I Chapter 269 Section 10

[21] California Codes Penal Code Section 22010-22090

[22] Williamson L.J., L.A. Weekly, Sports, Nunchucks Are Banned in California...Except in Martial Arts Schools, Where They're All the Rage, 11/15/2012. Retrieved 1/24/2013. url: http://blogs.laweekly.com/arts/2012/11/nunchucks_martial_arts_karate.php

[23] Anne Marie Helmenstine, Ph.D.; How to Make Napalm B: Chemical Synthesis of a Gelled Sol; About.com Chemistry http://chemistry.about.com/od/advancedscienceprojects/a/How-To-Make-Napalm-B.htm; Retrieved January 27, 2013

[24] Title 26, Subtitle E, Chapter 53- Machine Guns, Destructive Devices, and Certain Other Firearms

[25] Linder, Douglas O. "Selected Documents: Jury Verdict Form (October 17, 1931)". Al Capone Trial. University of Missouri–Kansas City. Retrieved January 27, 2013

[26] Kleck, Point Blank p. 25

[27] Burger, Warren E. (January 14, 1990). "The Right To Bear Arms: A distinguished citizen takes a stand on one of the most controversial issues in the nation". Parade Magazine: 4–6

[28] Lynyrd Skynyrd. "Saturday Night Special." *Nuthin' Fancy*. MCA, 1975. Audiocassette.

[29] "Saturday Night Specials". NRA Institute for Legislative Action. April 21, 1999. https://www.nraila.org/articles/19990421/saturday-night-specials. Retrieved December 13, 2015

[30] *Are there laws on cheap handguns in your town?* Frontline. PBS.

http://www.pbs.org/wgbh/pages/frontline/shows/guns/maps/state.
html. Retrieved December 27, 2015

[31] *"Hot Guns: Ring of Fire".* Frontline. PBS. Retrieved December
14, 2015

[32] Peter Harry Brown, Daniel G. Abel. *Outgunned: Up Against the
NRA-- The First Complete Insider Account of the Battle Over
Gun Control.* p.162 ISBN 9781451603538

[33] Freudenberg, Nicholas (21 January 2014). *Lethal But Legal:
Corporations, Consumption, and Protecting Public Health.*
Oxford University Press. USA. pp. 48–52. ISBN 978-0-19-
993720-2.

[34] Harrison, Geoffrey. Lethal Weapons (Great Debates: Tough
Questions / Smart History. (2013) Norwood House Press. ISBN
1599535920

[35] Robert Sherrill, *The Saturday Night Special*, Charterhouse,
1973, ISBN 978-0-88327-016-5, p. 280.

[36] Eichelberger, Erika. *Dem Bill Would Ban "Saturday Night
Specials".* Mother Jones. March 5, 2013.
http://www.motherjones.com/mojo/2013/03/luis-gutierrez-junk-
gun-ban-saturday-night-special. Retrieved December 13, 2015

[37] Judge dismisses suit against gun makers. The Washington
Times. July 21, 2003.
http://www.washingtontimes.com/news/2003/jul/21/20030721-
113731-5952r/. Retrieved December 14, 2015

[38] Webster, Daniel W., Vernick, Jon S. and Hepburn, Lisa M.
*Effects of Maryland's Law Banning "Saturday Night Special"
Handguns on Homicides.* September 13, 2001.
http://aje.oxfordjournals.org/content/155/5/406.long. Retrieved
December 14, 2015

39 *Design Safety Standards Policy Summary.* Law Center to Prevent Gun Violence. December 1, 2013. http://smartgunlaws.org/gun-design-safety-standards-policy-summary/#footnote_5_5929. Retrieved December 13, 2015

40 DOJ Guns used in Crime. Bureau of Justice Statistics. July 1995. http://www.bjs.gov/index.cfm?ty=pbdetail&iid=947. Retrieved December 14, 2015

41 McCarthy, Erin. *Why the Glock Became America's Handgun.* Popular Mechanics. January 12, 2012. http://www.popularmechanics.com/military/weapons/a7445/why-the-glock-became-americas-handgun/. Retrieved December 14, 2015

42 Lynyrd Skynyrd. "Gimme Back My Bullets." *Gimme Back My Bullets.* MCA, 1976. Audiocassette.

43 Hofstadter, Richard: America as a Gun Culture. American Heritage Magazine, October, 1970

44 Wikipedia. United States military casualties of war. http://en.wikipedia.org/wiki/United_States_military_casualties_of_war. Retrieved December 27, 2015

45 Firearm Owner's Protection Act of 1986, P.> No. 99-308, 100 Stat. 449 (1986), as amended. Background checks on individuals who purchase firearms from an FFL have been required since passage of the Brady Handgun Violence Prevention Act (Brady Act) in November 1993. The NICS provides any FFL an immediate contact for information as to whether a prospective purchaser is a "prohibited person" under 18 U.S.C § 922 (g) or (n) or state law.

46 *Following the Gun: Enforcing Federal Laws Against Firearms Traffickers* p.41

[47] ATF Order 3310.4B, Firearms Enforcement Program, Chapter K, Section 143(ee)

[48] Ref: "ATF P 5300.4 - Federal Firearms Regulations Reference Guide 2005 General Information discusses "straw purchase" on p. 165

[49] "Interview with an inventor of the KTW bullet". Guncite.com. Retrieved October 24, 2013

[50] Kleck Armed reference on page 177

[51] NCGS § 14-34.3

[52] ORS 166.350(a)

[53] SC Code 16-23-520

[54] VA Code 18.2-308.3

[55] *Ban these 'cop killer' bullets.* Los Angeles Times. March 12, 2015. http://www.latimes.com/opinion/editorials/la-ed-ammo-atf-delays-ban-on-armor-piercing-bullets-20150312-story.html. Retrieved December 27, 2015

[56] Lucas Sullivan. Feds to Dayton: Lower police recruit passing score. Dayton Daily News. February 16, 2011. http://www.daytondailynews.com/news/news/local/feds-to-dayton-lower-police-recruit-passing-score/nMpG2/. Retrieved February 11, 2013

[57] Mike Parker. Man hunt for ex-soldier who shot police chief's daughter and killed policeman. Express. February 10, 20136. http://www.express.co.uk/news/world/376732/Man-hunt-for-ex-soldier-who-shot-police-chief-s-daughter-and-killed-policeman. Retrieved February 11, 2013

[58] Dorner manhunt: Officers opened fire on mother, daughter. February 9, 2013. http://latimesblogs.latimes.com/lanow/2013/02/cops-opened-fire-on-mother-daughter-during-dorner-manhunt.html. Retrieved February 11, 2013

[59] Rostker, Bernard D., Lawrence M. Hanser, William M. Hix, Carl Jensen, Andrew R. Morral, Greg Ridgeway and Terry L. Schell. Evaluation of the New York City Police Department Firearm Training and Firearm-Discharge Review Process. Santa Monica, CA: RAND Corporation, 2008. http://www.rand.org/pubs/monographs/MG717.html. Also available in print form.

[60] Baker, Al. *A Hail of Bullets, a Heap of Uncertainty*. The New York Times. December 9, 2007. http://www.nytimes.com/2007/12/09/weekinreview/09baker.html?_r=0. Retrieved December 14, 2015

[61] David Ariosto. Police: All Empire State shooting victims were wounded by officers. CNN. August 26, 2012. http://www.cnn.com/2012/08/25/justice/new-york-empire-state-shooting/. Retrieved December 14, 2015

[62] Wilson, Michael; Halbfinger, David M.; Otterman, Sharon (August 24, 2012). "Long Before Carnage, an Office Grudge Festered". New York Times. Retrieved December 14, 2015

[63] Statistics on the Dangers of Gun Use for Self-Defense. May 11, 2015. http://smartgunlaws.org/dangers-of-gun-use-for-self-defense-statistics/. Retrieved December 11, 2015

[64] Arthur L. Kellerman et al., Injuries and Deaths Due to Firearms in the Home, 45 J. Trauma 263, 263, 266 (1998)

[65] Garen J. Wintemute, *Guns, Fear, the Constitution, and the Public's Health*, 358 New England J. Med. 1421-1424 (Apr. 2008)

[66] Linda L. Dahlberg et al., *Guns in the Home and Risk of a Violent Death in the Home: Findings from a National Study*, 160 Am. J. Epidemiology 929, 935 (2004).

[67] David Hemenway, *Private Guns, Public Health* 78 (2004).

[68] Branas, Charles C. et al. "Investigating the Link Between Gun Possession and Gun Assault." *American journal of public health* 99.11, (2009): 2034. *PMC.* Web. 28 Dec. 2015.

[69] See David Hemenway, *Policy and Perspective: Survey Research and Self-Defense Gun Use: An Explanation of Extreme Overestimates*, 87 J. Crim. L. & Criminology 1430, 1432 (1997).

[70] Gary Kleck & Marc Gertz, *Armed Resistance to Crime: The Prevalence and Nature of Self-Defense with a Gun*, 86 J. CRIM. L. & CRIMINOLOGY 150, 174 (1995).

[71] Marty Langley & Josh Sugarmann, *Firearm Justifiable Homicides and Non-Fatal Self-Defense Gun Use: An Analysis of Federal Bureau of Investigation and National Crime Victimization Survey Data*, Violence Policy Center 1, 9 (Apr. 2013), at http://www.vpc.org/studies/justifiable.pdf.

[72] Marty Langley & Josh Sugarmann, *Firearm Justifiable Homicides and Non-Fatal Self-Defense Gun Use: An Analysis of Federal Bureau of Investigation and National Crime Victimization Survey Data*, Violence Policy Center 1, 2 (Apr. 2013), http://www.vpc.org/studies/justifiable.pdf.
See also, Federal Bureau of Investigation, U.S. Dept. of Justice, *Crime in the United States, 2009, Expanded Homicide Data Table* 15,

http://www2.fbi.gov/ucr/cius2009/offenses/expanded_information
/data/shrtable_15.html.

[73] David Hemenway, Deborah Azrael & Matthew Miller, *Gun Use in the United States: Results from Two National Surveys*, 6 Inj. Prevention 263, 263 (2000).

[74] Kellermann, Arthur L.MD, MPH, et al. "Injuries and Deaths Due to Firearms in the Home." Journal of Trauma, Injury, Infection, and Critical Care 45 (1998): 263-67

[75] Branas, (2009) see Wellford CF, Pepper JV, Petrie CV. Firearms and Violence: A Critical Review. Washington, DC: National Academies Press; 2005:6, & Weiner J, Wiebe DJ, Richmond TS, et al. Reducing firearm violence: a research agenda. Inj Prev. 2007;13: 80–84.

[76] The 2.5 million estimate is the result of a telephone survey conducted by Florida State University criminologist Dr. Gary Kleck, see Hemenway, David, "The Myth of Millions of Annual Self-Defense Gun Uses: A Case Study of Survey Overestimates of Rare Events," *Chance* (American Statistical Association), Volume 10, No. 3, 1997

[77] http://www.vpc.org/studies/justifiable.pdf

[78] http://www.vpc.org/studies/justifiable15.pdf

[79] Latin for "friend of the court." Frequently, a person or group who is not a party to a lawsuit, but has a strong interest in the matter, will petition the court for permission to submit a brief in the action with the intent of influencing the court's decision. Legal Information Institute.
https://www.law.cornell.edu/wex/amicus_curiae.
Retrieved December 17, 2015

[80] Kleck, Armed, p. 306

[81] John Lott and David B. M. Mustard, "Crime, Deterrence, and Right to Carry Concealed Handguns," JOHN M. OLIN LAW & ECONOMICS WORKING PAPER NO. 41 THE LAW SCHOOL THE UNIVERSITY OF CHICAGO (1997)

[82] Aneja A, Donohue JJ, Zhang A. The Impact of Right-to-Carry Laws and the NRC Report: Lessons for the Empirical Evaluation of Law and Policy. American Law and Economics Review. 2011;13(2):565-632

[83] Carlisle E. Moody, Thomas B. Marvell, Paul R. Zimmerman, and Fasil Alemante. *The Impact of Right-to-Carry Laws on Crime: An Exercise in Replication.* Review of Economics & Finance. December 9, 2013. Article ID: 1923-7529-2014-01-33-11. http://www.bapress.ca/ref/v4-1/1923-7529-2014-04-33-11.pdf. Retrieved December 14, 2015

[84] CA Welf & Inst Code § 8102 (2013)

[85] Berenson, Alex & Broder, John M. Police Begin Seizing Guns of Civilians. September 9, 2005. The New York Times. http://www.nytimes.com/2005/09/09/us/nationalspecial/police-begin-seizing-guns-of-civilians.html. Retrieved December 28, 2015

[86] Mark Follman et al., More Than Half of Mass Shooters Used Assault Weapons and High-Capacity Magazines, Mother Jones (Feb. 27, 2013), at http://www.motherjones.com/politics/2013/02/assault-weapons-high-capacity-magazines-mass-shootings-feinstein.

[87] *Analysis of Recent Mass Shootings.* Everytown for Gun Safety (Mayors Against Illegal Guns.) August 20, 2015. http://everytownresearch.org/reports/mass-shootings-analysis/. Retrieved December 28, 2015

[88] High-Capacity Ammunition Magazines are the Common Thread Running Through Most Mass Shootings in the United States. http://www.vpc.org/fact_sht/VPCshootinglist.pdf

[89] Kleck Armed p178

[90] Lacy, Marc & Herszenhorn, David M. In Attack's Wake, Political Repurcussions. January 8, 2011. The New York Times. http://www.nytimes.com/2011/01/09/us/politics/09giffords.html?_r=0. Retrieved December 28, 2015

[91] Americans for Responsible Solutions. http://americansforresponsiblesolutions.org/about/

[92] Newcomb, Alyssa and Zak, Lana, *Giffords, Kelly Say 'Enough' to Gun Violence on 2nd Anniversary of Tucson Shooting.* ABC News, January 8, 2013, http://abcnews.go.com/US/giffords-kelly-gun-violence-Second-anniversary-tucson-shooting/story?id=18145328#.UO2VZ3eAp8H. Retrieved December 17, 2015

[93] Kleck Point Blank p.77;

[94] Fackler, Martin L., J. A. Malinowski, S. W. Hoxie, and A. Jason. 1990. "Wounding Effects of the AK-47 Rifle Used by Patrick Purdy in the Stockton, California, Schoolyard Shooting of January 17, 1989." *American Journal of Forensic Medicine and Pathology* 11:185-9

[95] Watters, Daniel: "The 5.56 X 45mm Timeline: A Chronology of Development", The Gun Zone, 2000–2007. http://www.thegunzone.com/556dw-8.html. Retrieved December 21, 2015.

[96] Dean, Paul. Anatomy of a Bullet Wound : People are shot in Southern California every day. But, experts say, few of us

comprehend a bullet's impact. Here, the last 58 seconds in the life of a gunshot victim. Los Angeles Times. January 14, 1990. http://articles.latimes.com/1990-01-14/news/vw-403_1_gunshot-wounds/3. Retrieved December 28, 2015.

[97] Hague Convention Declaration III – On the Use of Bullets Which Expand or Flatten Easily in the Human Body July 29, 1899.

[98] Sherriff's demo of how magazine size makes very little difference. February 28, 2013. https://www.youtube.com/watch?v=MCSySuemiHU. Retrieved December 28, 2015

[99] Candiotti, Susan. Source: Colorado shooter's rifle jammed during rampage. July 22, 2012. http://www.cnn.com/2012/07/22/us/colorado-shooting-investigation/. Retrieved December 28, 2015.

[100] Stokols, Eli. Herpin explains why it was 'good thing' Holmes had large ammo magazine. February 14, 2014. http://kdvr.com/2014/02/12/herpin-a-good-thing-that-james-holmes-had-100-round-magazine/. Retrieved December 28, 2015

[101] Boston's Gun Bible, Boston T. Party ISBN 978-1-888766-06-6, Javelin Press, Durango, CO, April 2002

[102] "Assault rifle." Encyclopædia Britannica. 2010. Encyclopædia Britannica Online. 3 July 2010. Britannica.com. Retrieved December 17, 2015.

[103] "Machine Carbine Promoted" Tactical and Technical Trends. No. 57, April 1945. Archived: Lonesentry.com. http://www.lonesentry.com/articles/ttt07/stg44-assault-rifle.html. Retrieved December 18, 2015

[104] https://translate.google.com/#de/en/Sturmgewehr

[105] http://www.thefreedictionary.com/automatic+weapon

[106] http://www.thefreedictionary.com/machine+gun

[107] http://www.thefreedictionary.com/submachine+gun

[108] http://www.thefreedictionary.com/machine+pistol

[109] http://encyclopedia.thefreedictionary.com/Semi-automatic+weapon

[110] Ingram, Carl (April 9, 1985). "Restricting of Assault-Type Guns Okd by Assembly Unit". Los Angeles Times. Archived from the original on December 18, 2015

[111] Assault Rifle - "any of various automatic or semiautomatic rifles with large capacity magazines designed for military use" Merriam-Webster.
http://www.merriam-webster.com/dictionary/assault%20rifle. Retrieved December 28, 2015

[112] Assault - "*1 a* : a violent physical or verbal attack; *b* : a military attack usually involving direct combat with enemy forces; *c* : a concerted effort (as to reach a goal or defeat an adversary); *2 a* : a threat or attempt to inflict offensive physical contact or bodily harm on a person (as by lifting a fist in a threatening manner) that puts the person in immediate danger of or in apprehension of such harm or contact — compare battery 1b; *b* : rape 2 " Merriam-Webster.
http://www.merriam-webster.com/dictionary/assault. Retrieved December 28, 2015

[113] Kleck,Gary. Targeting Guns: Firearms and Their Control. Transaction Publishers. ISBN 9780202369419 pxiii

[114] *ArmaLite*, "1952-1954" https://armalite.com/history/1952-1954/. Retrieved December 23,2015

[115] BRIAN ROSS, JAMES GORDON MEEK, MEGAN CHRISTIE, ALLAN LENGEL, JOSH MARGOLIN, MATTHEW MOSK and ALEX HOSENBALL. Good Morning America. December 8, 2015. https://gma.yahoo.com/clues-san-bernardino-terror-attack-man-bought-assault-171528445--abc-news-topstories.html#. Retrieved December 9, 2015

[116] Hitchman, Norman A ; Forbush, Scott E ; Blakemore, Jr, George J. *Operational Requirements for an Infantry Hand Weapon.* June 19, 1952

[117] Beekman, Christian. *Here's why the US military is replacing the M16.* October 28, 2015. Business Insider, Military & Defense. http://www.businessinsider.com/heres-why-the-us-military-is-replacing-the-m16-2015-10. Retrieved December 18, 2015

[118] *Gun Fight.* Barbara Kopple. April 13, 2011. HBO. 1:00:33

[119] Canadian Sniper's World Record Kill. CBC Sunday Report. September 9, 2007. Military.com http://www.military.com/video/operations-and-strategy/afghanistan-conflict/canadian-snipers-world-record-kill/112356016400. Retrieved December 17, 2015

[120] Friscolanti, Michael. "We were abandoned". Maclean's. May 15, 2006. http://www.macleans.ca/news/canada/we-were-abandoned/. Retrieved December 17, 2015

[121] Sheridan, Michael (May 3, 2010). *"British sniper Craig Harrison (The Silent Assassin) breaks record, kills target from 1.5 miles away".* Daily News. http://www.nydailynews.com/news/world/british-sniper-craig-harrison-silent-assassin-breaks-record-kills-target-1-5-miles-article-1.444566. Retrieved December 17, 2015.

[122] *Henderson, Charles (2003). Silent Warrior (2003 ed.). Berkley Books. ISBN 0-425-18864-7* p181.

[123] Christopher S. Koper with Daniel J. Woods and Jeffrey A. Roth. An Updated Assessment of the Federal Assault Weapons Ban: Impacts on Gun Markets and Gun Violence, 1994-2003. Report to the National Institute of Justice, United States Department of Justice June 2003

[124] Ibid p96.97

[125] Ibid p17

[126] Ibid p17

[127] Ibid p80

[128] Ibid p92

[129] Ibid p80

[130] Ibid p11

[131] Ibid p83

[132] Hawkins, Awr. A majority of Americans oppose an "assault weapons" ban for the first time in 20 years of New York Times' polling on the topic. Brietbart. December 11, 2015. http://www.breitbart.com/big-government/2015/12/11/majority-americans-oppose-assault-weapons-ban-first-time-20-years-nyt-polling/. Retrieved December 17, 2015, see http://www.nytimes.com/interactive/2015/12/10/us/politics/times-cbs-news-poll.html?_r=0

[133] Sportsmen for Obama. https://www.youtube.com/watch?v=kBHkMADXnOw. Uploaded October 2, 2008

[134] Lutz, BJ. Obama Mentions Chicago's Gun Problem During Debate. NBC5 Chicago. October 16, 2012. http://www.nbcchicago.com/blogs/ward-room/second-presidential-debate-obama-romney-chicago-gun-violence-174503261.html. Retrieved December 28, 2015

[135] Farley, Robert. Did Obama Flip-Flop on Gun Control?. FactCheck.org. February 5, 2013. http://www.factcheck.org/2013/02/did-obama-flip-flop-on-gun-control/. Retrieved Decmeber 20, 2015

[136] http://www.washingtonpost.com/news/post-politics/wp/2015/10/01/full-text-obamas-remarks-about-mass-shooting-at-oregon-community-college/,
Full text: Obama's remarks about mass shooting at Oregon community college, Washington Post

[137] 3 Law Library of Congress, supra note 8, at 11 (citing Home Office, Firearms Act 1968 Proposals for Reform, Cmnd. 6, No. 261 (1987), ¶ 25).

[138] Shotgun is defined in section 1(3) of the Firearms Act 1968, c. 27 as "(a) . . . a smooth-bore gun (not being an air gun) which – (i) has a barrel not less than 24 inches in length and does not have any barrel with a bore exceeding 2 inches in diameter; (ii) either has no magazine or has a non-detachable magazine incapable of holding more than two cartridges; and (iii) is not a revolver gun[.]"

[139] The Firearms Rules 1998, SI 1998/1941, ¶ 5(1) & sched. 2, http://www.legislation.gov.uk/ uksi/1998/1941/schedule/2/made.

[140] Id. ¶ 7(1).

[141] Id. ¶ 6(2).

[142] Firearms Act 1968, c. 27 § 28(1A),
http://www.legislation.gov.uk/ukpga/1968/27/section/28.

[143] Firearms Act 1968 § 28(1B),
http://www.legislation.gov.uk/ukpga/1968/27/section/28.

[144] Scott, Eugene. *Obama: It's 'insane' that people on the 'no-fly' list can buy guns.* CNN. December 5, 2015.
http://www.cnn.com/2015/12/05/politics/barack-obama-guns-congress/. Retrieved December 9, 2015

[145] *Transcript: President Obama's address to the nation on the San Bernardino terror attack and the war on ISI.* CNN. December 6, 2015. http://www.cnn.com/2015/12/06/politics/transcript-obama-san-bernardino-isis-address/index.html. Retrieved December 9, 2015

[146] The Brady Campaign To Prevent Gun Violence: Our History.
http://www.bradycampaign.org/our-history. Retrieved January 2, 2016

[147] Harris, Richard. *A Reporter at Large: Handguns.* New Yorker, July 26, 1976.
http://www.newyorker.com/magazine/1976/07/26/handguns. Retrieved December 17, 2015

[148] Folkart, Burt A. *N.T. Shields; Gun Control Leader.* Los Angeles Times. January 26, 1993. http://articles.latimes.com/1993-01-26/news/mn-1795_1_handgun-control. Retrieved December 14, 2015

[149] Bruce, John M., Wilcox, Clyde. The Changing Politics of Gun Control. 1998. Rowman & Littlefield. 9780847686155. p.54] [H.R. 4445 (100th): Undetectable Firearms Act of 1988 http://www.govtrack.us/congress/bills/100/hr4445

[150] Charles Gordon, Lawrence Gordon, Joel Silver, & Renny Harlin. (1990) Die Hard 2. United States: 20th Century Fox

[151] Charley Reese, Brady Bill Ii: A Conspiracy To Deprive Honest Americans Of Liberty. Orlando Sentinel. March 10, 1994. http://articles.orlandosentinel.com/1994-03-10/news/9403100004_1_license-fee-brady-ii-handgun-control. Retrieved December 15, 2015

[152] *"What's The Difference Between A Fully Automatic and a Semi-Automatic Assault Weapon? About 3.5 Seconds.".* Brady Campaign. February 26, 2009. Archived from the original on July 25, 2011. http://web.archive.org/web/20110725101039/http://blog.bradyca mpaign.org/?p=693. Retrieved December 15, 2015

[153] http://www.bradycampaign.org/about-brady

[154] Kellerman (1998)

[155] http://www.bradycampaign.org/our-impact/campaigns/keep-crime-guns-off-our-streets

[156] Bureau of Alcohol, Tobacco, and Firearms, *Commerce in Firearms (2000). p23. Table 13*

[157] Sarkar, Saurav. *Why Do Nearly One in Five Crime Guns in Chicago Originate at Just Four Gun Dealers?* September 22, 2015. http://www.bradycampaign.org/blog/why-do-nearly-one-in-five-crime-guns-in-chicago-originate-at-just-four-gun-dealers. Retrieved December 16, 2015

[158] Grimaldi, James V.; Horwitz, Sari (October 24, 2010). "Industry pressure hides gun traces, protects dealers from public scrutiny". Washington Post. Retrieved December 16, 2015

[159] *" Brady Center blamed for $200K legal fee ruling against Aurora victim's parents"* Legal Solutions Blog. Thomson Reuters. June 26, 2015. http://blog.legalsolutions.thomsonreuters.com/current-awareness-2/brady-center-blamed-for-200k-legal-fee-ruling-against-aurora-victims-parents/. Retrieved December 16, 2015

[160] Following the Gun. Note 17

[161] Federal Denials Reasons Why the NICS Section Denies. FBI. https://www.fbi.gov/about-us/cjis/nics/reports/federal_denials.pdf Retrieved December 16, 2015

[162] Keep Guns Out of Criminals' Hands. http://www.bradycampaign.org/our-impact/campaigns/keep-guns-out-of-criminals%E2%80%99-hands] [Bureau of Justice Statistics. http://www.bjs.gov/index.cfm?ty=pbdetail&iid=5157

[163] Nra.org. https://home.nra.org/about-the-nra/. Retrieved December 28, 2015

[164] Dennis A. Henigan. For the NRA, It's All About Fear. Huffington Post. March 4, 2011. Url: http://www.huffingtonpost.com/dennis-a-henigan/for-the-nra-its-all-about_b_857526.html. Retrieved February 11, 2013

[165] LaPierre, Wayne. NRA: Why 'universal' checks won't work. USA Today. February 10, 2013. http://www.usatoday.com/story/opinion/2013/02/10/wayne-lapierre-nra-universal-checks/1907427/. Retrieved December 28, 2015

[166] Charley Reese. Brady Bill II: A Conspiracy To Deprive Honest Americans Of Liberty. March 10, 1994. Url: http://articles.orlandosentinel.com/1994-03-10/news/9403100004_1_license-fee-brady-ii-handgun-control. Retrieved February 11, 2013

Chapter VIII

[1] Franklin, Benjamin & Franklin, William Temple. *Memoirs of the life and writings of Benjamin Franklin* (1818) London : H. Colburn. See https://archive.org/details/templefranklin02franrich

[2] *Donald Trump urges ban on Muslims coming to US.* BBC. December 8, 2015. http://www.bbc.com/news/world-us-canada-35035190. Retrieved December 12, 2015

www.ingramcontent.com/pod-product-compliance
Lightning Source LLC
LaVergne TN
LVHW091213080426
835509LV00009B/968